P9-CJL-815

YOUR WORK MATTERS TO GOD

DOUG SHERMAN AND WILLIAM HENDRICKS

NAVPRESS (A)*
A MINISTRY OF THE NAVIGATORS
P.O. BOX 6000, COLORADO SPRINGS, COLORADO 80934

The Navigators is an international Christian organization. Jesus Christ gave His followers the Great Commission to go and make disciples (Matthew 28:19). The aim of The Navigators is to help fulfill that commission by multiplying laborers for Christ in every nation.

NavPress is the publishing ministry of The Navigators. NavPress publications are tools to help Christians grow. Although publications alone cannot make disciples or change lives, they can help believers learn biblical discipleship, and apply what they learn to their lives and ministries.

© 1987 by Doug Sherman and William Hendricks
All rights reserved, including translation
Library of Congress Catalog Card Number:
87-62854
ISBN 08910-92242

Unless otherwise identified, all Scripture quotations in this publication are from the *New American Standard Bible* (NASB), © The Lockman Foundation, 1960, 1962, 1963, 1968, 1971, 1972, 1973, 1975, 1977. Another translation used: the *Holy Bible: New International Version* (NIV). Copyright © 1973, 1978, 1984, International Bible Society. Used by permission of Zondervan Bible Publishers.

NOTE: Throughout this book, wherever the masculine pronouns are used, they should be understood as indicating both genders, unless the context implies otherwise.

Printed in the United States of America

CONTENTS

AUTHORS

Doug Sherman is the founder and president of Career Impact Ministries (CIM), a Christian organization that helps business and professional people integrate their faith into their careers.

After graduating from the Air Force Academy with a B.S. in engineering management, Doug served as an instructor in the Advanced Jet Training program, a position he held until he left the Air Force to attend Dallas Theological Seminary, where he received a Th.M.

Doug and his wife, Jan, live in Arlington, Texas, and have three children.

William Hendricks is the executive director of CIM. He received a B.A. in English literature from Harvard University, an M.S. in mass communications from Boston University, and an M.A. from Dallas Theological Seminary. Before joining Doug at CIM, he worked as a consultant in communication and media production.

Bill lives in Dallas, Texas, with his wife, Nancy, and their two daughters.

PREFACE

In 1974, Seward Hiltner wrote that Christianity needs a theology of work—and quickly. Unfortunately, though, constructing theology is a process that, like the great cathedrals of Europe, happens not over months and years, but over generations. Yet the urgency of Hiltner's suggestion has done nothing but increase in the decade and more since he made it.

This book was born out of that sense of urgency. In our opinion, Christianity is logjammed on this issue. Every day, millions of workers go to work without seeing the slightest connection between what they do all day and what they think God wants done in the world. For example, you may sell insurance, yet you may have no idea whether or not God wants insurance to be sold. Does selling insurance matter to God or not? If not, you are wasting your life. Yet without a clear theology of work, you have no way to answer the question, and therefore no basis to provide ultimate meaning to your job.

Imagine an entire Church made up of workers in this predicament. What sort of impact could such a Church have on its culture? Could it inspire a generation with a compelling vision for life? Or would it instead be dismissed as a triviality, fit only for one's private life, inappropriate and irrelevant in the marketplace?

We think your work matters deeply to God. So it is for you, the everyday worker, that we have written this book. This may seem odd to some. Why address a theology of work to the layperson? Wouldn't it make more sense to hammer this out at the seminary level, where scholars can smooth out the wrinkles, and professors can teach it to future pastors?

Undoubtedly research and reflection at this academic level must take place. Here and there, it is taking place. And we look forward with anticipation

7

to seeing the fruit of this labor. But in the meantime, workers like you desperately need a comprehensive view of work that links your work to God. This book attempts to do that.

HOW TO READ AND USE THIS BOOK

Like most business and professional people, you probably have very little time for the reading you must do, let alone for the reading you'd like to do. Consequently, you may be looking for ways to get the point of this book without reading it cover to cover. Naturally we think all of it is "must" reading, but then what authors wouldn't?

It might help you, then, to know the plan of our argument. Part I talks about the many serious problems that come from not having a biblical view of work. Chapter 1 introduces this issue, and Chapters 2-4 look at three inadequate perspectives on work that many Christians hold.

In Part II we present a theology of work that we believe corresponds to the Scripture's overall teaching. This is the core of the book, the basic message. We argue that biblically, your work matters to God. If you can only afford to read part of the book, read this part.

Part III then examines a number of practical implications that flow out of this view: implications for job selection, dealing with conflict, income and lifestyle, leisure, relationships on the job, even your relationship to your church. As you'll see, the concept that God cares about your work makes a practical difference both on and off the job.

Our hope is that this will be something of a handbook for you, a resource you can use over the years. We hope that you will pull it down off the shelf when you face particular career issues and need insight or when you need stimulation for your thinking.

Of course, our ultimate goal is life-change: We want God's truth about work to make a real difference in how you live your life. It certainly has for us and for many others.

THE AUTHORS

By the way, when you start reading Chapter 1, you will notice that we use the first person singular: "I," "me," "my," etc. The voice you hear is Doug's. And yet, this book has two authors.

We chose to write in this way because we wanted to capture the sense of immediacy and drama that we feel about this issue. Such a mood is best conveyed by a single narrator. Nevertheless, be certain that everything here represents both of our thinking and convictions. This has been very much of a joint venture. And an extremely stimulating and enjoyable one at that.

ACKNOWLEDGMENTS

Many, many people have contributed in ways known and unknown to the writing of this book. Some of those whom we would especially thank include: Bill Robertson, Jerry Roberts, Ray Blunt, Ray Bandi, Jeanne Hendricks, Jim Dethmer, Bill Garrison, Norman Geisler, Wayne Hey, Frank Tanana, Howard Hendricks, Dan Smick, Pat Booth, Rick Nutter, John Maisel, Kent Graeve, Dave Bertch, Bob Hendricks, Bob Buford, Fred Smith Jr., Ralph Mattson, Doug Coe, Ford Madison, Lynn Anderson, Dick Halverson, Rick Adams, Mike Reilly, Bob Savage, and Doug Holladay.

We also deeply appreciate the work of Kathy Yanni at NavPress, along with John Eames, Steve Eames, Volney James, and Jon Stine. Nor could this book have come about without the assistance of Jean Taft, and especially Karolynn Simmons, whose "magic fingers" turned choppy copy into properly processed prose.

DOUG SHERMAN
WILLIAM HENDRICKS

PART I
HOW CHRISTIANS VIEW WORK

CHAPTER 1

BETWEEN TWO WORLDS
The Need for a Biblical View of Work

You might as well know up front that I'm a born fighter. Not that I carry a chip on my shoulder or delight in getting my nose bloodied. But I'm a man who loves to embrace a cause and prevail. In this book my cause is the worker, particularly the worker who, at least in his private life, calls himself a Christian.

Why I should perceive this person as a cause will soon become evident, if it is not so already. During the past ten years I have put my time in on the street, listening to and talking with workers. Much of that talk has had to do with the bold promises of Christ, and whether or not they—and He—have any relevance to the workplace. As these people have discussed the things that mean the most to them, I've discovered that the issue of faith and work is a raw, open nerve for many.

Perhaps it is for you. Perhaps one or more of the following expresses your situation:

1. You may go to work unaided and unchallenged by the Word of God.
2. You may be unclear as to how to take advantage of the resources of Christianity for day-to-day work problems and decisions.
3. You may be bored by your work and see no lasting value in it. Indeed, you may feel that only through your religious life do you find any purpose and meaning.
4. You may be skeptical as to the relevance of Christianity to the rigors of the secular work world.
5. You may struggle with the cost of integrity and need inspiration to keep your "ethical edge."

6. You may embarrass the cause of Christ by living an inconsistent life-style at work.
7. You may not be challenged to influence coworkers for Christ.
8. You may struggle with how to put work in its proper perspective and balance the many demands that compete for your time.
9. You may lack an integrated life purpose that spans the public and private arenas.
10. You may lack a sense of dignity in your day-to-day work, and thus your life.

I think these are critical needs that we dare not ignore. And that is why I have written this book. I want its message to make a difference in your life—and in your work. I want to convince you that your work matters to God. I want to affirm that as a worker you matter to God. I want to challenge you to live an ethically distinctive, Christlike lifestyle on the job. And I want to suggest practical strategies you can use toward that end.

But before we get to that, I want to look behind the needs mentioned above and consider the larger context that explains where they came from. Let me begin with the circumstances under which I first began to notice a tension between the world of faith and the world of work.

LIFE IN THE FLIGHT ROOM

Every profession has its clubhouse. Surgeons have their scrub rooms. Athletes meet in locker rooms. Teachers gather in lounges. Performers chat in dressing rooms.

In such places the conversation sometimes centers on the work and sometimes on the lives and interests of the workers. But always the talk reveals what it means to live life as a member of that profession.

When I was a fighter pilot at Webb Air Force Base in Big Spring, Texas, my hangout was the flight room. That's where the other flight instructors and I met before and after our missions.

We were quite a club! If you are familiar with the movie *Top Gun*, you know our world. It was a high-tech, high-stress society of supersonic flight and superhuman legend. In the air, we'd push our students, ourselves, and our aircraft right to their limits. Back in the flight room, recounting our exploits, we'd push the truth much further!

This ceaseless attempt to top each other extended to all things. And you'd think that such competition would have torn us apart. But it actually brought us together. It's what enabled us to fly at 500 knots, three feet apart, communicating by head and hand signals and, as much as anything, by feel.

Imagine, then, what happened on those rare occasions when a chaplain would enter the flight room. The atmosphere suddenly changed. The talk stopped. Everyone looked up. The invader faced a squadron of stares that seemed to ask, "What are you doing here? What's the matter? Did something happen? Did somebody 'ding in'? Why else would a chaplain be here?"

In short, most of the clergy seemed terribly out of place in our flight room. I'm sure anyone would have. But the tension seemed more pronounced with them. Somehow I felt that they just didn't understand our world. Their issues and interests seemed so distant from ours that we struggled even to communicate.

Of course, we pilots felt just as out of place whenever we entered their world—their sanctuaries illumined by stained-glass windows, their ancient hymns, their rituals, their creeds, their homilies on God and Christ and goodness and love. Their work somehow seemed on a higher plane (so to speak). Very remote from dogfights and flight plans and check rides.

They seemed to have different heroes, too. Among pilots, if you can't be the top gun, then you envy the one who is. But aside from skill, I also knew of pilots whose faith made a noticeable difference in their performance, attitude, and lifestyle—individuals who were good men as well as good pilots. Yet very few of the chaplains ever mentioned these men. Instead, they praised people who had left the service to become ministers and missionaries.

This left me with an odd feeling that most of my life, given as it was to flying, didn't matter to God. After all, if the men who supposedly spoke for God thought so little of my world, then God must think likewise. For this reason, most of my comrades dismissed the clergy and religion and God as irrelevant.

TWO WORLDS

I'm afraid this situation is all too common. As I have talked to hundreds of workers—in business and the professions, in the military, in government, in education, and in the ministry—I invariably detect a tension between the world of work and the world of religion.

Of course, some would say that's as it should be. "You can't serve God and Mammon," they will remind me, as if in work one can never serve God, and in religion one can never serve Mammon—dubious assumptions, I think. But this does not explain the tension; it merely reinforces it.

Instead, I believe that the tension suggests an abnormality: As Christians we have over many years allowed a chasm to grow between our faith and our day-to-day work, a chasm that God never intended.[1]

Forgive me if this seems to state the obvious. But so often the obvious goes unstated and therefore unchallenged. Yet even a casual observer can't help but notice the many clues to the fact that Christianity and the world of work have parted ways. The tension that occurs when religion enters the workplace is only one of the more apparent.

A DEAFENING SILENCE

Another obvious clue is the scarcity of resources for Christians who want to apply their faith on the job. An organization I founded, Career Impact Ministries, polled about 2000 people who call themselves Christians and who regularly attend church. We asked each of them, "Have you ever in your life heard a sermon, read a book, listened to a tape, or been to a seminar that applied biblical principles to everyday work issues?" More than ninety percent replied no.

A friend of mind recently checked these findings in a novel way. He attends a rather large, prestigious church on the East Coast. He obtained a catalog of the church's cassette tapes listing every message from Sunday morning and evening services, Wednesday evening prayer meetings, and all major seminars and meetings during the last five years. He scanned the entire catalog, cover to cover. However, he claims that with one or two possible exceptions, not one of the titles spoke to issues of the workplace—not one in five years of preaching and teaching.

Next time you visit a bookstore, religious or otherwise, look for titles about how Christianity applies to the workplace. You certainly won't find many, if any.

All of this suggests that the Church has grown virtually silent on the subject of work. This is remarkable, given the strong emphasis that the Reformers placed on it, and given the comprehensive view of life and work brought to America by the Puritans.[2]

By contrast, I find a disparity today between the emphases of most Christian teaching and the way most people live. The average person spends anywhere from forty to seventy-five percent of his life in work or work-related tasks. Let's say sixty percent.[3] He may spend another thirty or thirty-five percent on his family and personal interests. And perhaps he spends as much as five or ten percent on church or religious activities.

Yet most Christian teaching addresses these areas in precisely the opposite proportions: a very heavy emphasis on religious matters, some help in regard to marriage and family, but little that speaks directly to the workplace. The result: millions of people go to work every day unaided, disillusioned, and unchallenged by the Word of God.

This silence is deafening! It leaves workers quite unclear on how to take advantage of the resources of Christianity for their day-to-day work problems and decisions. In fact, they wonder not just how their faith applies on the job, but *whether* it applies at all.

So all of this strongly suggests that the world of work and the world of religion, once bound together in a seamless whole, have been torn apart. And there are other more subtle clues that all is not well between them.

PURPOSELESSNESS

For one thing, many workers in the modern marketplace feel increasingly bored with their jobs and with life. This is the subtext of all the glitzy beer, hamburger, and travel commercials that show hardworking laborers building America and solving its problems. They portray the workplace not as it is but as we wish it could be—an engrossing, challenging, even uplifting human drama in which each of us performs our strategic role and fulfills a personal mission.[4] Instead, for many work is "just a job." Its value begins and ends with a paycheck.[5]

This was not always the case. I won't argue the probability that most of humanity has always found work to be mostly hard and routine, and probably futile as well. But wherever Christianity has gone, it has "etched a halo, as it were, around man's daily labor." For slaves and carpenters it reinterpreted work into divinely appointed tasks by which God is glorified and people's needs are satisfied.[6]

In other words, it brought meaning to the workplace. Why, then, in a culture so profoundly influenced by Judeo-Christian values, by the Protestant Reformation, and by the Puritans, has that meaning evaporated for so many?

Wherever I turn, I find Christians replying that it is because our culture has retreated from Christian values. This is unquestionably true. But it may also border on blaming the victim. Could it not also be said that Christianity has retreated from our culture? In any case, the fact remains that whatever messages of hope and significance Christianity has to offer, they are not getting through to the work force.

MORAL SCHIZOPHRENIA

A related fact of our time is the widespread compromise of ethics in the marketplace. It is now common to speak of the decline of ethics in business and government. But whether our condition today is worse or better than it once was is to my mind irrelevant. What matters is whether we do what is right *today*. All the evidence suggests that we do not.

Naturally, some will say that is because of the increasing complexity of ethical issues; we are facing questions and choices no one has ever faced before. I don't doubt it. But that cannot account for the widespread abuse in matters that are unquestionably wrong.

In December 1983, the Princeton Religion Research Center published a landmark survey conducted for *The Wall Street Journal* by the Gallup Organization. The researchers measured a wide range of moral and ethical behaviors, such as calling in sick when not sick, cheating on income tax, and pilfering company supplies for personal use. The results were disappointing, to say the least.[7]

But what the researchers found most startling was that there was no significant difference between the churched and the unchurched in their ethics and values on the job. In other words, despite the fact that more and more people attend churches, churches seem to be having less and less of an impact on the moral fiber of their people, at least in the workplace. To quote the researchers:

> These findings . . . will come as a shock to religious leaders and underscore the need for religious leaders to channel the new religious interest in America not simply into religious *involvement* but into deep spiritual commitment.[8]

To my mind, living out a deep spiritual commitment begins in the small, day-to-day moral choices we make. For if we cannot do what is right in little matters like pilfering and abusing lunch hours, what hope do we have of achieving moral victories in more complex issues?

The Gallup survey suggests that our culture is now setting the rules for Christians at work. As a result, many workers live with a moral schizophrenia. At church they swear allegiance to values informed by creeds and Scriptures. But at work they bow down to idols of expediency and career success. Moral camouflage has become *de rigueur* in the workplace.

CAREERISM

Another sign that religion and work have given up on each other is the careerism of our generation. By careerism I mean the idolatry of career, such that it establishes one's self-worth, becomes the controlling center of one's life, and is the last in a series of priorities to go.

The key to interpreting this development is the baby boomers, some of whom have earned the title "yuppies."[9] Actually, the advent of the yuppies may be the biggest non-story of the century. Since the early '80s, the press and its cousins, the demographers and marketing researchers, have made a big to-do about yuppies, as if they came out of nowhere. But what else would one expect from a generation of children who grew up in a relatively affluent society, whose parents sent them to college so that they could get good jobs, who married (more or less), and who proceeded to get good jobs and live two-income lifestyles?

What makes a yuppie or any other person a careerist, though, is if he or she exalts work to a sacred level—which is to say, if he or she exalts self to a sacred level. For to the careerist, duty to self is the greatest of the commandments. But what could be more self-expressive than work? Of all human endeavors, work holds the greatest potential for honoring and incarnating one's self.

Consequently, the career becomes untouchable. Marriage, children, friendships, even morals if necessary, must accommodate themselves to career demands or else be left behind.[10]

Who can adequately account for careerism, which is something of a new religion, particularly for many in the baby boom? Whatever the explanation turns out to be, this phenomenon is surely symptomatic of a society awash in secularization, a gradual subtraction of God from the culture, and a repudiation of religion as irrelevant. In other words, this generation lives by a new set of rules. The old rules said, "Deny yourself." The new rules say, "Fulfill yourself." The old rules said, "Love the Lord thy God." The new rules say, "Love the lord thy self."

Daniel Yankelovich very aptly describes this as a cultural tug-of-war. The rope is the answer to the question, "Who or what determines the morality of what I need and want?" Christianity answers, "God does." The careerist answers, "I do." Naturally, I think the Christians are championing the truth. But people like the careerist are ending up with the culture.[11]

THE IRRELEVANCE OF RELIGION

All of this suggests that religion is now irrelevant in the work world. That was the conclusion of so many of my pilot friends: Christianity just didn't work in the workplace.

I find that most professionals, and especially most men, hold a mild skepticism toward the faith. They feel that something abstract like faith can't stand the rigors of the street. They attend church on Sunday, and so forth. But religion is a sort of weekend hobby, like golf or fishing. Come Monday, it's time to put away those toys and get back to the "real world."

This situation was noticed more than forty years ago by Dorothy Sayers, an author and professor in England. In April 1942, she delivered an address at Eastbourne, England, entitled, "Why Work?" In answering that question she said the following:

> In nothing has the Church so lost her hold on reality as in her failure to understand and respect the secular vocation. She has allowed work and religion to become separate departments, and is astonished to find that, as a result, the secular work of the world is turned to purely self-ish and destructive ends, and that the greater part of the world's intel-ligent workers have become irreligious, or at least, uninterested in religion. But is it astonishing? How can any one remain interested in a religion which seems to have no concern with nine-tenths of his life?[12]

No wonder Christians have so little impact on our culture. Yet in my view, this is an outrage in a society desperately in need of moral champions.

Sociologists and psychologists have correctly observed the increasingly self-directed nature of our culture.[13] Their studies suggest that the career has become far more than a means of paying the bills. It has taken on many of the roles once played by religion. Meanwhile, religion, according to one historian, has become privately engaging but socially irrelevant.[14]

BRIDGING THE GAP

The gap between faith and work is serious. And I could describe many serious implications of it for the Church, our society, and even for other cultures around the world.

But the person most affected by it is you, if you are a Christian worker. For it falls to you to somehow bridge the ever-widening chasm between the truths of Christianity and the realities of the workplace. You normally have three alternatives to consider.

First, you can commute back and forth between two worlds, between two realities—your public life at work, and your private life at home and at church. This may be what most Christians do. However, to pull it off requires some deft psychological juggling.

It helps if you set up an unspoken, unholy contract with your pastor—something I've observed all too frequently among Christians. In this arrange-ment, the pastor is encouraged to preach to his utmost the great doctrines of the faith. He is even encouraged to grow prophetic and inveigh against the evils of society, against the sins of the government, against the injustices of multinational corporations—just as long as he avoids applying the Word to the work life of the businessperson. That's off-limits.

In exchange, the businessperson agrees to support the pastor and the programs of the church politically, financially, and by participation. This arrangement works well because it enables many to do as they please in the workplace and yet still feel square with God. Work need not hinder religion; and religion certainly need not matter at work.[15]

Even so, it often takes too much psychological energy to shuttle back and forth between two such disparate worlds without feeling tension. Consequently, a second alternative is for you to discount the value of your work and yourself as a worker in deference to the higher realm of religion. In other words, you conclude that your work doesn't matter to God, not nearly as much as church and ministry and "spiritual" things.

I'll discuss this much more in Chapter 3. But let me mention two serious implications of choosing this alternative. First, it destroys your dignity as a worker. If sixty percent or more of your life doesn't count to God, then you don't count to God. If your work has no value, then you have no value. At best you become a second-class citizen in the Kingdom of God.

A more tragic outcome is guilt. I spoke in Houston once on the dignity of everyday work. After the meeting a man came up to me. He was fifty-five, a retailer of locks and security systems. Tears were in his eyes, but a smile was on his face. He told me, "Doug, you have no idea of the guilt you have released me from today. For thirty-five years I thought that if I were really to be on the cutting edge for God, I would need to go to the mission field. And yet I never felt like I had the ability or inclination to do that. Today you have given me a whole new vision for my life."

I wish his story were unique. But in my experience, it is all too common.

Of course, a third alternative is to discount not the value of work, but the value of religion. I am afraid that this is the long-term consequence of the gap between the two. For the work world is not a neutral setting. It has a definite point of view. And more importantly, in the paycheck it has a foolproof way of motivating you to cooperate, if not to agree, with its point of view. Consequently, in any battle between religion and work, work will tend to win hands down.

ELIMINATING THE GAP

None of these alternatives seems satisfactory to me, because the gap between religion and work is itself unsatisfactory to me. The presence of such a significant chasm means that we have allowed a major category of life—

work—to slip out from under the auspices of Christ's lordship.

This will not do, because Christ is Lord of all of life. If He is not, if He only presides over what we do on Sunday or at home, if He is only an ideal, if Jesus is merely a name in a book we read to our children—then He really isn't our Lord at all. He doesn't really matter in what matters most to most of us: our work.

But Jesus *is* Lord. And as such, He is not interested in merely bridging the gap, but in eliminating it altogether. We must bring the entirety of our lives back together under Him.

I have found that when people do that, it transforms not only their work but even their outlook on life. Some of the benefits people have described include:

1. A new and refreshing sense of dignity and meaning in work. The simple idea that God cares immensely about what you do all day lends awesome value to your job.
2. An encouraging sense of destiny and calling in work. As you'll discover, God has designed you to accomplish certain kinds of work. Thus, you can go to your job with a deep conviction that you are there for a purpose.
3. Motivation to pursue a lifestyle of ethical distinction on the job. Knowing that you and your work matter to God and that you have a Boss in heaven provides stimulation to pursue moral integrity and a Christlike character.
4. A comprehensive view of life that relates work to spirituality. You'll discover how to bring your work and your faith together, along with the other areas of your life, creating a meaningful whole and thus escaping spiritual schizophrenia.
5. A new respect for the faith in light of its contribution to work. The discovery that Christianity addresses work and work issues—issues that matter to you—will cultivate an elevated appreciation for the resources God has provided.
6. Answers to many questions you may have about your relationship to your church. You'll gain insight into your status and contribution as a layperson, and into how and where you express your commitment to Christ.
7. Hope! Once you discover how much God cares about you and your work, you'll be eager to learn what He has to say about the particulars of your job. This should encourage you, because it means that you don't have to "go it alone" as a believer in a secular workplace. You'll act from the confidence that God and His resources are with you.

YOUR WORK MATTERS TO GOD

Life-changing benefits like these have happened for many people. I know because I'm one of them. In fact, this book is in many ways a statement of my own journey in the faith.

Shortly before entering the Air Force Academy in Colorado Springs, I had decided to become a Christian. Not a church-goer. Not just a good person. And definitely not a religious fanatic. Rather, a believer and follower of the Jesus of the New Testament.

From the beginning, it had seemed self-evident to me that if Christianity were both true and relevant, then it had to make a difference in how I lived in the everyday work world—without taking me out of that world.

I was so convinced of this that I and the other pilots who shared my beliefs began to meet in order to study and discuss how our faith might apply on the flight line. We were determined to be both fighter pilots and Christ-followers *at one and the same time.*

Later I went to graduate school to find out what the Bible and Christians through the years have had to say about these issues. I discovered that God is a Worker and has created us in His image as His coworkers. I learned that as Christians we are actually employees of Christ. And on this basis I concluded that what we do all day is of great importance and value, certainly to God.

Moreover, I found that the Scriptures make a practical difference in the many day-to-day issues we all face on the job. Issues like stress, priorities, relationships, ambition, and compromise. Issues like profit motive and debt structure, partnerships and bankruptcy. Issues like participation in evil, office politics, lawsuits, and negotiation. These are the arenas where faith must prove its value. Otherwise it will mean as little to work as a hymnal.

But of course, on the street this lofty view of work is not well-known, even among Christians. Instead, most workers have opted for one of three sub-biblical attitudes that I want to briefly cover in Chapters 2, 3, and 4.

Some people view their work in purely secular terms; work and God are mutually exclusive. Others have adopted what I call a Two-Story view, in which work has no intrinsic value. And others regard work as merely a platform for evangelism. As we'll see, these attitudes are sub-biblical; they are not completely at odds with Scripture, but they are not wholly in line with it either.

This is unfortunate because I believe most Christians sincerely want to please God with their lives. However, since work is such a major part of life, and since these people are operating on less than the whole of God's truth in that major part, their view of work actually undermines their intentions.

As we evaluate these views, you may be surprised to find the extent to which they have influenced your own attitudes about your work. If so, that would be helpful as a preparation for the material in Part II. It may also help to explain some of the tensions you may feel between your faith and your vocation.

In Part II, I'll develop the idea that your work matters to God. I'll argue that work has been given great value by God, and that the Christian has more reason than anyone else to work with a sense of purpose and satisfaction. I'll also explain the impact of sin on work.

Finally, in Part III, I'll set forth a number of important implications that flow out of this view of work. These include implications for where you work, how you work, how much you work, and even what you do with the money you make from your work.

So let's turn to consider what I call the secular view of work.

NOTES: 1. Actually, this split is probably part of a much larger schism in our culture between faith and the secular society. See, for example, Martin Marty, *The Modern Schism: Three Paths to the Secular* (New York: Harper & Row, 1969), or Stephen Charles Neill and Hans-Rudi Weber, ed., *The Layman in Christian History* (Philadelphia: The Westminster Press, 1963), pages 250f.

2. The Church has not been totally silent on work. However, one must do a good bit of hunting to locate helpful material. Most of it is buried in obscure places: such as Carl F.H. Henry's extremely seminal chapter, "The Christian View of Work," in his book, *Aspects of Christian Social Ethics* (Grand Rapids, Mich.: Baker Book House, 1964); or Dorothy Sayers' speech, "Why Work?" in a collection entitled *Creed or Chaos?* (New York: Harcourt and Brace, 1949).

   In addition, a number of helpful contributions have come from writers in the Roman Catholic tradition, and the World Council of Churches. More recently, laypeople themselves have started to address this topic. See the "Suggested Reading" section for more information.

   As for the Reformers' and Puritans' views on work, see Doug Sherman, "Toward a Christian Theology of Work," Th.M. Thesis, Dallas Theological Seminary, 1984.

3. Actually, it makes little difference how much or how little one works. In our culture, work dominates the rest of life. It determines where we live, who our friends will be, and how we'll spend our time.

4. See Neil Postman, *Amusing Ourselves to Death* (New York: Peguin, 1985), pages 27-28.

5. See Studs Terkel, *Working* (New York: Pantheon Books, 1972), pages xi-xxiv, for an excellent description of the feelings and perceptions of workers about the workplace.

6. See Henry, *Aspects of Christian Social Ethics*, page 32.

7. "Ethical Behavior Seen Declining," *Emerging Trends*, Volume 5, Number 10 (1983), pages 3-5.

8. "Ethical Behavior Seen Declining," page 5.

9. Or, "Dinks," which stands for "double-income, no-kids." Bill calls them "dinkys": "double-income, no-kids-yet."

10. I will say more about this in Chapter 2. But one of the best summaries of careerism and its tragic effects is Douglas LaBier, *Modern Madness* (Reading, Mass.: Addison-Wesley Publishing Company, Inc., 1986), pages 25-36.

11. See Daniel Yankelovich, *New Rules* (Toronto: Bantam Books, 1982), pages 244-245.

12. Sayers, *Creed or Chaos?*, page 56.

13. See Yankelovich, *New Rules*; Bellah et al, *Habits of the Heart* (Berkeley, Calif.: University of California Press, 1985); Lasch, *The Culture of Narcissism* (New York: Warner Books, 1979); and LaBier, *Modern Madness*.

14. Theodore Roszak, *Where the Wasteland Ends* (New York: Doubleday, 1973), page 449.

15. See Richard Lovelace, *Dynamics of Spritual Life: An Evangelical Theology of Renewal* (Downers Grove, Ill.: InterVarsity Press, 1980), pages 207, 225.

CHAPTER 2

GOING FOR IT!
The Secular View of Work

I n Chapter 1, I described a chasm that has opened up between the world of work and the world of religion. One of the most far-reaching consequences of that chasm is that many workers are left free to assume that what happens on the job makes not the slightest bit of difference to God, if there even is a God. Another way to say this is that God is irrelevant at work. Work exists on its own. It is purely secular.

Of course, it is somewhat simplistic to speak of "a secular view of work," as if there were only one, and as if such a view were well-defined. The reality is that workers bring a multitude of perspectives to their jobs that defy easy classification.

And yet I think we can detect some broad themes that blow through the work world, especially as it exists in urban areas. One unifying feature among them is the notable absence of God in the system. To that extent, many workers, perhaps most in our society, hold a fairly secular view of work.

In this chapter I want to explore some of these themes. I'll mention five, though there are unquestionably many more. Then I want to briefly show why these views are inadequate for the Christ-follower. You may be surprised to find the extent to which you have bought into one or more of the following ideas.

1. The ultimate purpose of work is to fulfill yourself.
As I pointed out in the last chapter, sociologists and psychologists have noted for some time the increasingly self-directed nature of our society. Daniel Yankelovich goes so far as to suggest that "the struggle for self-fulfillment in today's world is the leading edge of a genuine cultural revolution."[1]

25

On the street this idea translates into a morbid preoccupation with one's "needs." Listen as Yankelovich goes on to describe Abby, a woman who typifies today's quest for self-fulfillment:

> In talking about herself she refers to her "emotional needs," her "sexual needs," her "material needs," her "need to be challenged intellectually," her "need to assert herself." When she discusses her "unfilled potentials" and her "need to keep growing," she seems to take these metaphors literally—almost as if she believes the process of filling her unmet needs is like filling a set of wine glasses at a dinner party: the more needs filled, the greater the self-fulfillment.[2]

To the careerist, work becomes a uniquely intoxicating spirit with which to fill up the glasses and liven up his party/life. His career may contribute significantly to others. But whether it keeps him coming back for more depends on the contribution it makes to himself. The paycheck worth working for is not simply money, but meaning—personal meaning and significance.

A goal worth fighting for. Studs Terkel perceptively describes the workplace as a venue of violence—violence "to the spirit as well as to the body. It is about ulcers as well as accidents, about shouting matches as well as fistfights, about nervous breakdowns as well as kicking the dog around."[3]

Why would anyone keep going back into such a world? What could compel someone to endure such an assault on his personhood? We gain a clue from, of all people, Rocky Balboa, who as a fighter embodies the careerist vision and articulates its ultimate slogan: "Go for it!"

The "it" means—what? A boxing championship? Lasting fifteen rounds, "going the distance"? The adulation of an adoring woman? Defiance—a refusal to "throw" the fight? All this and more for Rocky. His battle, like ours, is to authenticate himself: "It" means whatever it takes to make certain that "self" really does exist and really does matter.

Obviously this is a highly subjective and elusive goal. Consequently, if you are a careerist, you define your goal, your "it," the outcome you want, no matter how ephemeral or senseless that may appear to others. What matters is that "it" makes sense to you. And like Rocky, you will endure incredible wear and tear on your body and soul because, in the end, you are fighting for yourself.

Master of your fate. Whether or not you achieve "it" ultimately depends on you. Your destiny lies within yourself. No one else can achieve "it" for you.

This is the recurring theme promoted in the marketplace today by a host of popular, high-priced motivational speakers and consultants. They pitch inspiring formulas that promise to help you get what you want.

They are fond of asking, Do you have what "it" takes? To get what you want, you have to want "it" badly enough. In other words, success depends on your intensity of desire. For instance: "You can never have riches in great quantities *unless* you can work yourself into a white heat of *desire* for money, and actually *believe* you will possess it."[4]

And yet "it" doesn't fall from the sky into the laps of dreamers. No, these prophets of positive thinking tell us that to get what you want you have to work hard and/or work smart. Success depends on your energy or your intellect, your strength or your smarts.

"It" requires determination ("There are many starters, but few finishers"); discipline ("Creativity is two percent inspiration and ninety-eight percent perspiration"); the right goals ("If you aim at nothing, you'll hit it every time"); savvy ("Success in life comes not from holding a good hand, but in playing a poor hand well"); perseverance ("Tough times never last; tough people do"); vision ("Some men dream dreams and ask, Why?; I dream dreams and ask, Why not?"); self-confidence ("Believe in God, and you're halfway there; believe in yourself, and you're three-quarters there"[5]). There is no end to the qualities that supposedly account for success. But all of them reflect human power to somehow "Go for 'it'" and get the job done: "Our rewards in life will depend on the quality and amount of contribution we make."[6]

2. Success in life means success in work.

Almost everyone I know sees a close connection between the success of his work and the success of his life. I think this is normal and valid. But many today see personal success almost exclusively in terms of success at work:

> Careerism has become the main work ethic of our times. At root, careerism is an attitude, a life orientation in which a person views career as the primary and most important aim of life. An extreme but not uncommon expression of this is found in the comment of a man who told me that he feared dying mainly because it would mean the end of his career.[7]

Likewise, a man might be a virtual alcoholic, his second or third wife may have just walked out on him, his kids might be on drugs, and his subordinates might hate his guts—yet if he is successful in his business, we still regard him as a successful person. In fact, he likely thinks of himself that way. And why not? People still crave his endorsement, his money, his name, or his participation.

It's on the company. Of course, the majority of us work in fairly large organizations made up of many divisions and many layers of bureaucracy. Consequently, "To be a success at work means to advance up the hierarchy of such corporations by helping the corporation make a good profit. But how is this kind of success related to a more fundamental kind of success in life?"[8]

The answer is that the upwardly mobile corporate executive is no longer an "organization man." Instead he or she is a person who uses the company hierarchy as a vehicle for his or her own agenda. As we saw before, that agenda usually relates to self-expression and self-fulfillment.[9]

The "career path." Furthermore, today's corporation must accept the fact that its workers, especially its white collar workers, have broadened the definition of "career" to include virtually all of life. People speak of a "career path" that maps out their personal destiny.

"The implication is that career should be equivalent with our identity." It even includes non-work categories. And the extent to which we have a "fulfilling" career is the extent to which we may regard ourselves as successful.[10]

3. You can tell how successful someone is by his material wealth, his professional recognition, or his positional status.

This follows from the principles above. I find that every career has its symbols of success that tell an individual and his associates that he's "made 'it.'" As a cadet in the Air Force, success to me meant the number of stars on an officer's shoulder. To many football players, success means a Super Bowl ring. To some lawyers, success means making senior partnership or having one's name added to the marquee. And in Washington, D.C., success means mounting a picture of oneself with the President, signed by the Chief Executive.

Such tokens are neutral in themselves. They are probably even valuable and useful. But for some people, they are not only well-deserved symbols of career achievement, but actually badges of personal worth. If you think this overstates the case, consider two tragic illustrations:

> One senior executive jumped off the roof of his building when he
> walked into work one morning and discovered that his desk had been
> moved. A chemist who failed to receive a grant for a research project
> returned to his lab one night, concocted a poison, and drank it, dying
> where he felt most at home. And most betrayed.[11]

These are extreme cases, to be sure. Yet they are not uncommon. And such extremes highlight in graphic terms what is inherent in more common and acceptable expressions of a secular view of work.

If you can't buy happiness, buy pleasure. Along these lines, I am constantly amazed at how easily we confuse money with happiness. Often when I speak on the subject of success, I ask my audience, "How many of you think you would be fundamentally happier if you made twice as much income as you do right now?" Everyone laughs nervously and nods, catching the point, but invariably someone adds, "Make it three times as much and you've got a deal!"

Obviously money is necessary for us to purchase what we need. And most of us would accept the view that "you can't buy happiness." Yet how hard some of us work to prove that adage wrong! We think that if we could only have this or that thing, *then* we would be satisfied.

Americans have always made a strong connection between money and survival. But today, with the rise of careerism and the phenomenon of the two-income family, money means something more. It is the door to the enjoyment of life: "One needs money for possessions, for travel, for leisure, for the 'full, rich life.'" It is also valued as a symbol of social worth.[12]

The look. However, even though most of us would still define success in terms of riches, fame, or power, our actions show that what matters to us is not these things themselves, but what they say about us. They say we are successful, and that means more than being successful (whatever that means). Image counts more than substance.[13]

Og Mandino cites "the brilliant" Howard Whitman, who has written: "There are two main criteria of success: 1. Do others think you are a success? 2. Do you think so?"[14] Here we have success as determined by human opinion: What you are matters nothing in comparison to what others and you *think* you are. This arrangement has all the objectivity of a beauty contest.

But in the judging, whose vote counts more—yours or your associates'? Whitman tries to argue that ultimately only you can pronounce yourself a success. But, he warns, "It cannot be composed of outward signs or appearances, but only of intangible personal values stemming from a mature philosophy."[15] This is positive think-speak for "Do your own thing, and damn what anybody else thinks!"

It is curious, though, how astonishingly similar the "intangible personal values" of today's careerists have become. The more everyone does his own thing, the more everyone does the same thing—and evaluates success the same way. A certain watch, a certain car, a certain club, a certain address: Having them does not mean you are a success—but who cares? Others will *think* you are. And isn't that one of the two main criteria of success? In fact, in this view, isn't that really *the* main criterion of success?

Performance value. A final observation worth noting here is that when we base personal significance on career success and its rewards, it profoundly affects our perspectives on people. We begin to value others for their performance, for what they can contribute—especially for what they can contribute to our success.

Of course, the workplace is understandably a very task-oriented arena where performance counts. We hire people who can serve a particular function in the enterprise. But the secular worker often applies this utilitarian approach outside the workplace to life in general.

I have heard a father, for instance, complain that his son won't "amount to" anything. Upon investigation, however, I find that the father is highly motivated and successful in finance and deal-making, while the son has a far more artistic bent. You see what has happened. The father has, first of all, decided to evaluate (or devaluate) his son according to the young man's deficiency in the father's area of expertise. Furthermore, he seems far more interested in what his son *does* than in who he *is*. And I can tell you that the relationship is unhealthy, in that the two have built nothing between them that has to do with something besides their work. Performance is all that matters.

4. You've got to do whatever it takes to get the job done.

Expediency is probably the value most universally designed into the workplace. Whatever the task, it is defined in terms of the overall objectives of the enterprise as ordained by the needs of one's market.

For example, if you run a company that bulldozes paths for highways, expediency demands that you do or not do certain things. It demands that instead of hiring ninety-pound weaklings to run the equipment, you get guys who look like the front line of the Chicago Bears. It demands that instead of warehousing your machines in midtown Manhattan, you find a low-rent space with easy access to an interstate. Instead of issuing navy blazers and wingtips to your crews, you hand out coveralls and work boots.

In short, the nature of your business defines what you do and how you do it. Success demands expediency. It is not simply the case of the ends justifying the means, but of the ends dictating them. No one would question this type of expediency.

But what happens if expediency becomes the *only* value used in making decisions? Suppose doing *what* it takes to get the job done becomes doing *whatever* it takes to get it done? Are there any limits to expediency? For an increasing number of workers, the answer seems to be no, especially in the area of ethics.

Recently a lawsuit was brought against a major manufacturer of baby food. The company had put sugar water in bottles and sold it as 100 percent apple juice to a large number of parents. One of the lawyers in the case confided to a relation of mine that this type of activity "is the tip of the iceberg."

No wonder *Time* magazine, always on the lookout for a newsworthy trend, recently ran a cover story entitled, "What Ever Happened to Ethics?"[16] Surveying a landscape of scandal from Boesky to the Bakkers to the Iran-Contra fiasco, the magazine declared that America "finds itself wallowing in a moral morass," and wondered whether we are not wandering in a "values vacuum." Likewise, Malcolm Forbes notes that:

> The hottest topic on Wall Street today isn't the spectacular gyrating and heady climb of the Dow Jones industrials. The most widespread concern about Wall Street is over its standards, ethics, morality— triggered by the multi-$billions made from illegal machinations.[17]

What accounts for these ethics of expediency? The answer is obviously complex. But consider two aspects: the nature of the workplace today, and the implications for values of the cult of self-fulfillment.

The jungle. At the beginning of creation, work may have started out in a garden. But in our generation it has ended up in a jungle.

Christopher Lasch points out that middle-class society has in many ways taken on the character of the ghetto, whose language it has adopted.[18] He means that we have become preoccupied with personal survival in a dangerous world.

As a consequence, work has become warlike, as workers seek competitive advantage over others. To survive and prevail requires "intimidating friends and seducing people." Consequently, distractions such as moral scruples must be left behind when one enters the jungle. A sort of moral Darwinism rules there: Survival depends on doing not what is right, but what works.

Imagine a person driven by a quest for self-fulfillment, whose entire self-concept rides on the success or failure of his work. In such a jungle, it seems predictable that he will do *whatever* it takes to achieve his goals:

> What is good is what one finds rewarding. If one's preferences change, so does the nature of the good. Even the deepest ethical virtues are justified as matters of personal preference. Indeed, the ultimate ethical rule is simply that individuals should be able to pursue whatever they find rewarding, constrained only by the requirement that they not interfere with the "value systems" of others.[19]

This nullifies lasting commitment to anyone or anything outside of oneself. If a relationship (spouse, child, friend, subordinate) stands in the way, one sacrifices it. If a boss or board obstructs one's progress, one goes to work undercover. If legal or moral issues prove bothersome, one compromises them. All on the basis of expediency.

Such a principle is purely secular in that the individual himself not only sets his goals, but sets his rules as well. He sees no authority or value system higher than himself to which he will ultimately submit.

5. "I just go to work to earn a living."
On the face of it, this seems like a harmless, normal statement that any responsible wage earner might make. In fact, one of the major reasons any of us goes to work is to provide for ourselves and for our families. Indeed, as we'll see in Part II, this is one of the reasons God has given us work and expects us to work.

But is earning a living a good enough reason by itself to justify work? As I have said, there is a legitimate self-interest in wanting to gain a livelihood. But if that were the only reason one were to work, it would reduce one's job to a purely self-directed activity. This is inadequate from a biblical point of view, as we will see in Part II.

I also know workers who use this very rationale to justify highly suspect business practices and opulent lifestyles. "I'm just trying to provide for my family," one man told us. "Providing" for him required fraudulent deals, deception with investors, funny arithmetic with the government, and unfair dealings with employees. "Providing" for his family meant a prestigious German automobile, furs for his wife, private schools for his children, and expensive vacations overseas. Providing for the family? Who was he trying to kid?

EVALUATION

It would be nice to think that any Christ-follower could see the problems inherent in the five perspectives mentioned above. But this is far from likely. In the first place, these and similar ideas have become so commonplace that they sound normal and are virtually assumed without question. This passive acceptance indicates how much our culture has adopted a secular worldview.

Furthermore, many Christians have also adopted this same worldview without even knowing it. Oh, sure, on Sunday, as we saw in the last chapter, they go to church and affirm New Testament doctrines and creeds—teaching that is directly opposed to the secularism of our day. Yet what difference does it make? For on Monday they switch gears and act the part of secular workers.

Consequently, it is necessary to offer some critique to the secular view of work. So let me begin with the positive. One of the best things we can say about the attitudes mentioned above is that they motivate workers from a positive direction. In other words, they present work as something worthwhile.

This is no small contribution. For billions of workers throughout history and throughout the world today, and even for many millions in our society, work seems terribly burdensome. It is oppressive or boring, like a curse on the back of mankind.

So it comes as good news that work might actually be a path toward a better life. The hope of personal prosperity is an amazing stimulus that taps unimagined reservoirs of human energy.

And without question, some have prospered who have adopted the secular view. Not all, but some. And those who get written up in magazine and newspaper articles or appear on "Lifestyles of the Rich and Famous" serve as inspiring heroes for countless others who are still "on the way up."

But these positive features are more than outweighed by at least three negative aspects.

1. The secular view of work expects more of work and self than work and self can deliver.

Imagine that I invent a game called "I Win." The objective of the game is for me to win. And the way for that to happen is for me to score points. I score points whenever I determine that points should be awarded. Furthermore, I set the rules of how the game will be played. And the playing field will correspond to whatever dimensions I deem appropriate at a given moment.

You would likely view such a game as nonsense. The arbitrary nature of the scoring, rules, and field of play render it absurd. And there is no objectivity to the game, nothing outside of myself that defines or interprets it. Indeed, this is not really a game so much as a pointless exercise in self-indulgence.

Yet this is the "game" that the careerist plays through work. By making self-fulfillment his goal, he turns work into a highly subjective enterprise. After all, what does it mean to "fulfill" himself? Only he can say. What proves meaningful to someone else will not satisfy him. Furthermore, what fulfills him today may not tomorrow. Consequently, he is constantly redefining the terms under which he finds himself, his work, and the rewards of work to be acceptable.

This arrangement has all the appearance of a psychological Mobius strip. The careerist uses work to define himself, yet he himself assigns whatever meaning and purpose his work ends up having. In short, he has invented a way of life in which he must be both cause and effect.

Is this realistic? Not unless both humans and their work are capable of delivering far more than we have yet seen from them throughout history. Yankelovich comments:

> On traditional demands for material well-being seekers of self-fulfillment now impose new demands for intangibles—creativity, leisure, autonomy, pleasure, participation, community, adventure, vitality, stimulation, tender loving care. To the efficiency of technological society they wish to add joy of living. They seek to satisfy both the body *and* the spirit, which is asking a great deal from the human condition.[20]

This is an understatement! Yankelovich himself goes on to describe the severe limitations of adopting a self-fulfilling posture toward life and work. It puts the careerist in a triple bind. First, the subjective nature of fulfillment presents a person with an infinity of possibilities about what to do with his life. But how does someone know how to make the right choices?

Second, self-fulfillment sounds great in a growing economy in which one is making substantial money. But how does it relate to economic downturns and deprivations? When one's family is starving, doesn't it seem self-indulgent to worry about how one "feels" toward whatever work one can find?

Third, a preoccupation with how work affects self makes a person less effective in contributing to life, not more. This is because he never gets beyond himself, never considers life and others objectively. He becomes the measure of all things.[21]

All of this translates into a very dark side for many workers. The quest for self-fulfillment turns into a tortuous descent into self-destruction. One of the best surveys of this condition and its causes comes from Douglas LaBier. In his book *Modern Madness*, he notes the following as some of the symptoms of the pathological outcome of careerism:

Loss of self. By equating self-worth with career success, the careerist builds his life on a very shaky foundation. Any setback or change in the workplace acts like a psychological earthquake, damaging if not demolishing his sense of identity and value. This leads to some obvious tragedies such as suicide, and to some less obvious ones as we will see below.[22]

I would especially point out the spiritual tragedy, though. The careerist seeks to gain the world, but ends up losing his own soul. By seeking to save himself through work, he loses himself instead.[23]

Compromise of integrity. Earlier we looked at the careerist's ethics of expediency. LaBier points out that in the individual this registers as a vague sense of self-betrayal, a gradual chipping away of integrity. This is particularly true for the corporate worker:

> The price of successful careerism is feeling trapped and caught as they navigate upward through layers of hierarchy, fueled by visions of recognition, power, and position that lie just ahead. But smack in the midst of their career steeplechase they find themselves semiconscious of criticisms about themselves and what they do in their work. Particularly, values which disturb them and leave them feeling uncertain and anxious about what to do that would help.[24]

A related condition is the feeling of having sold out for position and comfort over time. One corporate manager describes a recurring dream in which "I'm running in a marathon race, and all the other runners are people I recognize from my office. Then all of a sudden I realize that I don't know why we are all in the race, or where the finish line is."[25]

This reminds me of a student I once trained. In the middle of an extended flight, I observed that he was drifting off course. So I asked him if he knew where he was going. He replied, "No sir—but we're sure making good time!" The same could be said for the careerist.

Inflated notions of importance. Having placed enormous demands on work, the careerist must somehow deal with the reality that his job is a bit less significant than he would like it to be. This is particularly problematic for many corporate workers, whose positions seem somewhat minor or expendable.

One strategy for coping with this is to inflate the importance of what one is doing all out of proportion to its true value. Consequently we find some workers battling for power, puffing up the strategic nature of their contribution, or becoming preoccupied with applause and appearance.[26]

Hopelessness and stagnation. It may take a while, but many workers eventually realize the futility of careerism. Unfortunately, by the time they discover this they are in over their head and see no escape:

> They see no alternatives which might be more fulfilling but also realistic. This underlies much of the joylessness and semi-depression that has become so rampant in our society. The feeling that no one can really win; that there is no way out. Though well-adapted to our high-tech, fast-track culture, many feel emotionally numb and without a sense of purpose or overall framework for guiding their lives.[27]

Rage. LaBier reports that those who work with the psychological problems of today's workers observe an extremely high degree of anger and hostility. Many successful executives, for instance, enter therapy because they are brimming with anger and hate their jobs. They feel that they have reached a level in their careers at which they don't have anything else, and consequently they experience tremendous rage.[28]

Sometimes the roots of such anger lie in the soil of fundamental, lifelong unhealthiness. But not all angry workers are emotionally sick. Nor do all of them express their anger in obvious ways:

> Anger at the workplace is often masked by other behavior or symptoms, like violence, depression, physical problems, passivity, or sabotage. And there is no question that it has tremendously destructive effects on the person, emotionally and physically. For example, anger has been linked with cancer, chronic headaches, and heart disease. There is some evidence that chemicals released into the body during the experience of anger and rage can literally wear down the system. Some people can be described as "anger junkies" because they know it is destructive, yet they can't stop it. They feel addicted to it.[29]

Alcoholism and drug abuse. One way to cope with the problems caused by the self-defeating demands of careerism is to narcotize the pain:

> Typical, now, among some fast-track careerists is the extensive use of cocaine, particularly among people in high-pressured careers, such as financial areas like securities, commodities, and the financial service industries. In a survey by a national drug treatment service, 75% of the workers reported using drugs at work, of whom 83% use cocaine. Twenty-five percent reported using drugs every day. The survey also found that corporate executives and other high-paid professionals use twice as much cocaine as those who make less. In fact, alcohol and cocaine have become the twin escape routes of the '80s, providing artificial aliveness to the inner dead, and mellowed-out numbness to the self-betrayed.[30]

Loneliness. It seems obvious that anyone who turns work into the self-indulgent game of "I Win" will sooner or later find himself alone in the world. This happens because the careerist pays scant attention to forming and maintaining relationships. After all, career matters more than people. As a consequence, many of the careerists comprise the twenty-five percent of the population that live alone, and the fifty percent of marriages that fail. Along the same lines, twenty percent of all children now live with only one parent.[31]

By the way, it is worth noting the close connection between the careerist's loneliness and his view of freedom. Freedom has always been prized by Americans. But the careerist defines it to mean the right to pursue his personal destiny exclusive of all outside authorities and values. This means the right to be left alone by others. Or conversely, the right to walk away. In practice, this freedom to be left alone results in being left alone.[32]

In short, the secular view of work is an inevitably self-defeating approach toward life. It demands that the person accomplish feats that, according to Christian theology, only God can do. This brings us to a second flaw in the secular position.

2. The secular view of work tends to make an idol of career.
You may think of an idol as a little figure of stone or wood that some faraway pagan bows down to. But anthropologists define an idol as anything that is sacred such that it defines our self-worth, becomes the controlling center of our life, and is the last in a series of priorities to go.[33]

By this definition, work has become an idol for many in our culture. How about you? Does your work define who you are? Pamela Pettler has written a brilliantly funny little book called *The Joy of Stress*. See if you can find yourself in this section entitled "They're Getting Ahead of You":

A True Story
One day in late 1969, in the research library of the University of California at Berkeley, a young man went berserk. He ran through the library, shouting hysterically at his astonished fellow students, "Stop! Stop! You're getting ahead of me!"

He was arrested. But what was his crime, really? *Being in the wrong decade.* As we all know, the sixties era, and its childish preoccupation with peace, good sex, and battered VW buses, was little more than a black mark, a shameful demerit in the History of Stress.

Now, of course, in the stress-filled eighties, this concept of "getting ahead of me" has regained its rightful place of importance. In fact, it is one of the basic precepts of stress.

Simply stated, *people are getting ahead of you.* All the time.

While you're at your desk, people working out at the gym are getting ahead of you.

While you're at the gym, your co-workers are getting ahead of you.

If a friend gets a promotion at work, she has gotten ahead of you.

If a colleague reads a book you haven't read, he has gotten ahead of you.

The entire U.S. swim team has gotten ahead of you.

While you're reading this book, *everyone* is getting ahead of you.

The beauty of this concept is that it can be applied across the board, anywhere, anytime.

On the road? Drivers of more expensive cars have gotten ahead of you.

Watching TV? All the writers, actors, and technical crews have gotten ahead of you.

At Marine World? The *dolphins* have gotten ahead of you.

Always judge yourself, and your intrinsic moral worth, in terms of specific achievements as compared to others.

Always judge any situation in relation to how much the people involved have gotten ahead of you, and in what ways.[34]

The work world bristles with comparisons! And you and your intrinsic moral worth are constantly measured by your accomplishments in relation to those of your coworkers. As the authors of *Habits of The Heart* put it, "However we define work, it is very close to our sense of self. What we 'do' often translates to what we 'are.'"[35]

If your work controls your identity, it probably controls everything else in your life. A 1981 *Psychology Today* study on "Money and Self-Esteem" discovered that one's career is probably the most important influence on one's perception of "quality of life." It means more than having a good social life, parenting, money, or having fun. In fact, this study found it to mean twice as much as religion in its influence on life.[36]

And why not? For where we work determines where we live, who our friends will be, and how we'll spend our time. Work has therefore become a priority for most of us, and the number-one priority for many of us. In fact, I recently read an article suggesting that career has replaced sex as the main interest for people in our society.[37]

As we saw earlier, many workers today are sacrificing themselves on the altar of work. They tolerate immensely harmful symptoms such as anger, chemical dependencies, and loneliness in a blind pursuit of self-fulfillment through career success. This may be pathological—but it is also idolatrous! Such a person *worships* his career as though it were a god.

But like all idols, work is impotent in the face of true human need. As Psalm 115:4-7 puts it:

Their idols are silver and gold, the work of man's hands. They have mouths, but they cannot speak; they have eyes, but they cannot see; they have ears, but they cannot hear; they have noses, but they cannot smell; they have hands, but they cannot feel; they have feet, but they cannot walk; they cannot make a sound with their throat.

In other words, idols are powerless. And work as an idol is just as powerless. Worst of all, those who worship work as an idol are defenseless in the face of true need. In the psalmist's words, "Those who make them will become like them, everyone who trusts in them" (Psalm 115:8).

I have seen this happen. I have sat with grown men, exceptionally powerful men in business, and watched them weep as they told me their tragic stories, some with personal lives shattered, others with families in shambles, perhaps their character debased or their business in doubt or their circumstances out of control. None of their professional accomplishments, none of the machinery of their companies, none of their wealth is of the slightest help. They are in deep trouble and their god is impotent.

I grieve with such men and women. They have chosen the wrong god. Of course, I also respect the fact that the same thing could happen to me as to anyone. It happens when we take God's gift of work and begin to worship and serve it rather than Christ. This brings us to a final flaw in the secular view of work.

3. The secular view of work leaves God out of its system.

This is really the flip side of what I just described. You may be able to avoid turning your job into a idol. But nothing is gained by that if you still leave God at home. Either way, a major category of your life is being lived apart from Him, and that is unacceptable if you intend to be a Christ-follower.

Of course, you may just assume that God takes no interest in what you do all day. Consequently, you never think about relating your work to Him. If so, you'll be interested to find that just the opposite is the case. Your work matters to God, and because it does, it is of critical importance that you not leave Him out of it. I will expand on this idea in Part II, and that material will serve as a further response to the secular view of work.

CONCLUSION

Before leaving this discussion, though, I want to stress again that you don't have to be a nonChristian to have a very secular attitude toward work. In fact, I find that a majority of Christians I know have bought into many of the values of our secular culture. I hope that in pointing out some of these values and their deficiencies, I will challenge you to examine your own posture toward your career. As we're going to see, God has so much more for us than working merely for our own agendas.

However, the secular view is not the only one that separates work and God. Some of the most deeply religious Christians have adopted an alternative that I call the Two-Story view, which I'll discuss in the next chapter.

NOTES: 1. Daniel Yankelovich, *New Rules* (Toronto: Bantam Books, 1982), page xix.
    2. Yankelovich, *New Rules*, pages 50-51.
    3. Studs Terkel, *Working*, page xi.
    4. Napoleon Hill, *Think & Grow Rich* (New York: Fawcett Crest, 1937), page 37.
    5. Denis Waitley, *Seeds of Greatness*, (Old Tappan, N.J.: Fleming H. Revell, 1983), page 199.
    6. Waitley, *Seeds of Greatness*, page 71.
    7. Douglas LaBier, *Modern Madness* (Reading, Mass.: Addison-Wesley Publishing Company, Inc., 1986), page 25.
    8. Bellah et al., *Habits of the Heart*, page 22.
    9. Often at the expense of others' similar agendas. See Christopher Lasch, *The Culture of Narcissism* (New York: Warner Books, 1979), pages 119f.
   10. LaBier, *Modern Madness*, pages 25-26.
   11. LaBier, *Modern Madness*, page 27.
   12. Yankelovich, *New Rules*, page 53.
   13. Lasch, *The Culture of Narcissism*, pages 116-120.
   14. Og Mandino, *Og Mandino's University of Success* (Toronto: Bantam Books, 1982), page 10.
   15. Mandino, *University of Success*, page 11. Whitman cites Faulkner, Schweitzer, Gandhi, and Thoreau as his examples of successful individuals with a "mature philosophy." One wonders how books like Mandino's and those of similar writers (Napoleon Hill, Clement Stone, Denis Waitley, Michael Korda) produce or promote anything remotely approaching the philosophical maturity of such men. The contrast between the values and practices of these two groups couldn't be more extreme. For instance, Whitman (mis)quotes Thoreau's proverb that "a man is rich in the proportions of things he can let alone." This is like finding the phrase, "Jesus loves the little children, all the children of the world," in *Mein Kampf*. Whitman is quick to recognize this inconsistency, so he qualifies his statement with an understatement, "This is not to say that poverty should be the goal . . . ." I should say not!
   16. *Time* (May 25, 1987), pages 14-29.
   17. Malcolm Forbes, "Fact and Comment," *Forbes* (July 13, 1987), page 33.
   18. Lasch, *The Culture of Narcissism*, pages 129f.
   19. Bellah et al., *Habits of the Heart*, page 6.
   20. Yankelovich, *New Rules*, page 8.
   21. Yankelovich, *New Rules*, page 56.
   22. LaBier, *Modern Madness*, page 27.
   23. Luke 9:23-26.
   24. LaBier, *Modern Madness*, page 27.
   25. LaBier, *Modern Madness*, page 28.
   26. LaBier, *Modern Madness*, pages 28-29.
   27. LaBier, *Modern Madness*, page 30.
   28. LaBier, *Modern Madness*, page 31.
   29. LaBier, *Modern Madness*, pages 31-32.
   30. LaBier, *Modern Madness*, page 35.
   31. LaBier, *Modern Madness*, page 35.
   32. Bellah et al., *Habits of the Heart*, page 23.
   33. J.A. Walter, *Sacred Cows* (Grand Rapids, Mich.: Zondervan Publishing House, 1979).
   34. Pamela Pettler, *The Joy of Stress* (New York: Quill, 1984), pages 22-25; permission to quote from Pamela Pettler and William Morrow & Company, Inc./Publishers.
   35. Bellah et al., *Habits of the Heart*, page 66.
   36. Carin Rubinstein, "Money and Self-Esteem," *Psychology Today* (May 1981), page 31.

37. The specific context was a *Wall Street Journal* item on the closing of the Playboy Club in New York City. The article quotes a writer, Barbara Ehrenreich, as saying, "People today are more interested in their cars and their careers than they are in sex." The article continues, "In an era of aggressive careerism—by both sexes—the company no longer gets much mileage out of the so-called Playboy philosophy." See *Wall Street Journal* (September 12, 1985), page 1.

CHAPTER 3

YE CANNOT SERVE GOD AND MAMMON
The Two-Story View of Work

I n the last chapter we looked at a view of life that exalts work and dismisses faith. Now I want to examine a view that disparages work as the enemy of faith. As we'll see, this view sounds very noble and spiritual. Yet it rests on some very unbiblical premises. And it produces some very unbiblical results. Let's begin by describing what I call a Two-Story view of work.

THE MISSIONARY'S TESTIMONY

Perhaps the easiest way to come to terms with this view would be to illustrate it. Maybe you've heard testimonials similar to the one paraphrased below:

> Thank you for the opportunity to speak on the issue of missions, and why I think every committed Christian should be involved in full-time service to God.
>
> Let me share with you a little bit of my background. Prior to attending seminary, I was a businessman involved in the sale of drill presses. These drill presses were used in some of the more sophisti-cated machine shops.
>
> During the early years of business, I realized it took a lot of time to get the business going, and that limited my involvement in church. But as time went on, I found more and more of an interest in serving God. As I became more heavily involved, I began to reflect on my life and what I was doing in my day-to-day work. I became gripped by the fact that my whole life was given to a business that puts holes in metal—holes that are later filled up with screws!

The Things That Last

While I was thinking about this, I began to think of the things that last for eternity. This was prompted by a sermon my pastor gave one day on the two things that last for eternity—the Word of God and the souls of men.

As I pondered the significance of these things, I began to think about how meaningless my life was, given to making holes in metal which will someday be filled up with screws. Not only did this occupation seem meaningless, but the thought dawned on me that someday the whole earth will be destroyed, as it says in 2 Peter, and all the elements of the earth will melt—if it doesn't rust before then! The utter futility of my life as a businessman led me to start considering the ministry. I wanted to invest my life in things that will really last.

As I thought of this, I began to think about some of the frustrations I felt as a "part-time" servant of God. I was only able to attend church and be involved in the program on Wednesday nights, Sunday mornings, and Sunday nights. I realized that I was not only part-time, but I was also serving God only in my tired hours. And I felt He was worthy of something much more.

A Career Change

This led me to a very important decision concerning my career. Was I going to have a life given principally to something as futile as putting holes in metal, or to something that would really count? I began to consider what business is all about, and I realized that my whole motive for being in business was self-centered. I was principally in it to provide an income for myself and all the comforts I and my family wanted. Ultimately, I realized that my orientation was one of greed. I was just in it for myself.

Furthermore, I saw that I lived in a business culture dominated by self-centered and greedy thinking. And I knew that I could not continue to be around it without picking up the same values that that culture had. Self-centered values oppose every line of the Bible. I knew I wanted to be different and to live a different lifestyle.

Well, as if these things had not been enough to convince me, the final thing that struck me was a challenge I heard from a prominent Christian leader. He told me that as a minister of the gospel, I had the highest calling on the face of the earth!

As I thought about this, I could see why he would say that. Without question, the program of God in the world today is to save sinners and to sanctify saints. Drilling holes in metal is far removed from that work. In fact, if I wanted to be on the front line as a participant in God's work, and not just a spectator, I needed to give my life work to the things that really count.

Because of these reasons, I chose to go into full-time work for God.

A Challenge

Today I would challenge you to do the same. Sometimes I think that the ministry is one of the ways God has of filtering out uncommitted people. It's like Jesus told the rich, young ruler: "Sell all and follow Me." I realize that some must stay behind and make enough money to support the full-time people. And I'm grateful for them. But the fact remains, full-time servants are on the cutting edge of God's work!

Well, what about you? *You* don't have to be addicted to mediocrity! *You* don't have to live a half-hearted commitment to Christ! Jesus said in John 6:27, "Do not work for the food which perishes, but for the food which endures to eternal life." This is our Savior's exhortation to make our lives count! In light of this admonition, I challenge you to surrender yourself to a full-time life of service and ministry.

To be sure, this man's testimony paints an extreme. Obviously not all missionaries or ministers feel this way; far from it. But he is not a straw man, either. Bill and I have both heard pitches like this many times. Perhaps you have, too. Sadly, he displays a view of work that is all too common among many Christians, even if not articulated in quite this way. He holds a "two-story" view of life and work. Let's examine this view.

SUMMARY

Like this missionary, many people believe that the only part of life that "really counts" to God is the part committed to religious activities like Bible reading, prayer, church activity, and the like. Day-to-day work itself has no *intrinsic* value.

By no intrinsic value I mean no inherent worth, nothing about it that recommends it as a worthwhile or noble human activity. It contributes nothing to the work God is doing, which is, of course, the only important work. If it has any "value" at all, it is only to meet survival needs. And of course those were needs caused by man's fall (Genesis 3), so that work is an unfortunate consequence of sin, and takes place among sinners in a sinful world. Indeed, work is like a punishment in that it has no more value than the "work" of prison inmates, who do certain jobs within the prison but contribute nothing significant to the larger society.

Given this perspective, work is actually a self-oriented activity. At best, a person works merely to preserve his own life and that of his family. At its worst, sinful people, consumed by covetousness and desire, use work and its profits to heap up luxuries and pleasures in a frenzy of greed.

Work is thus considered "secular." It has no concern with God. In many ways, it even becomes an enemy to what God really wants done in the world. It takes away from worship, prayer, church activity, evangelism, and family life, which are "sacred" categories. In short, work is something to finish and get out of. There is no inherent dignity to it.

Of course, few people would articulate this attitude in such a hard-boiled manner. But I submit that, in the right context, many of us would find ourselves in basic agreement with these statements—especially if they were isolated and hidden in a sermon, a book, a devotional guide, or some other religious format.

Of course, you may subscribe to these beliefs yourself. Or, even if you would not wholly agree with them, you may generally accept them as representing the way things are. Or you may be like many laypeople I meet who, upon hearing statements like the above, sense that something is wrong, but cannot quite put their finger on it—especially when the person making the statements is like the missionary, in that he backs up his claims with impressive Scripture passages.

In short, this view sounds so biblical, so spiritual. But is it? Does it adequately represent God's mind on the issue of work? I think not. Let me show why.

EVALUATION

The problem with this view is not that it fails to consult Scripture, but that it reads Scripture through a pair of glasses that distort its message. In other words, this view brings a number of unwarranted assumptions to the text— and to life.

Let me mention four of these assumptions: (1) God is more interested in the soul than in the body; (2) the things of eternity are more important than the things of time; (3) life divides into two categories, the sacred and the secular; and (4) because of the nature of their work, ministers and other clergy are more important to God's program than the laity.

Before we examine these assumptions, notice that each of them is a "two-story" view. By two-story, I mean a system that sets up a dichotomy or hierarchy among things. Things are separated into two categories, one of which is inherently superior.

So in the four cases just mentioned: the soul is superior over the body; the eternal over the temporal; the sacred over the secular; and the clergy over the laity. Overall, the Two-Story view of work distinguishes between work that matters to God (work that deals with the soul, with the eternal and sacred things, essentially the work of "ministry") and work that has little if any value to God (secular, everyday work).

Let me address each of these two-story hierarchies. I want to show that they are assumptions not warranted by Scripture. This will set the stage for Part II, where I'll present a very different view of work, a view I believe is more faithful to the Bible's meaning. It is important, though, to recognize the flaws in this two-story view of life. Otherwise, we'll keep reading the Bible through glasses that distort its truth.[1]

1. The Soul-Body Hierarchy

The two-story view assumes that God is far more interested in the soul than in the body. I can understand why. Relating to God, after all, is largely an unseen thing that takes place in our "inner person." Consequently, we tend to promote inner activities that nurture that relationship—"soul-activities," such as prayer, meditation, Bible reading, and the like.

But how does our body fit into our relationship with God? I am hard-pressed to find anyone addressing that question. In fact, I suspect that many Christians would regard such a question as meaningless or irrelevant. For the majority assume, like the missionary, that God's primary interest is in man's soul. It is this inner life, they feel, that connects us to God and that we must cultivate.

Implications for career. In short, our teaching generally exalts the soul and neglects the body. As a consequence, I find that we subtly rate careers by the extent to which they contribute to the soul. Careers in ministry come first, because they supposedly give themselves to "the souls of men and the Word of God."

Then come careers in the "helping professions"—counselors in psychology and psychiatry, doctors (especially general practitioners of the Marcus Welby stripe), teachers, nurses, social workers, perhaps mothers. These are not involved as exclusively as ministers in "soul-work," but they certainly cultivate the inner life more than the third group.

The third group are the laborers and also the people whose primary goal (supposedly) is money. The farmer, the truck driver, the assembly-line worker, the repairman—these people deal with physical things and "work with their hands" (a description that presumes that they leave their minds at home, I guess). The money people are those bankers, stockbrokers, real estate developers, and entrepreneurs who traffic in all that green stuff—and we know how evil that can be![2] In short, we exalt work for the soul. Work for the body has little if any intrinsic value.

What is man? But this is a seriously flawed way of looking at things. In particular, it is an extremely sub-biblical view of the nature of man. It assumes that man is somehow made up of parts, a "soul" and a "body." But this is not how Scripture portrays man:

> Then the LORD God formed man of dust from the ground, and breathed into his nostrils the breath of life; and man became a living being. (Genesis 2:7)

This passage teaches us that God created man as a *unit*. Man is not two parts (a soul and a body), or three parts (spirit, soul, and body) or even one-and-a-half parts (a soul imprisoned in a body). Man is not a soul that inhabits a body, nor a body animated by a soul. He is a *soul-body unity*.

In other words, God does not deal with you just as a soul. When He created you, He created all of you, as a soul and as a body—as an entire being. In fact, throughout Scripture, words such as "body," "soul," "spirit," "flesh," and "heart" are used (and used interchangeably) to describe the diversity of the human being. But such terms never lose sight of the unity of the whole person.[3]

So, to offer just one illustration, Paul urges us "to present [our] bodies a living and holy sacrifice" to God.[4] What does he mean? The most reasonable explanation is that we are to surrender all that we are to God's will. Doubtless Paul uses the term "body" in this context because of his metaphor of a sacrifice. One sacrifices bodies on an altar. But he obviously has the entire person in mind here.

Consequently, there can be no hierarchy of the soul over the body. Whatever contributes to the soul contributes to the person, and whatever contributes to the body contributes to the person. Whatever contributes to a person contributes to the person as a whole.

So if you work as a physical therapist, a coach, a barber, a clothier, or in some other body-oriented occupation, you should take heart. Your work is not spiritually inferior because it concerns itself with the body. In fact, you may instinctively realize the intricate relationship between the "outer" and the "inner" person.

The psychiatrist does. He knows that physiochemical processes deeply influence behavior and moods. And yet he also realizes that in many treatments, drugs will have little impact on healing without the additional therapy of counseling.

As we will see in Part II, God desires to see the broad range of mankind's needs met, not just the spiritual. If God were only interested in soul-work, then He needn't have created a physical universe. He needn't have placed Adam and Eve in a garden "to cultivate it and keep it." He needn't have sent Christ in a human body. And He needn't bother to resurrect the body after death.

But God meets the needs not just of souls but of people. And as we'll see in Part II, your daily work, no matter what it is, can be used of God to serve people.

2. The Eternal-Temporal Hierarchy

Many Christians assume that the things that really matter are the things that pertain to eternity. In fact, they would say that what happens here and now has meaning and significance only in light of eternity.

Perhaps you've heard the familiar refrain: "There are only two things that last for eternity: the Word of God and the souls of men. Therefore, if you want your life to really count, then you need to give yourself to building the Word of God into men." Or as a popular hymn puts it:

Turn your eyes upon Jesus,
Look full in His wonderful face,
And the things of earth will grow strangely dim
In the light of His glory and grace.[5]

In light of eternity, this view asks, what ultimate value could there possibly be in working for "the food which perishes"? To give one's life to the manufacture of an automobile, or the advertising of toothpaste, or the buying and selling of real estate, is in essence to give oneself to a world that is passing away. By contrast, a life given to God's work has intrinsic value because it concerns itself with what ultimately matters.

What is real? This concept of eternity and its implications for work are fairly widespread among Christians today. Yet is eternity what "really counts" to God? Is it the ultimate reality? Scripture suggests otherwise. It distinguishes between a seen world and an unseen world, and calls the seen world "temporal" and the unseen world "eternal."[6] So there are apparently two aspects or two "sides" to reality.

But the Bible goes on to declare that *both* time and eternity are very real and very important to God. The natural universe is just as real as the supernatural universe. One is not "ultimate reality" while the other is "just reality." Both exist with absolute certainty, though of course each exists and operates according to its own set of laws and principles. This is evident from Genesis 1:1: "In the beginning God created the heavens and the earth."

Here we have the eternal and the temporal side by side. An eternal God exists and creates a time-space universe. The eternal God is real; the universe He creates is just as real. The universe is not a "shadow" of eternity. It is a completely real dimension called the time-and-space universe.

"Ultimate" reality. And yet there is a sense, of course, in which eternity is the *ultimate* reality, in that it will be our final destiny. In this sense ultimate means "the last in sequence" or "eventual." Because we start our existence in time and end up in eternity, eternity is our eventual or ultimate destiny.

On this basis, shouldn't eternity take priority over time? Knowing that eternity is our destiny, shouldn't that inform everything we do today? I think so. I think that is why God has gone to such extraordinary lengths to warn us: We must choose *now* whether that destiny will be with God or apart from Him.

That is why those of us who are Christians, those of us who know about this ultimate destiny and about what Christ did to make it possible to spend that destiny with God, ought to do everything we can to urge people to choose *now* to prepare for that destiny.

Careers and eternity. Does "doing everything we can" mean quitting our secular jobs and becoming evangelists? Some, like the missionary, would say it probably does. Others would say no, but use your job primarily as a platform for evangelism. I'll discuss the latter point of view in the next chapter.

As for the former, I think it is mistaken.[7] It automatically assumes, first of all, that holding down a secular job isn't "doing everything we can." But in fact it may be.

If God has created you with a certain design, say as an architect, and placed you in a given opportunity, perhaps in a city that needs buildings, then working as an architect to the glory of God comes far closer to "doing everything you can" than quitting your job to become an evangelist. Why? Because building buildings to the glory of God *now* is one of the principal means God has given you of telling everyone that your life looks ahead—and theirs should, too—toward an eternity, a destiny, with God.

I'll have more to say about this in Parts II and III. But this idea of our work itself as a means of pointing the way to God has largely been lost in our culture. We need to reclaim it. I don't think anyone would have preferred that Handel or Bach had quit writing music and become evangelists. Or that William Wilberforce had quit Parliament and become an evangelist. The work of men like these has surely been used mightily of God to point people's eyes toward eternity, even though it was not principally evangelistic.

Evangelism and daily life. But the view that we should all quit our secular jobs and become evangelists also assumes that doing evangelism is "doing everything we can." But in fact, doing evangelism, as crucial as that is, isn't doing everything we can do—or should do.

As any legitimate vocational evangelist knows, people are persuaded toward accepting the gospel not only by what we say, but by how we live our lives. So "doing everything we can" involves not only evangelism, but also a lifestyle consistent with our evangelism.

Yet in saying this, I don't want to just toss out a cliché. For that, I'm afraid, is what the idea of a distinctive Christian lifestyle as it relates to evangelism is becoming—a cliché. All the evidence suggests that despite unprecedented numbers of people converting to Christianity, the faith is having little impact on the lifestyle of its converts.

No doubt many factors account for this. Yet I wonder if one of them isn't the point under discussion: Don't we subtly communicate that evangelism is the most important thing in the Christian life? And doesn't that imply that salvation is the most important thing in the world? It's as if everything after that is icing on the cake. After all, whatever we don't get finished in this life we can always take care of in eternity, right? So if our lifestyle isn't all it could be, well, we'll leave that to eternity.[8]

In response, may I suggest that evangelism is only the most "important" in the sense that the first step of a long journey is the most "important," for it means getting started. But it is not the whole journey. In fact, it takes the traveler only one small step toward his destination.

And our destination, as believers, is Christlikeness. We are extremely foolish if we assume that Christlikeness is something we need not worry about until eternity. Indeed, God warns us that the choices we make *now*, and how we live *now*, may well determine how much we are like Christ once we are with Him.

As for evangelism and lifestyle, I would only add two thoughts that I'll develop later in Part III. First, I believe that the workplace is the most strategic arena for Christian thinking and influence today. And second, our greatest need in the workplace right now is for Christians whose lifestyle and workstyle are so unique and so distinctive that coworkers will want to know why.

To recap: I've said that the Scriptures portray a temporal reality and an eternal reality, which are both very real. As humans, we start out in time, but we end up in eternity. Therefore, what we do now and how we live now should be with a view toward that eternal destiny. This makes evangelism important, but not all-important in the sense of quitting our job to become an evangelist. Instead, each of us must seek to please God by whatever means He gives us, not only as a witness to others, but as a preparation of ourselves for an eternity with Christ.

What has value? There remains, however, the question of eternal value. The missionary said that he left his job selling drill presses because he wanted to give his life to what "really counts," to the things of eternity. He would view the work of the architect that I mentioned earlier as fairly insignificant. After all, he only designs buildings that will pass with time.

Why do the missionary and many like him look at life this way? Doubtless because as humans we tend to see a strong connection between *duration* and *value*. The longer something lasts, the more value it has, we feel. For this reason many Americans are driving Mercedeses, BMWs, and Toyotas rather than American-made cars. Their perception is that these foreign cars will return greater value over time than their domestic cousins.

But suppose the duration of something stretches to infinity; suppose it lasts forever. In that case we would say it has ultimate value, eternal value. The DeBeers family, in fact, uses this very idea in its famous slogan, "a diamond lasts forever." Eternal duration presumes eternal value.[9]

This connection between duration and value seems generally reasonable. But we get into trouble when we jump categories, as the missionary has, and impose the quality of "everlastingness" as a criterion of value for temporal things.

If we do that, then we have to say that God's work of creation has no value. Why? Because it won't last into eternity.[10] He has already pledged to destroy it someday, and to create a new heaven and earth in its place. Hence, if "only the things of eternity count," then God's work of creation doesn't "count." But that is absurd.

The missionary is on solid ground when he says that drill presses and the holes they drill have no eternal value. Obviously when the salesman dies and goes to be with the Lord, the drills won't really matter one way or the other.

But to say therefore that they have no value is nonsense, because they have all the value they need, given the category—time—for which they were created. Those drills may punch holes in airplane engine parts, and thus help produce transportation for people and goods. They may put holes in air conditioning equipment used by schools, hospitals, businesses, or churches. They may produce parts for satellites, for automobile engines, for ships, for microscopes, for farm equipment, for watches, for printing presses, for hydro-electric generators.

Those drill presses could have great value, given their function and their use *in time*. But it would be a category mistake to require them to last for eternity in order to have value. They would have to last for eternity to have eternal value, but not to have temporal value.

Remember what we said earlier about both sides of reality being very real. Things that exist in time are very real and can have very real value in time.

What "really counts"? This is all well and good, the missionary might respond. It's true that drill presses may have great value in time. But don't we want to give our lives to things that will have great value in eternity? If I lead some person to salvation in Christ, I'll be able to look on the fruit of my labor for the rest of eternity. But the architect who puts up a building must someday watch that building pass away. And in eternity he'll have little if anything to show for his earthly labor. Wouldn't he rather give his life to what really counts?

But I would reply that he actually is giving his life to what "really counts"—what counts both in eternity and in time. What will ultimately matter in eternity is our faithfulness right now with the resources and responsibilities God has given us.[11]

So the architect who designs buildings to the glory of God, who works with integrity, diligence, fairness, and excellence, who treats his wife with the love Christ has for the Church, who raises his children in godly wisdom and instruction, who urges nonChristian coworkers and associates to heed the gospel message—in short, who acts as a responsible manager in the various arenas God has entrusted to him—this man will receive eternal praise from God. That is what really matters in eternity.

In time, meanwhile, what "really matters" to God is that the various needs of His creation be met. One of those needs is the salvation of people, and for that He sent Christ to die and He sends the Church to tell the world about what Christ did.

But in addition to salvation—obviously a need with eternal implications— mankind has many other needs. Just because many of them are temporal needs does not diminish their importance to God, nor does it diminish the value of the work done to meet those needs. In fact, God thinks they are important enough to equip a variety of people with various abilities to meet those needs. Furthermore, in meeting the legitimate needs of people, a worker is serving people who obviously have eternal value. In other words, the product of the work may be temporal but those who benefit from the work are eternal.

So we find that whether or not the product of our labor lasts into eternity, our labor is full of eternal implications. No matter what our work is, God takes it seriously because He takes us seriously. In Part II I'll explain much more about how everyday, temporal work matters to God.

For now we need to realize that as humans we stand, as it were, with one foot in time and one foot in eternity. "God has made everything appropriate in its time," Ecclesiastes says, but "He has also set eternity in [people's] hearts."[12]

Bound as we are for an eternal destiny, we should live our lives now with a view toward that destiny.[13] That's why the Lord Jesus taught us to pray that the Father's will might be done *on earth* as well as in heaven. After all, why should God entrust eternal responsibilities to us if we have proven unfaithful in temporal ones?

3. The Sacred-Secular Hierarchy

This hierarchy builds from the idea that a deeper and higher reality exists beyond the time-space universe and that this higher realm is where God is. Through religion, we can enter this holy realm and enjoy communion with God. Thus we live in a tension between "secular" demands and desires (work, hobbies, politics, errands) and the higher, "sacred" categories of religion (prayer, worship, church activities, ministry).

However, in light of our critique of the eternal-temporal hierarchy, I hope you can immediately spot the flaw in this secular-sacred dichotomy. It lies in the premise of a deeper and higher reality.

All of life relates to God. It is true that there are two "sides" to reality: a seen world we call the time-space universe, and an unseen world we call eternity. But as we said earlier, the seen, temporal world is just as real as the unseen, eternal one. There is no "ultimate reality" or "higher realm" that lies beyond the universe.

Consequently, there is no distinction between the secular and the sacred. At any moment, no matter what we are doing, we are relating to God either properly or improperly. Thus we need to distinguish, not between secular and sacred, but between sin and righteousness.

In other words, you can go to church and pray (a "sacred" category) and yet still be in sin. You may recite a creed or partake of the elements yet retain hateful thoughts toward someone who has wronged you. Or sit there and dream about your ambitions, and how fulfilling them will give you esteem, power, or money. Or skip on the offering because some church leader has said something that offended you.

On the other hand, you can go to work in an office where the atmosphere is very "secular"—the conversation is littered with profanity, the jokes are off-color, the work is often slipshod, the politics are wearisome. And yet, like Daniel or Joseph in the Old Testament, you can keep your own conversation pure and your behavior above reproach. You can do your work with integrity, even if others do not. You can honor and obey God in a very worldly environment.

In short, God's interest is not simply that we do holy activities but that we become holy people. Not pious. Not sanctimonious. Not other-worldly. But pure, healthy, Christlike.

What is "sacred work"? This has profound implications for you if you are employed in "secular" work. As I'll discuss at length in Part II, your work, assuming it is legitimate, is an extension of God's work. But that raises your occupation to a "sacred" responsibility!

We usually think of "sacred" work as belonging to the pastor or the missionary. But that is a two-story distinction. By contrast, Scripture shows that God's work, while it includes the work of these ministers, goes far beyond it, far beyond this "sacred" activity.

God's work is at least as broad as creation. Using people (both believers and unbelievers), He works to maintain and order that creation. Hence, an engineer who designs a bridge or a sewage treatment plant actually accomplishes God's work of providing for humanity's needs. He does so whether or not he acknowledges it. Likewise, God uses human governments to work out justice and civil order.

So here we have "sacred" work—sacred because it is God at work—being accomplished through everyday people in their daily occupations.

Of course, I should point out that as a Christ-follower, you have an even greater responsibility to approach your work as a God-honoring task. Ephesians 6 teaches that Christ is your ultimate Boss. And you will answer to Him for the work you do.

In short, Christ Himself has done away with the sacred-secular dichotomy. He is Lord of all, and He desires that we live all of life in a way that honors and pleases Him.[14]

4. The Clergy-Laity Hierarchy

To a large extent, this hierarchy is simply the expression of a two-story view of life in terms of human careers. It is the minister, according to this view, who has a "higher calling." He is the person who, in a vocational way, keeps us in touch with God. His work is principally "soul work." He deals with eternal matters, and does so in a sacred context.

But of course if you disallow the foundational two-story hierarchies, as I do, then you also dismantle the hierarchical view of the clergy. One of the grave errors, I believe, in the two-story view of clergy-laity is that it rests on dubious assumptions.

And yet for nearly 2000 years, the Church for the most part has operated with a belief that clergy have some sort of "higher calling." Even since the Reformation, most Protestant laypeople regard their pastors and other clergy as having a special status, a unique prestige and position in the cause of Christ. The assumption is that somehow God regards them and their work differently from everyone else.

A deafening silence. Nothing I say will do much to change this situation. But I do not find any notion of a "higher calling" in the New Testament. I realize that this is an argument from silence. But one would expect that if God invariably extends a unique, special, higher call to those in "full-time" ministry; if pastors, evangelists, and missionaries enjoy a special status in the Church; if those who officiate at worship services are like priests in an Old Testament sense—all of which are two-story assumptions—one would expect the New Testament to clearly say so.

But it does not! This silence is especially deafening[15] given the elaborate and detailed specifications spelled out for the Old Testament religious system. But in the New Testament, such specifics are lacking. Instead, we read only general principles, many of which are descriptive rather than prescriptive.[16]

There are definitely positions of leadership mentioned in the New Testament Church. But there is a marked emphasis away from regarding such leaders as a hierarchy over other Christians.[17]

New clergy. In light of this, we might ask: What exactly is the clergy's function? And what is the laity's? Let me answer the second question first. The laity's task, according to the New Testament, is to do God's work. The passage most quoted in this regard is Ephesians 4:11-12:

> He gave some as apostles, and some as prophets, and some as evange-lists, and some as pastors and teachers, for the equipping of the saints for the work of service, to the building up of the body of Christ.

"Saints" here refers to *all* believers. To them belongs "the work of service." In other words, God's work belongs to you as a layperson.

Now when I say "God's work," I don't mean just church work or religious work or work that the clergy could do. The work of service, God's work, goes considerably beyond these categories, even though we tend to limit it to them.[18]

But if you are a sales representative in computer software, then your job and how you do it is tied up with God's work. If you are a naval officer on a ship, your command and how you perform it is tied up with God's work. If you are a career homemaker, your work in the home with your husband and children and how you do it is tied up with God's work.

I'll discuss this considerably more in Parts II and III. But for now, consider 1 Peter 2:9-10:

> You are a chosen race, a royal priesthood, a holy nation, a people for God's own possession, that you may proclaim the excellencies of Him who has called you out of darkness into His marvelous light; for you once were not a people, but now you are the people of God; you had not received mercy, but now you have received mercy.

This describes you and me as Christ-followers. Peter calls us a royal priesthood.[19] A priest is a person authorized to stand between God and people. He performs sacred duties, the holy work, and in many ways stands for God. But Peter says we are all priests, we are all "clergy."

Where then do we function as priests? Peter says we do it out in society "among the Gentiles" (1 Peter 2:12); in human institutions (2:13); in employer-employee relationships (2:18f); in marriages (3:1f.); and so forth. These are the arenas in which people, both Christians and nonChristians, need a priest, someone to stand between them and God as an agent of reconciliation and hope.

The point is, we need laypeople to do the work of God wherever the work of God needs doing. Some of it undoubtedly needs doing at church. But in this book I want to emphasize that so much of it needs doing in the workplace.

We need a "new clergy"[20] in the workplace to function as God's agents, to accomplish His work. That is why your career matters so much to God.

For centuries the Church has subscribed to Peter's idea of a universal priesthood, but in my view she has kept the priests locked up in the Church. She has communicated that laypeople function as priests primarily within a local church setting, doing church work.

This works well enough when the Church as an institution has cultural and political influence in a society. But in our culture, as in much of Europe, the Church is having a diminishing impact. She is becoming irrelevant in the face of overwhelming human need.

I believe the answer lies in unleashing the laity to accomplish God's work wherever it needs doing. This is what Elton Trueblood had in mind when he said that while the first Reformation gave the Word of God back to the people of God, today we need a second Reformation to give the work of God back to the people of God.[21]

Producing new clergy. What, then, is the task of the "professional" clergy? To produce and equip new clergy. That is the emphasis of the Ephesians 4 passage just quoted. If laypeople are to do God's work, ministers are to equip them, prepare them, support them, and in every way aid them in that work.

For this, the clergy should receive the honor and respect appropriate in light of their service. And obviously their position requires that they be given the necessary authority and remuneration to execute their tasks.[22]

I'll discuss this more in Chapter 14. But if you are a member of the clergy, your greatest challenge today may be to equip the laity, the new clergy, for the work God has for them. And if you are a layperson, your greatest challenge may be to redefine your life and your commitments as a priest of God, as a member of the new clergy, God's agent performing God's work wherever it needs doing.

LIFE IN A TWO-STORY WORLD

It remains for us to ask what practical difference the Two-Story view makes for work and workers. I'll mention four tragic results; there are certainly many more. The point, though, is that this view rests on premises that are just as sub-biblical as those of the secular view. Not surprisingly, it creates or at least provides a climate for a number of serious problems.

1. Guilt and a diminished sense of dignity.

The first problem is guilt. Earlier I mentioned a man who had labored for thirty-five years under guilt for not having gone into missions. Why guilt? Because he had been told that God is interested in the souls of men, but this fellow worked with his hands. He had been told that only the things of eternity will last, yet his job was to secure temporal possessions. He had been told that missionaries have the highest calling in God's program, but he had never felt "called" or qualified to be a missionary. Result: a belief that God disapproved of his life and work. In other words, guilt.

Coupled with guilt is the terrible violence the Two-Story assumptions do to the dignity the Bible assigns to everyday work and to the worker. They render "secular" jobs meaningless. If you run an advertising agency, develop real estate, manufacture aluminum siding, type correspondence, pump gas, whatever—these jobs supposedly concern themselves only with temporal affairs. According to this view, they have no ultimate, lasting value. Certainly not before God.

But that means that sixty percent of your life is meaningless, that it doesn't matter to God. Yet if that is so, then you don't matter to God. To do something that matters, you must disengage from your work to participate in the things that "count"—ministry to people, Bible reading, prayer, church.

But of course you can only do these things part-time (unless you quit your job and go into "full-time" Christian work). So you are really just a part-time Christian, "just a layperson," just a second-class citizen in the Kingdom of God.

But what motivation does this view give you as a worker to return to your job on Monday? Your work won't last. It is insignificant in God's sight. So why pour energy and emotion into it? Why pursue excellence or try to achieve great things or seek increased profits? These are the cares of the world! And what an evil world it is!

This brings us to a second practical implication of the Two-Story view.

2. Withdrawal from the work world.

Having divided life and the world into "sacred" and "secular" categories, the Two-Story adherent tends to withdraw from anything he regards as "secular." Some, like the missionary quoted earlier, pursue the ministry on this basis.[23]

I recall a friend in the ministry telling me that he had to reprimand one of his employees for not completing some work on time. "You'd never get away with this kind of thing in a secular job," my friend told the person, to which he replied, "Hey, why do you think I went to work for a ministry?"

Other Christians abandon the culture to set up their own counter-culture of Christian schools, Christian clinics, Christian garages, Christian beauty salons, Christian fitness centers, Christian theme parks—complete with a Christian Yellow Pages.

This was foreseeable. Two-Storied views always give rise to a retreat from the culture by the spiritually fastidious. And while other factors are certainly at play here, at least some of these refugees are the modern counterpart to the first-century ascetics.

3. Moral compromise.

Faced with a sacred-secular dichotomy, not everyone opts for the sacred. As we saw in the last chapter, many Christians adopt a very secular outlook on life. This often includes ethical compromise. And why not? The Two-Story assumptions are impotent to inspire moral excellence. If I tell you that your daily work has no value to God, then I'm giving you no reason to honor Him in your work. Result: You might as well do as you please. And that is precisely what has happened. According to the Gallup survey mentioned in Chapter 1, churchgoers display an appalling lack of ethical distinction on the job.

4. Skepticism about the relevance of Christianity.

In the last chapter I mentioned the skepticism with which so many people view religion. They feel that it can't stand the rigors of the street. The Two-Story view does nothing to convince them otherwise. By dismissing work as something that doesn't matter to God, it disqualifies itself as having anything meaningful to say about work. In other words, it renders itself irrelevant to the discussion. As a result, workers start looking elsewhere to find meaning between Sundays.

Some find all the dignity they need at work. And why not? Studies like *In Search of Excellence* show that many businesses today recognize and respond to the fact that a job means everything to the employee—status, worth, income, esteem, relationships. Perceptive management at these excellent companies operates from no Two-Story fallacies. Clear instructions, unequivocal praise, well-timed, restrained correction, and other strategies tell the employees: You matter. You're needed. We trust you. You're okay. With good news like that, who needs religion?

Others look no further than the pop-psychology columns of the newspaper for a message that speaks their language. How to find a job. How to keep a job. How to negotiate a raise. How to plan for retirement. Dress for success. Affairs at work. Your management style. Coworkers who smoke. Daycare and guilt. Discovering your stress level. And so forth.

Much of this literature is harmless filler, flawed by clichés and pumped up with hopelessly idealistic advice. Some, however, is much more dangerous, promoting anti-biblical and/or unhealthy approaches to life's problems. But regardless of the quality of the analyses, one thing is certain: The average person pays far more attention to these articles than to most sermons, certainly more than to sermons that presuppose a Two-Story view of life. Why? Because these columns address the issues of the street.

CONCLUSION

Despite its religiosity, the Two-Story view of work and life is wholly inadequate. It rests on sub-biblical assumptions and produces sub-biblical results. It debilitates the Christian worker. But worst of all, it silences God's voice at the very time and place where our culture most needs to hear Him:

> Christianity has the answer—if it only cares, or dares, to listen—the answer to the problems of our age. But why does it keep silent? Or why does it just say to people who are increasingly estranged from biblical language and thought patterns, "have faith, have faith," without really answering the chilling questions being cried out in agony. Jesus saves: indeed, but that means not only saving your soul out of the shipwreck of this world! His saving grace redeems us here and now,

and gives answers to the problems of today. He is able to redeem us, really and truly, not just "spiritually" in a narrow sense.[24]

Does Jesus redeem our work, really and truly? In Part II I will argue that He certainly does. But first we need to look at one more view of work that many Christians hold. In some ways it is a subset of the Two-Story view. However, it says that work has at least some value as a platform for evangelism.

NOTES: 1. Though I will not develop it here, this discussion is based on the thesis that a Two-Story view of life has been with the Church since its earliest days. The apostles did not subscribe to such assumptions. But their successors borrowed heavily from Greek philosophy, which is very dualistic. These Greek ideas, clothed in biblical language, have, for the most part, been passed down unchallenged to succeeding generations of Christians. As a result, most of us today bring assumptions to the biblical text, assumptions based on a worldview articulated by Plato, Aristotle, Plotinus, and other Greek thinkers.

"Well, that doesn't apply to me," you may respond. "I've never read Greek philosophy. Or even if I did read it, I never really bought into it." No matter. If you were born and raised in Western Civilization, you have been deeply influenced by ideas that trace back to the Greeks, if not for their origin, at least for their articulation. Our beliefs about education and scholarship, government and politics, law and justice, and even leisure and sports all contain ideas rooted in Greek thought.

Likewise, if you have been around much Christian teaching, you've undoubtedly been influenced by at least some Greek ideas. Nothing overtly or purely pagan. But I suggest that Christianity in our culture has absorbed from its tradition a number of subtle beliefs that trace back to Greek philosophy.

Now I am not "down" on philosophy. Nor am I "down" on the Greek philosophers, for they have provided us with many insights into philosophical questions. Nevertheless, reading the Bible through their eyes—through Greek glasses—can severely distort the truth of God's Word. We will think that the Bible says things it does not say, and overlook important things it does say.

The result will be a distorted view of life. And also a distorted view of work. Wearing Greek glasses, one would tend to ignore or disparage everyday work. That is how work looks when viewed through these lenses.

See, for example, William G. T. Shedd, *A History of Christian Doctrine* (Minneapolis, Minn.: Klock and Klock Christian Publishers, 1978 reprint), I, pages 51-74; or Colin Brown, *Philosophy and the Christian Faith* (Downers Grove, Ill.: InterVarsity Press, 1968), pages 13-17.

2. By the way, the athlete fits into this category because he makes so much, and because he is a part of the entertainment industry. Of course, if he even hints at being religious, we're likely to promote him to the first category!

3. See G. C. Berkouwer, *Man: The Image of God* (Grand Rapids, Mich.: Eerdman's Publishing Company, 1960), page 200; George Eldon Ladd, *A Theology of the New Testament* (Grand Rapids, Mich.: Eerdmans Publishing Company, 1974), pages 457f; and Hans Walter Wolff, *Anthropology of the Old Testament* (Philadelphia: Fortress Press, 1981).

4. Romans 12:1.

5. Chorus to "O Soul, Are You Weary and Troubled?" by Helen H. Lemmel, 1922.

6. See 2 Corinthians 4:18.

7. Just as the view that says evangelists have the most important work is mistaken.

8. I am not pummeling a straw man here, no less a figure than Charles Haddon Spurgeon proclaimed: "Your one business in life is to lead men to believe in Jesus Christ by the power of the Holy Spirit, and every other thing should be made subservient to this one object; if you can but get them saved, everything else will come right in due time." "Soul-Saving Our One Business" in *The Soul Winner: How to Lead Sinners to the Savior* (Grand Rapids, Mich.: Eerdmans Publishing Company, 1963), page 269.

Frankly, I'm not sure that Spurgeon (or preachers and teachers who proclaim a similar message) intended his comments to sound as extreme as they do. In the heat of the moment, a speaker may make such a statement, but later upon reflection realize that it deserves qualification.

9. I'm not saying this is automatically so—just that this is human perception.
10. Mark 13:31, 2 Peter 3:11-13, Revelation 21:1.
11. Matthew 25:14-30, Luke 16:10-13, 1 Corinthians 4:1-5.
12. Ecclesiastes 3:11.
13. This is the point of 2 Corinthians 5:9-10, which warns us that temporal work has eternal consequences. The same could be argued from Ephesians 6:8.
14. The key passages for this idea are 1 Corinthians 10:31 and Colossians 3:27.
15. Or, if you prefer, this vagueness is especially puzzling.
16. For more on this, see Robert John Hendricks, "The Pragmatic Implications of Dispensational Theology for Ecclesiology," Th.M. Thesis, Dallas Theological Seminary, 1982.
17. See, for instance, Matthew 23:1-12; 1 Corinthians 3:5-9; 4:1; 12:18,25; 2 Corinthians 4:7; Galatians 2:6.
18. And have done so for at least most of this century, according to Dr. Howard Grimes. See his intriguing review of the layperson's role in the United States in Stephen Charles Neill and Hans-Rudi Weber, ed., *The Layman in Christian History* (Philadelphia: The Westminster Press, 1963).
19. See Exodus 19:5-6.
20. I am indebted to Lynn Anderson, a Church of Christ pastor in Abilene, Texas, for this term.
21. See Elton Trueblood, *Your Other Vocation* (New York: Harper, 1952), pages 21-22.
22. Galatians 6:6, 1 Thessalonians 5:12-13, 1 Timothy 5:17-18, Hebrews 13:17.
23. I am by no means saying that everyone in ministry today holds a Two-Story view of life. Many do not. However, many do.
24. H. R. Rookmaaker, *Modern Art and the Death of a Culture* (Downers Grove, Ill.: InterVarsity Press, 1970), page 222.

CHAPTER 4

THE STRATEGIC SOAPBOX
The Mainstream Model of Work

So far we have seen two views of work that promote a wide gap between the world of work and the world of religion. The secular view makes career the dominant focus of life, and leaves God out of the picture. By contrast, the Two-Story view maintains a hierarchy of "sacred" activities over "secular" pursuits, including work. Thus it sees no inherent dignity or lasting eternal value in everyday work. Before considering an alternative view from the Scriptures, we need to briefly consider one other view of work that many Christians hold. I call it the Mainstream Model.

THE MAINSTREAM MODEL

The Mainstream Model argues that Christians participate in the mainstream of the culture primarily to set up strategic opportunities to share the gospel message with friends and associates. Obviously a major part of the mainstream is the workplace. So according to this widely held view, Christians should work in secular jobs primarily as a strategy for evangelism.

Evangelism here means confronting nonChristians with a clear presentation of the facts of the gospel and an invitation to accept those facts. At a minimum, it requires apprising the unbeliever of his separation from God due to his sinful condition; of the atoning death of Christ on his behalf; and of the need to place faith in Christ's death as the basis for salvation and a new relationship with God.

Those who hold the Mainstream view of work and life base their worldview on the Great Commission. The Great Commission is the last commandment Jesus spoke to His disciples before He ascended into heaven. All four

Gospels conclude and Acts opens with some form of this command. However, the version quoted most often is found in Matthew 28:19-20:

> Go therefore and make disciples of all the nations, baptizing them in the name of the Father and the Son and the Holy Spirit, teaching them to observe all that I commanded you; and lo, I am with you always, even to the end of the age.

Jesus makes it very clear that His disciples are to go throughout the world and make disciples of all the nations, baptizing people and teaching them to obey Scripture.

Did they obey Him? Absolutely! The explosive growth of the New Testament Church clearly indicates that they and others took this commission quite seriously. As Paul said, "Woe is me if I do not preach the gospel . . . . I do all things for the sake of the gospel."[1]

The adherents of the Mainstream Model take this commission just as seriously. In fact, they feel that all of life should be "keyholed" through this command. In other words, *everything* should be seen in light of how it contributes to evangelism. Anything that takes away from evangelism is an enemy of God's work, and anything that contributes to it is an ally.

Hence, according to this view, your work could be an ally if you use it as an evangelistic opportunity. However, your work itself is of only secondary importance. Your primary task is to proclaim the gospel. As one flight attendant says, "The Great Commission is what we're called to. It is the number-one reason that God put us here. We need a job just to make our house payments and pay the bills."[2]

Work is thus seen as utilitarian, a fairly insignificant means of survival while engaging in a far greater end. Only the mission to reach a lost and dying world gives final meaning and purpose to life.

"This is preferable to spending our lives merely in a 'survival mode,'" explains a San Diego-based vice president of a financial services company. "We want to do more than survive in our jobs; we believe God has called us to make an impact. He has equipped us to see impact. Matthew 28:19 records God's commission to us: As you are going (through life and its problems), make disciples."[3]

And where would be better than the workplace to make disciples, argue the more perceptive Mainstream adherents? In neighborhoods of rear-entry garages and high transience, relationships are, at best, difficult to build. But in the workplace, Christians have direct and unimpeded access to nonbelievers.

"Evangelism is easy for lay people," says a Denver secretary, "because we already have our mission field. We don't have to search for people to talk to about Christ; we can just be natural and alert for opportunities."[4]

In other words, work serves as a platform from which you as a believer can declare your faith. It is a necessary means to the greater end of evangelism.

This view affects your perception of relationships with coworkers. Though you obviously recognize their function or role in the organization—boss, subordinate, manager, assistant —you pay far more attention to them as souls for whom Christ died.

The secretary explains, "My purpose is to plant spiritual seeds and develop relationships with the people I work with. I don't have many opportunities to share Christ in the midst of a busy work day, but I *can* ask my co-workers to go out to lunch or meet after work. As I get to know them, I can then ask, 'Has anyone ever explained to you how you can have a relationship with God through Christ?' If they are interested, they know I'm available to share what I know."[5]

Such relationships might sound boring or contrived. But many Mainstream adherents find great meaning and stimulation in such encounters. "The challenge of reaching coworkers with the news of Christ adds momentum and excitement to living,"[6] says the financier. In fact, "I believe that if a person isn't having fun doing evangelism — on the job and off — in America, then he or she isn't doing it right."[7]

In short, if you adopt this Mainstream Model for your life, you redefine your job description. You are no longer a doctor, a teacher, or a salesperson. Rather, you become an evangelist in the field of medicine, education, or marketing.

Sounds compelling! The Mainstream Model seems to have come up with a way of life that honors the Great Commission and offers us a meaningful cause, a purpose for living. And it gets results. Churches and organizations that teach it and whose members practice it have grown dramatically in the past two or three decades.[8]

So if you hold the Mainstream view, you would likely conclude that:

1. Your "secular" career is valid, but should be seen primarily in light of its strategic evangelistic value.
2. You should limit your time at work so as to maximize evangelistic efforts.
3. All of your decisions about career planning should be made on the basis of how they will impact your evangelism of people.
4. Evangelists and missionaries probably hold the most significant position in the Kingdom of God. This is because all of their life is given to

the very spiritual work of evangelism.
5. The work of God in the world today is primarily evangelistic. The only reason God meets physical and emotional needs of people is merely to sustain them so that they can either hear the gospel (for nonChristians) or share the gospel (for Christians).

AN EVALUATION OF THIS VIEW

To argue against the Mainstream position appears to be arguing against the Great Commission. Indeed, to even question it sounds to many like a devilish, subversive activity.

So let me begin by mentioning the positive contributions of the Mainstream Model. Above all else it honors the New Testament emphasis on evangelism. In fact, I think the Mainstream view has helped the Church begin to recapture the sense of priority that we as Christians should attach to evangelism.

Furthermore, it recognizes how essential the worker is to this cause. Our main contact with unbelievers is at work. Therefore, our primary strategies should focus there.

The Mainstream view also recognizes how crucial it is for us as workers to live Christlike lives on the job. Without this lifestyle, our lips will have little impact in sharing the message of Christ.

So let me preface my evaluation of this popular view by emphatically stating: *Evangelism should be a priority!* For the Church in general and for every Christian in particular.

But should it be our only priority? That is, should it be so central to our Christian faith that it virtually defines how we should live and how we should interpret life? Should we regard evangelism as the ultimate issue against which all decisions should be weighed? Should all of life be "keyholed" through the Great Commission?

Here is where I part company with the Mainstream view. I would never argue against evangelism. Quite the contrary, I insist on it. But I do argue against an extreme view that sees *all* of life and work in light of gospel proclamation. Let me suggest three reasons why the Mainstream Model is inadequate.

1. The Great Commission is broader than evangelism.
In the first place, the Great Commission itself does not support the Mainstream position. This may surprise you, but consider the text itself. Though often cited, it is not always read *in full*.

Then Jesus came to them and said, "All authority in heaven and on earth has been given to me. Therefore go and make disciples of all nations, baptizing them in the name of the Father and of the Son and of the Holy Spirit, and teaching them to obey everything I have commanded you. And surely I am with you always, to the very end of the age." (Matthew 28:18-20, NIV)

There are many observations we could make about this passage. I'll mention three. First: *The Great Commission is primarily about discipleship, and only secondarily about evangelism.* The main command here, the main verb, is "make disciples."

But this leads to a second observation: *Discipleship is more than evangelism.* It includes evangelism, but it extends beyond it. This is clear from the two tasks that flow out of the command to "make disciples." Jesus describes discipleship in terms of "baptizing" and "teaching." I would include evangelism under the "baptizing" part of discipleship. But discipleship goes on into "teaching," into a lifestyle of obedience to Christ.

So Jesus commands His disciples to make disciples, first by evangelizing and baptizing, and then by teaching. But third, notice the content and the result of that teaching. The content has to do with Jesus' own teaching: "everything I have commanded you." And the result of such teaching is obedience, or life-change. Hence, the commission implies that *discipleship includes* first a response of faith to the gospel and then *a response of obedience to Christ's commands.*

Now in Matthew's Gospel, the words "everything I have commanded you" may point to the five other great discourses in that book.[9] One of those discourses, for example, is the Sermon on the Mount (chapters 5-7). But note that this sermon deals with far more than gospel proclamation. In fact, one of its main topics is work. In other words, the Great Commission not only includes evangelism, but it includes teaching people to put Christ first in their work as well as in the rest of their lives.

New Testament discipleship. I believe that this understanding of the Great Commission is borne out by the rest of the New Testament. Jesus' disciples and Paul wrote these texts, and what they wrote suggests that this is how they understood the Great Commission.

First, we find them in the book of Acts, principally going and proclaiming the gospel everywhere.[10] Result: Thousands responded, and thousands were thus *baptized.* Thus the disciples obeyed the first part of the commission.

But Acts also records that, following baptism, the new converts "were continually devoting themselves to the apostles' *teaching,*" among other things.[11] What was the content of that teaching? We find out in the New Testament books following Acts.

In those books, as in the Sermon on the Mount, we find out that obedience to Christ involves every aspect of life (including work, which is a major category). As Paul says in Colossians 3:17, "*Whatever* you do in word or deed, do all in the name of the Lord Jesus, giving thanks through Him to God the Father."

Thus the disciples obeyed Christ's commission by making disciples through a process of gospel proclamation and life-changing instruction.

And so I conclude that the Great Commission involves far more than evangelism. It includes evangelism. But it also includes teaching people to put Christ first in their lives—including their work. And putting Christ first in work involves far more than evangelism, as we will see.

The greatest command? For the sake of argument, however, let's suppose that the Great Commission *does* place a hierarchy on evangelism. In that case I would ask, why should this command assume preeminent status, such that evangelism would determine everything we do? There is no inspired text that places the heading "The Great Commission" in front of Matthew's final paragraph. Such a title is a fairly recent development.

Is the Great Commission the greatest of Christ's commands? Curiously, when asked almost the same question, Jesus replied:

> "'Love the Lord your God with all your heart and with all your soul and with all your mind.' This is the first and greatest commandment. And the second is like it: 'Love your neighbor as yourself.' All the Law and the Prophets hang on these two commandments." (Matthew 22:37-40, NIV)

So if we want to "keyhole" Scripture through Jesus Christ's greatest command, we should turn to Matthew 22, not Matthew 28. But this is quibbling. We should obviously honor *all* of Christ's Word. All I am suggesting is that we keep the Great Commission in perspective with the rest of the New Testament.

To summarize, then, the Great Commission obviously includes evangelism. In fact, if we are not participating in evangelism, then we are not obeying Christ. But we can't say that our *only* or even our *primary* purpose in life is evangelism on the basis of the Great Commission, because the Great Commission does not say that or imply it. Instead, it tells us to evangelize *and* teach people to obey all of God's Word. And as we're about to see, God's Word shows us a lifestyle that is much broader than evangelism.

2. Life is broader than evangelism.

A second problem with the Mainstream Model is that it offers us too narrow a view of life. I often hear Christians say, "The only reason God has left me on this planet is to share my faith."

But is this true? Is evangelism God's *only* purpose for the believer? Not according to Ephesians. Three times in the first chapter of the book, Paul says that God's purpose in saving us is that we should live "to the praise of His glory" (1:6,12,14).

God's "glory" means who God is and what He has done. It was for His own glory that He created the universe in the first place. He chose to display in finite, time-and-space terms something of who He is and what He is like. Everything exists for God's glory, as a tribute and honor to Him. He is the only being worthy of such praise.

This is true even though His creation is now fallen. In fact, Christ's death and resurrection made it possible for us to return from sin to our original purpose for existence.[12] So God leaves us on this planet for the same reason He will someday take us to heaven—to bring glory to Him!

On this planet we can bring glory to Him not just when we evangelize, but when we eat, when we sleep, when we make love, when we think, when we sing, when we play, when we vote, and even when we work. Whatever we do, we should do it to the glory of God.

"This is all well and good," the Mainstream adherent might respond. "But you make life sound like a party. But it's not a party; there's a war on! People are slipping away every moment into a Christless eternity. So as C.S. Lewis asks, 'How can you be so frivolous and selfish as to think about anything but the salvation of human souls?'"[13]

The answer, of course, is that there is indeed a war on, but that the war must be fought on many fronts, of which evangelism is only one. A strategic one, to be sure. But if our *only* cause is evangelism, then I'm afraid we will ignore some of the other important battles God wants us to fight.[14]

The pentathlon. Let me change metaphors from warfare to athletics. In Europe, the most prestigious athletic event is the pentathlon. In our country we're familiar with the decathlon. But the pentathlon requires proficiency in five sports: horseback riding, pistol shooting, swimming, jogging, and fencing. If you want to win the pentathlon, you must excel in all five events.

Now the New Testament gives us as Christians a pentathlon of sorts. In Ephesians, as in the other letters of the New Testament, we are instructed how to bring glory to God in five broad categories of life: in our own personal and spiritual lives, in our church life, in our work, in our home life, and in our communities.

These are the arenas in which God expects us to live a distinctive lifestyle. For we must, in the words of the Great Commission, obey *all* that Christ has commanded us. This clearly includes evangelism. But concerning ourselves with tasks other than evangelism, far from being "frivolous and selfish," is in fact a matter of obedience.

A distinctive lifestyle. Moreover, I think we might find more nonChristians turning to Christ if we as Christians concentrated considerably more on a God-honoring lifestyle than simply on evangelistic strategies. Obviously we need both. But I think we are shooting ourselves in the foot if we try to witness apart from Christlike conduct.

I know, for instance, of a man who boasts of a Mainstream view of life. Consequently, he donates heavily to evangelistic ministries, takes associates to hear gospel presentations, and shares his faith regularly. Yet in his business dealings, the man is far more unethical than most of the people to whom he witnesses. On the street his integrity is a laughingstock! If I were one of his evangelistic prospects, I think I would ask him, "Why should I believe that your Jesus can change my life when I can't for the life of me see how He's made much difference in yours?"

If we are indeed in a war, then the most important thing we can do is obey our orders. But we cannot be selective about which ones we'll obey or concentrate on.

3. Work is more than just a platform.

A third problem with the Mainstream Model is that it demeans the dignity of everyday work. A classic Mainstream statement is, "I support myself by being a businessman, but my real calling is to share Christ with people in my industry."

But if you say that, it means that your work itself has no inherent value. It has only slight instrumental value: Your job simply provides you with a platform for evangelism, and it pays the bills.

Working for God. But this is not a New Testament concept. By contrast, work is actually one of your greatest opportunities to bring glory to God and to accomplish what He wants done in this world. In Part II I will summarize Scripture's lofty view of work.

For now, consider only one passage that highlights the significance of work to God:

> Slaves, obey your earthly masters with respect and fear, and with
> sincerity of heart, just as you would obey Christ. Obey them not only
> to win their favor when their eye is on you, but like slaves of Christ,

doing the will of God from your heart. Serve wholeheartedly, as if you were serving the Lord, not men, because you know that the Lord will reward everyone for whatever good he does, whether he is slave or free. (Ephesians 6:5-8, NIV)

Although addressed to slaves, this passage has profound implications for all believers who work. First, notice that God expects every employee to serve his employer as if that employer were Christ Himself: "just as you would obey Christ"; "like slaves of Christ"; "as if you were serving the Lord."

This means that you should put as much excellence into your job as you would into any evangelistic strategy among coworkers. It says that Christ is interested *in your work itself*.

Second, notice the emphasis on working with godly integrity whether or not the boss (or anyone else) is watching. Hence, more than a witness is at stake here. God expects wholehearted devotion to the task —something every employer, including God, appreciates and expects.

Finally, notice that Paul refers to the slave's work as "the will of God" and "good." The work referred to here was the most menial and insignificant of its day. Yet God viewed it with great dignity. As we'll see in Part II, the principle that emerges here is that daily work—even the slave's work—is an extension of God's work!

So if you have the idea that your job is *simply* a means to the greater end of evangelism, then you have devised a peculiar understanding of work, a view not found in the New Testament.

Losing out on a gift. And if you perceive your work *simply* as a platform for proclaiming the gospel, then you will come to work, not to work, but to proclaim the gospel. But this means that you must act as an outsider in the enterprise. You'll never fully participate, heart and soul, in the business's objectives. That's unfortunate, because God has much to offer us in our work.

In fact, I believe that if you adopt this Mainstream perspective, you may be destined for a somewhat sterile, utilitarian outlook on the job. Why? Because this is not only a narrow view of work, but of human life itself. People *need* work. They need its challenge, its product, its achievement, its aesthetic and emotional rewards, its relational dynamics, its drama, its routine, and its remuneration. Reduce the workplace to a soapbox, and you destroy a gift of God. For that is what work is—a gift![15]

More than a soul. I should also point out that the Mainstream Model undervalues not only work but the results of work as well. Occasionally someone will raise the argument, "Why pour millions of dollars into famine relief and medical care when what those people *really* need is the gospel! Why feed and clothe people if we're going to send them to a Christless eternity?"

But such a view assumes that the only legitimate needs of mankind are spiritual. Food, the product of farming, and medicine, the product of the health industry, are considered fairly meaningless inasmuch as they cannot meet these spiritual needs.

But man is much more than a soul in need of salvation. He is that. But he is also a body in need of food, clothing, shelter, and health; a mind in need of education, discovery, and creativity; a psyche in need of love, worth, esteem, and affection; and so forth. God desires to see that all of mankind's needs are met, and He provides workers who produce products and services designed to meet those needs. Furthermore, regardless of whether those needs are temporal or eternal, people themselves are certainly eternal.

To recap: The Mainstream position's greatest asset is its greatest liability. It promotes evangelism, which is superb. But by placing evangelism in a hierarchy over the rest of life, it displays a misinterpretation of the Great Commission, an unrealistic view of life, and a sub-biblical view toward work.

TENTMAKING

I should mention a recent development in evangelistic strategy related to the Mainstream position. This is the concept of "tentmaking." Tentmakers are those who use their vocation as an entree into some culture that would ordinarily be closed to Christian missionaries.

For example, I would never be able to live and work in Iran as the president of Career Impact Ministries. Iran is a Moslem country, vehemently opposed to Christianity. But suppose that somehow I learned that the Iranian Air Force needed people to train their pilots and that they didn't particularly care who did the training. Since I once did this very work, perhaps I could apply for a job and go live in Iran. But as a tentmaker, my "real" purpose in going would not be to train pilots but to share Christ with Moslems in Iran.

To the tentmaker, then, work is strategic. It opens doors that would otherwise remain closed to the gospel.

Paul the tentmaker. By the way, the term "tentmaking" derives from the apostle Paul's occupation. Paul manufactured tents in addition to his work as an itinerant preacher, evangelist, and church planter.[16] He offers two reasons for doing this.

Expediency. First, the central career question for Paul appears to have been, what would most further the gospel? In his case, he felt that having a "secular" job would help by producing an income. That income would allow him to avoid charging for his ministry and thus run the risk of being accused of making money off of the gospel.[17]

Tentmaking was thus a simple question of strategy. He explains this reasoning in 1 Corinthians 9. He does not appear to have valued this work for its inherent worth. Instead, he saw it as a means to his ultimate goal: to proclaim the gospel.

Now it is worth asking, if this perspective on life applied to Paul, should it not also apply to us today? The tentmaker would say it should. But this assumes a hierarchy of evangelism that I am not sure Paul held.

To be sure, Paul says, "I do all things for the sake of the gospel."[18] And we would expect him to: Proclaiming the gospel was his personal commission from the risen Lord. But for Paul to say that everything in *his* life was governed by gospel proclamation is not the same concept as the Mainstream view, which says that *everything in life* should be governed by gospel proclamation.

Example. We know this because of Paul's other reason for tentmaking: to serve as an example. In 2 Thessalonians 3, Paul says when he did this work he was serving as a model of the disciplined lifestyle that should characterize Christians. In fact, he strongly commands certain sluggards in the church "to work in quiet fashion and eat their own bread."[19]

In other words, while Paul himself focused his entire life on the ministry of the gospel, he did not make this single-minded focus normative for all other believers. Certainly he exhorted Christians to avoid offending their unsaved neighbors, because that might drive them away from Christ.[20] But nowhere in his letters does he urge people to slight their jobs in order to devote themselves to evangelism. Indeed, as we will see, he does just the opposite!

I have no quarrel with the concept of tentmaking. In fact, I think it is a creative way to penetrate hostile cultures for the sake of the gospel. But we must be sure that we operate from a biblical view of work, not one that compromises this important gift from God.

CONCLUSION

To avoid misunderstanding, I think I should repeat that I am not arguing against evangelism in this chapter. In the strongest terms possible, I insist that the New Testament places a high priority on this task. And I believe that the commission to evangelize extends to every believer.

However, if this priority becomes our only priority; if the commission becomes an unhealthy obsession; if the dignity that God assigns to daily work is compromised; if relationships become contrived; if the Great Commission becomes the lens through which all of Scripture and all of life is interpreted; in short, if evangelism becomes an extreme, then I think it is time to ask whether we are serving God or serving an inadequate view of life.

In Part II, I want to propose a view that not only creates a platform for evangelism, but accomplishes the much broader purposes God has assigned to our work. I invite you to consider this view with me.

NOTES: 1. 1 Corinthians 9:16,23.
2. "Evangelism on the Job," *Worldwide Challenge* (February 1987), page 60.
3. "Evangelism on the Job," page 59.
4. "Evangelism on the Job," page 62.
5. "Evangelism on the Job," page 62.
6. "Evangelism on the Job," page 59.
7. "Evangelism on the Job," page 57.
8. This is probably the dominant view of work in the "evangelical" wing of the Church, as one might expect.
9. One way to organize Matthew, in fact, is to see the book in six sections, with a discourse concluding each section. The five other discourses, then, would be 5:1-7; 9:35-11:1; 13:1-52; 18:1-19:2; and 24:1-26:2.
10. For example, Acts 8:4.
11. Acts 2:42.
12. Ephesians 2:8-10.
13. C. S. Lewis, "Learning in War-Time," *The Weight of Glory and Other Addresses* (Grand Rapids, Mich.: Eerdmans Publishing Company, 1977), page 45. This outstanding sermon by Lewis has much to say to the topic at hand. Lewis is addressing the question, Why should people pursue their studies when the threat of Hitler and the Nazis has become an overwhelming crisis at hand? In reply, Lewis also directly addresses the question, Why should we think about anything else but evangelism, given that all of mankind stands on the brink of either heaven or hell?
14. You may want to reread the section on the eternal-temporal hierarchy in Chapter 3.
15. See Ecclesiastes 5:18-19.
16. Acts 18:3.
17. See 1 Corinthians 9:1-23, especially verse 12.
18. 1 Corinthians 9:23.
19. 2 Thessalonians 3:12.
20. 1 Corinthians 10:32-33.

PART II
HOW GOD
VIEWS WORK

CHAPTER 5

YOUR WORK MATTERS TO GOD
Work Has Intrinsic Value

I n this and the next three chapters I want to champion one central idea—that your work matters to God.

By now I hope you can see what a significant concept this is. Work is not something we do apart from God, as the secular worker would view it. Work is not something beneath God's dignity or concern, as the Two-Story view believes. Nor is work a game that we play with nonChristians in order to accomplish a more important agenda, as the Mainstream advocate holds.

Instead, work is a major part of human life that God takes very seriously. In this chapter, I want to argue that work has intrinsic value—that it is inherently worth doing. In the next chapter, I'll suggest that work also has instrumental value, that it is a God-given means toward several important ends.

Then in Chapter 7, I'll tackle the tough reality of sin's impact on work: Is work a result of the curse? If work matters so much to God, why is it so burdensome? Finally, in Chapter 8, I'll discuss why you as a Christ-follower have more reason than anyone to go to work with a sense of purpose, freedom, and joy. In everyday work, you are actually serving Christ Himself.

Let's begin then by considering three good reasons why work has intrinsic value.

GOD IS A WORKER

How does God view the notion of work? Without question, He regards it as very significant. We can say this, first of all, because *God Himself is a worker.* You may have never thought of God in this way. But that is how He makes His first appearance in the pages of Scripture.

In Genesis 1, God is found *creating* the heavens and the earth. Genesis 2:2 calls this activity "work." It is the same word that is used for man's work in the Ten Commandments.[1]

Furthermore, since the time of Creation, God continues to work. It is true that after completing the Creation He "rested" from that work, that is, He stopped working on it. Nevertheless, Jesus declared to the Pharisees, "My Father is working until now, and I Myself am working."[2]

What is the ongoing work of God? First, He upholds the creation:

> In [Christ] all things were created, both in the heavens and on earth, visible and invisible . . . all things have been created through Him and for Him. And He is before all things, and in Him all things hold together. (Colossians 1:16-17)[3]

God also meets the broad range of needs that all of His many creatures have:

> He sends forth springs in the valleys;
> They flow between the mountains;
> They give drink to every beast of the field;
> The wild donkeys quench their thirst.
> Beside them the birds of the heavens dwell;
> They lift up their voice among the branches.
> He waters the mountains from His upper chambers;
> The earth is satisfied with the fruit of His works.
>
> He causes the grass to grow for the cattle,
> And vegetation for the labor of man,
> So that he may bring forth food from the earth,
> So that he may make his face glisten with oil,
> And food which sustains man's heart.
> The trees of the LORD drink their fill,
> The cedars of Lebanon which He planted,
> Where the birds build their nests,
> And the stork, whose home is the fir trees.
>
> The high mountains are for the wild goats;
> The cliffs are a refuge for the rock badgers.
> He made the moon for the seasons;

The sun knows the place of its setting.
Thou dost appoint darkness and it becomes night,
In which all the beasts of the forest prowl about.
The young lions roar after their prey,
And seek their food from God.
When the sun rises they withdraw,
And lie down in their dens.
Man goes forth to his work
And to his labor until evening.

O LORD, how many are Thy works!
In wisdom Thou hast made them all;
The earth is full of Thy possessions.
There is the sea, great and broad,
In which are swarms without number,
Animals both small and great.
There the ships move along,
And leviathan, which Thou hast formed to sport in it.

They all wait for Thee,
To give them their food in due season.
Thou dost give to them, they gather it up;
Thou dost open Thy hand, they are satisfied with good.
Thou dost hide Thy face, they are dismayed;
Thou dost take away their spirit, they expire,
And return to their dust.
Thou dost send forth Thy Spirit, they are created;
And Thou dost renew the face of the ground. (Psalm 104:10-30)

Furthermore, He is working out His purposes in history. This was Moses'
point in Deuteronomy 11:1-7:

You shall therefore love the LORD your God, and always keep His
charge, His statutes, His ordinances, and His commandments. And
know this day that I am not speaking with your sons who have not
known and who have not seen the discipline of the LORD your God—
His Greatness, His mighty hand, and His outstretched arm, and His
signs and His works which He did in the midst of Egypt to Pharaoh
the king of Egypt and to all his land; and what He did to Egypt's army,
to its horses and its chariots, when He made the water of the Red Sea

to engulf them while they were pursuing you, and the LORD completely destroyed them; and what He did to you in the wilderness until you came to this place; and what He did to Dathan and Abiram, the sons of Eliab, the son of Reubenite, when the earth opened its mouth and swallowed them, their households, their tents, and every living thing that followed them, among Israel—but your own eyes have seen all the great work of the LORD which He did.

And of course He accomplished the great work of atonement at the Cross. As Jesus explained: "My food is to do the will of Him who sent Me, and to accomplish His work" (John 4:34).
No wonder Psalm 111 says:

Praise the LORD!
I will give thanks to the LORD with all my heart,
In the company of the upright and in the assembly.
Great are the works of the LORD;
They are studied by all who delight in them.
Splendid and majestic is His work;
And His righteousness endures forever.
He has made His wonders to be remembered;
The LORD is gracious and compassionate.
He has given food to those who fear Him;
He will remember His covenant forever.
He has made known to His people the power of His works,
In giving them the heritage of the nations.

The works of His hands are truth and justice;
All His precepts are sure.
They are upheld forever and ever;
They are performed in truth and uprightness.
He has sent redemption to His people;
He has ordained His covenant forever;
Holy and awesome is His name.
The fear of the LORD is the beginning of wisdom;
A good understanding have all those who do His commandments;
His praise endures forever.

God is a worker. This alone gives us a clue that work itself must be significant, that it must have *intrinsic* value. For by definition, God can do nothing that is not inherently good, or else He would violate His own nature and character. The fact that God calls what He does "work" and calls that work "good" means that work has intrinsic worth.[4]

GOD CREATED PEOPLE AS WORKERS

We also find at the beginning of the book of Genesis that *God created man in His image as a worker.* This gives us a second reason why work has intrinsic value.

Most of us are already familiar with the profound and often misunderstood truth that man was created in the image of his divine Creator. But since God Himself is a worker, we would expect man, who is created in God's image, to be a worker, too. And that is precisely what the Genesis passage says about man:

> Then God said, "Let us make man in our image, according to our like-ness; and let them rule over the fish of the sea and over the birds of the sky and over the cattle and over all the earth, and over every creep-ing thing that creeps on the earth."
>
> And God blessed them; and God said to them, "Be fruitful and multiply, and fill the earth, and subdue it; and rule over the fish of the sea and over the birds of the sky, and over every living thing that moves on the earth." Then God said, "Behold, I have given you every plant yielding seed that is on the surface of all the earth, and every tree which has fruit yielding seed; it shall be food for you; and to every beast of the earth and to every bird of the sky and to every thing that moves on the earth which has life, I have given every green plant for food"; and it was so. (Genesis 1:26,28-29)

The concept of mankind ruling over the other creatures and subduing the creation and eating from the produce of the earth all point to man as a worker. Not only is God a worker, but man is a worker, too. In fact, Ecclesiastes 3:13 calls this work a gift of God: "Moreover, that every man who eats and drinks sees good in all his labor—it is the gift of God."

These and other passages of Scripture lend awesome dignity to your work. As a human created in God's image, you are inherently significant and when you work you are doing something that is very Godlike. It is not only God's work that is significant; human work is significant, too. It is something ordained by God. The fact that you work is, in the words of Genesis 1, "very good."[5] Intrinsically good. Valued by God.

GOD CREATED PEOPLE TO BE HIS COWORKERS

So man works because he is created in the image of God. But he was created not as a worker unto himself, but as a *coworker with God*. This puts a slight twist on what we have said so far, giving us a third important reason arguing for the inherent value of everyday work. The creation account says:

> And the LORD God planted a garden toward the east, in Eden; and there He placed the man whom He had formed. . . . Then the LORD God took the man and put him into the garden of Eden to cultivate it and keep it. (Genesis 2:8,15)

God planted the garden; man cultivated it. The first partnership!

What an incredible privilege. I often work with lawyers who are in line to become partners. Invariably they look on this as a tremendous honor and advantage. It usually means an increase in salary, perhaps their name on the shingle, maybe a bigger office—and usually longer hours, too! But it always means a rise in status.

But that is analogous to the privileged status we have as partners with God. To be facetious, I could put on my calling card: "God and Sherman, Partners." The point is that God conferred great dignity on us when He delegated to us much of the responsibility for managing the creation.

Whose work? Does this sound odd to you: an infinite God colaboring with finite humans? If so, it may be because of an issue often raised in Christian circles: How much of your life and work is your responsibility and how much is God's?

One extreme says everything depends on you; God takes a hands-off policy on human affairs. The other extreme says it doesn't matter how hard you work; nothing you do contributes to the work of God.

But certainly Genesis implies that you and God are meant to be *coworkers* throughout life. God "plants"; you "cultivate." That's a partnership.

Another way to look at this is to ask, Who took care of the garden of Eden? One view would say, Obviously Adam did. But the other view would say, No, God did; He merely used Adam as an instrument to meet the garden's needs.

But there is no reason why we couldn't say they *both* participated in this work.

To illustrate, when I was an instructor in the Air Force, I usually flew the T-38, a supersonic fighter trainer. This aircraft seated two: the student in front, and I, as the instructor, right behind him in back.

The purpose of my being there was to oversee his activity. He was to fly the mission from start to finish all by himself. And yet, I was still the commander responsible for the overall direction and fulfillment of that mission.

From voice check to engine start-up to taxi, through the airborne maneuvers and simulated dogfights, all the way to final approach, gear check, touchdown, and debriefing, the student was responsible for operating with precision.

Nevertheless, when it came time to record the flight, the mission was logged not only for the student as the pilot, but also for me as the aircraft commander. In other words, we both claimed time on the ride. That's the way the Air Force does it.

Now this is somewhat analogous to our partnership in work with God. As humans, we act as junior partners in what is ultimately God's work. Yet participation in that work makes it our work, too. We are colaborers with God in managing His creation.

Perhaps you feel that I am implying that God "needs" us to accomplish His work. Not at all. An omnipotent, sovereign Creator has no need. Rather, God chooses to have us participate in His plans.

The gift of work. But this means that work is actually a function of God's grace. Not surprisingly, then, work is called a gift in Scripture:

> Here is what I have seen to be good and fitting: to eat, to drink and enjoy oneself in all one's labor in which he toils under the sun during the few years of his life which God has given him; for this is his reward. Furthermore, as for every man to whom God has given riches and wealth, He has also empowered him to eat from them and to receive his reward and rejoice in his labor; this is the gift of God. (Ecclesiastes 5:18-19)

Work can be a wonderful gift! Having created us, God honors us by making us coworkers with Him.

Psalm 8 describes this partnership in vivid terms. The psalmist opens by praising the Creator for His being and character, and finally for His work.

He essentially asks, "In light of who You are and what You have done, God, of what significance is man?" The answer is that man has great dignity and value as God's coworker:

> Yet Thou hast made him a little lower than God,
> And dost crown him with glory and majesty!
> Thou dost make him to rule over the works of Thy hands;

Thou hast put all things under his feet,
All sheep and oxen,
And also the beasts of the field,
The birds of the heavens, and the fish of the sea,
Whatever passes through the paths of the seas.

BUT DOES THIS INCLUDE ALL WORK?

So we have seen three reasons why our everyday work is significant. The fact that God is a worker argues for it. The fact that people mirror God when they work argues for it. And the fact that people's work is an extension of God's work argues for it.

But how far can we press this? Are we to think that God smiles on *every* sort of "work" that humans do? Let me answer that by making three qualifying statements.

1. All legitimate work is an extension of God's work.
By legitimate work I mean work that somehow contributes to what God wants done in the world, and does not actively contribute to what He does not want done.

Naturally, it goes without saying that illegal work is therefore a corruption of God's work. The prostitute, the drug pusher, and the professional thief all "work." But they contribute nothing to what God wants done. Indeed, they destroy God's creation.[6]

There are other kinds of work that, although legal, are highly questionable in terms of ethics and morality. We'll discuss these at some length in Chapter 11.

The main thing to grasp, though, is that work itself as a human activity is a good, not an evil, thing given to us by God. Obviously evil affects work, but work itself is good, even when affected by evil.[7]

In this sense; work is a human activity much like sex, which has certainly been corrupted by people. And yet although there is so much evil linked to sex, the Bible insists that sex itself is an intrinsically good thing, something given to us as a gift from God.[8] Similarly, work can be used for ungodly purposes, but work itself remains inherently good.

This fact holds true for both Christians and nonChristians alike. Non-Christians also participate in God's work and should work because work is inherently worth doing. Yet, we cannot always expect such individuals to know or acknowledge God's perspective on their work. In fact, perhaps most nonChristians in our culture have been seduced by the secularism of our society and work primarily for self-driven ends. The same could be said of many Christians.

Nevertheless, in His sovereignty, God can and does use such people to accomplish His work. And whether or not people fulfill God's purpose for their work, that does not alter the fact that God regards work and workers as highly significant.

2. Because of sin, none of our work completely fulfills God's intentions.

I will have much more to say about this in Chapter 7. But for now we can say that God must certainly grieve when He looks at much of what happens in the marketplace, and at the conditions under which many workers continue to labor.

I can't imagine, for instance, that God thinks much of the many trivial pursuits that pass for occupations. For example, Bill once showed me a classified ad for a racetrack chaplaincy. When I saw it I thought, truth is stranger than fiction! What does a racetrack chaplain do, anyway? Preach to horses? Console losing bettors?

"You know, Doug, it might not be a horse track," Bill suggested. "It could be dogs! You know, whippets and greyhounds. If so, the chaplain would be administering last rites to rabbits!"

I must admit, on the face of it, I have a hard time taking a racetrack chaplaincy seriously. Of course, such a job might involve some type of ministry to jockeys and those involved in training horses and operating the facilities. Many professional sports teams have such a person involved, though usually part-time. But otherwise, if the chaplaincy were a mere figurehead, I would be hard-pressed to explain how such a job contributes to God's work in the world.

You can no doubt think of other jobs that seem to waste human and natural resources. For instance, is the best use of your life the creation or merchandising of so much of the kitsch sold in roadside shops—tumblers that say, "I'm a Pisces"; furry dice to hang from rear-view mirrors; bumper stickers that advertise one's sexual libido?

I'm not saying it is necessarily wrong to work with these items. I just think it is worth asking ourselves whether they are the *best* contribution we can make to God's work.

I also wonder whether God smiles on the way some workers are subjected to agonizing routine and monotony. Perhaps it increases efficiency to hire a worker to put the same bolt in the same nut in the same hole on the same assembly line, hour after hour, day after day. But is this what God had in mind when He gave man work in Genesis 1 and 2? Or does it reduce the worker—who is God's coworker created in His image—to a robot?[9]

3. The connection between the work we do and how it contributes to God's work is not always obvious.

You may wonder how your everyday work could possibly contribute to God's work. After all, isn't He mostly concerned with religious pursuits? I find that most "secular" workers feel this way, particularly those who deal with data and things as opposed to people. Workers in the "helping professions," such as psychologists, social workers, and many nurses, can usually imagine how their occupation might serve God. After all, by caring for humans in need, they are very Godlike in their work.

But suppose you are a cashier, a data processor, or an actuary. Suppose your job is to sit in a cherry picker all day and repair faulty traffic signals. Or perhaps you are an international currency trader for a bank and you sit in front of monitors all day, jumping in and out of the market, trying to score a few hundred extra dollars for the bank.

How could God possibly care about jobs like these? How could they in any way contribute significantly to His work in the world? The answer to these questions is the subject of the next chapter. You'll find that your work, no matter what it is, can serve a number of important purposes.

NOTES: 1. Exodus 20:9.
2. John 5:17. The resolution of this seeming contradiction lies in the nature of time and eternity. God's work is finished from an eternal perspective, but it continues from the temporal point of view.
3. See also Hebrews 1:3.
4. This is not to overlook the effect of sin on work. But just as each human has inherent dignity despite sin, so work has inherent value despite sin. By the way, the words used in Scripture calling work "good" refer to that which is intrinsically good. See, for example, Ephesians 4:28.
5. Some might argue that "very good" in Genesis 1:31 refers to God's work of creation, not man's work of ruling creation. But that won't do. The fact that man rules the creation is itself part of God's design, God's work. Therefore, man's rule, his work, is, along with the rest of the created order, "very good."
6. It is possible for laws to be passed against legitimate work such as gospel proclamation. In that case, the work would be illegal but would still contribute to what God wants done. The question is not so much the legality of the work as its morality, its relation to God's will.
7. Remember that we will consider the effects of sin on work in Chapter 7.
8. See, for instance, 1 Corinthians 7:17.
9. I am not demeaning the work of the factory laborer. On the contrary, I believe that the dignity of the factory worker itself demands conditions of work that respect his humanity.

CHAPTER 6

GOD'S WORK—YOUR WORK
Work Has Instrumental Value

I n the last chapter I argued that work is intrinsically valuable. This follows from the fact that God is a worker and has created mankind in His image as His coworker. This led to the observation that all legitimate work is an extension of God's work. But at the end of the chapter, we raised an important question: How can every worker discover the connection between his everyday work and how that work contributes to what God wants done in the world?

In other words, how does the professional athlete participate as a coworker with God? How does the retailer do God's work? How does the work of the backhoe operator, the bank teller, the journalist, or the mortgage banker contribute directly to God's work?

To begin to answer these questions, we need to see that there are at least five major reasons for the work God gives us. There may be other reasons besides these, but these are reasons clearly given in Scripture, and they are fairly comprehensive. These reasons show that work has broad instrumental value in addition to intrinsic value. In other words, it is a means to several ends:

1. Through work we serve people.
2. Through work we meet our own needs.
3. Through work we meet our family's needs.
4. Through work we earn money to give to others.
5. Through work we love God.

Now at a glance you should already be able to see some ways that your work contributes to God's work. At a minimum, your job provides you with an income to meet your needs, and, if you have a family, to meet their needs as well.

But is this part of God's work? Yes, but we are running ahead of ourselves. First we need to be very clear about what it is that God wants done in this world. Has He given us any clues beyond the creation mandate in Genesis 1 and 2? Indeed He has.

THE GREAT COMMANDMENTS

In Chapter 4, I mentioned that Jesus was asked which of God's commandments in the Old Testament was the greatest. Recall His response (Matthew 22:37-40, NIV):

> "Love the Lord your God with all your heart and with all your soul and with all your mind.' This is the first and greatest commandment. And the second is like it: 'Love your neighbor as yourself.' All the Law and the Prophets hang on these two commandments."

Love God. Love others. Love yourself. In the broadest and simplest terms, this is what God wants done in the world. This is the essence of His will for us. The New Testament, as well as the Old, flows in and out of these commands. In a way we could never do more than these commands. What matters is that we never do less.

So this is what God wants us to concentrate on. I want to point out that all five of the reasons for work flow out of these Great Commandments. In other words, when we fulfill the five purposes of work, we are fulfilling the Great Commandments. In fact, as we'll discover, work is one of our principal means of loving God, loving others, and loving ourselves. Consequently, our work can contribute to what God wants done in the world. Let's see.

THROUGH WORK WE SERVE PEOPLE

A friend of mine operates a pallet company. Pallets are the platforms used extensively in the transportation industries, designed to make it easier for forklifts to load and unload stacks of goods. My friend's company manufactures these pallets.

Now how could my friend's pallets possibly fit into the work of God in the world? Actually they are an important, albeit humble link in a complex chain that God uses to meet my needs and your needs. Those pallets are an indispensable part of the trucking industry—an industry that delivers ruby-red grapefruit from the Rio Grande Valley, boxes of cereal from Battle Creek, Michigan, and milk from Coppell, Texas, to a supermarket near my home.

All of these come together at my family's breakfast table. Before we eat, one of my children thanks God for the food. Why? Because He has brought to our table something we need.

We must recognize, however, that God has used a rather extensive system of workers to give us this food. He has used farmers to plant and cultivate citrus trees and wheat, and to raise dairy cows. We might also mention the scientists who have checked the food for purity, and the bankers who have arranged for the financing. Then, too, there are the dealers of farm equipment, and behind them the builders of that equipment.

Then we should remember the trucks and their drivers that God has used to haul this food our way. And we should appreciate the truck stop operators along the way who have provided diesel fuel and coffee. And, of course, someone had to lay down those miles of interstate that connect our country.

And finally, we should thank God for the supermarket employees, for the guy who carries the bag to our car, and for my wife who puts it all on the table.

By the way, did you notice my friend's pallets? They were tucked away under those crates of grapefruit, boxes of cereal, and gallons of milk. Though obscure, God used them to meet my family's needs.

Loving others through work. But are they significant? Yes, because meeting my family's needs is significant. It is Godlike. It is something He wants done. It is loving me and my family. Consequently, my friend is actually contributing directly to God's work in the world. Through his work, he is serving the needs of people like my family.

In a similar way, God uses your work to meet the needs of people. Sometimes this connection is fairly obvious. God clearly uses the surgeon to meet a physical need, the mother to meet an emotional need, the pastor to meet a spiritual need.

But sometimes the contributions are less evident, as with my friend who manufactures pallets. Or the engineer who writes micro-code for an integrated circuit. Or the comedian. Or the stockbroker.

Jobs like these often appear to be disconnected from anything that serves people. To find their contribution requires us to think broadly about the web of relationships God uses to meet human needs. We saw something of this complex system at play in the case of my friend's pallets. But we need to realize that God uses our work, whether or not anyone ever tells us, "I thank God for what you are doing!"

Works of art. This is important because some work contributes to life in very abstract, indirect ways. I'm thinking, for instance, of the work of the artist, the poet, or the musician. Some works of art seem to meet no apparent need. In fact, they are not designed to meet a need, but simply to exist as statements and phenomena unto themselves.

As a result, our culture tends to dismiss such work as pointless, wasteful, or self-indulgent. Yet note that the American worldview is highly utilitarian: things and people are valued not for their own sakes, but for what they can *do*, what they can *contribute*.

This probably stems from the materialist assumptions that pervade our thinking. But as a consequence, we have a demeaning view of the arts in our society. In fact, the art that gets funded is mostly art that has commercial value.[1]

This is a complex problem and I cannot discuss it in full here. But I would stress that the artist, too, can be a coworker with God, even if his work is undervalued by his culture. For God Himself is an Artist, a Creator, a Maker, a Craftsman. And He has fashioned many things that have little if any utilitarian value to mankind.[2] Like other workers, the artist and the musician must work "as unto the Lord, and not unto men."

God works in spite of us. By the way, let me add two qualifiers. First, I don't mean to imply that we always work from pure motives of service to others. We should, but the reality is that we don't. In fact, we often work from fairly selfish or egotistical motives. Nevertheless, God often manages to use us in spite of ourselves as His agents to meet the needs of others. If God did not work this way, very few human needs would be met.

Motives and career choices. Secondly, the fact that God intends for our work to serve others has definite implications for career choices. I'll say much more about this in Chapter 10. But for now let me stress that if you are in your job simply to serve your own ego or comfort, then you definitely need to change your reasons for working. And you may even need to change jobs.

THROUGH WORK WE MEET OUR OWN NEEDS
AND THOSE OF OUR FAMILY

It is not always noticed, but the Great Commandments include a legitimate self-interest: "Love your neighbor *as yourself.*" The idea is that each of us has a responsibility before God to care for himself as God's person. Not just physically, but spiritually, emotionally, relationally, morally, intellectually, and so forth.

Work is an important means toward fulfilling this responsibility. In 2 Thessalonians 3, Paul says that we should pursue gainful employment in order to provide for our needs:

Now we command you, brethren, in the name of our Lord Jesus Christ, that you keep aloof from every brother who leads an unruly life and not according to the tradition which you received from us. For you yourselves know how you ought to follow our example; because we did not act in an undisciplined manner among you, nor did we eat anyone's bread without paying for it, but with labor and hardship we kept working night and day so that we might not be a burden to any of you; not because we do not have the right to this, but in order to offer ourselves as a model for you, that you might follow our example. For even when we were with you, we used to give you this order: If anyone will not work, neither let him eat.

For we hear that some among you are leading an undisciplined life, doing no work at all, but acting like busybodies. Now such persons we command and exhort in the Lord Jesus Christ to work in quiet fashion and eat their own bread. (2 Thessalonians 3:6-12)

So we are actually commanded to work.[3] Furthermore, we are to work in order to provide for our families:

But if any one does not provide for his own, and especially for those of his household, he has denied the faith, and is worse than an unbeliever. (1 Timothy 5:8)

This is remarkably strong language! Failing to try to meet even the basic needs of one's family is denying the faith. Why? Because it directly opposes God's command to love those who are our own. In fact, it is to act worse than an unbeliever, because even pagans have the sense and decency to provide a livelihood for their families.

Fortunately, I find that providing for the family is one of the most important reasons why people go to work, as they explain it to me. In fact, because this motive is so common, many people fail to see it as a God-given reason for work. But that won't do. If you work to meet the legitimate needs of your family, then you are fulfilling something important that God wants done in the world.

Of course, the exact meaning of "providing" for the immediate family seems to vary from income to income. Some people seem quite able to sustain their spouse and children on a pittance. Others seem to think that "providing" involves extravagance and luxury. I'll have much more to say about this in Chapter 12, when we discuss the implications of these principles for income and lifestyle.

THROUGH WORK WE EARN MONEY TO GIVE TO OTHERS

So far we have said that through our work we can love others and love ourselves. We can love others by serving their needs through the goods we help produce or distribute, or through the services we help provide. And we can love ourselves by gaining an income to provide for our needs and the needs of our families.

But Scripture adds a purely benevolent purpose to work: to earn money in order to give it away to others. In fact, the overwhelming thrust of the Scriptures is that as God sees fit to prosper us, our abundance should begin to spill over and start benefiting others who, for a variety of reasons, are in need. For example, in Psalm 37:25-26, the writer looks back on his life and says:

I have been young, and now I am old; yet I have not seen the righteous forsaken, or his descendants begging bread. All day long he is gracious and lends; and his descendants are a blessing.

In other words, as God has prospered the righteous person and his family, it results in generosity toward others.

A similar idea appears in the New Testament. Writing to the Ephesians, Paul describes the radical change that takes place as a person turns from sin and pursues Christlikeness:

Let him who steals steal no longer; but rather let him labor, performing with his own hands what is good, in order that he may have something to share with him who has need. (Ephesians 4:28)

Because of a transformation of the person in Christ, this person no longer steals but gives instead. Christ causes a complete reversal in attitude and action. Notice, though, the idea of honest labor as the means by which the person comes up with enough abundance to share.

So giving some portion of your income away is a discipline and a privilege taught by Scripture. I believe every Christian, no matter what his level of lifestyle, should use part of his money to meet the financial and material needs of others.

The "others" that Paul has in mind in the Ephesians passage are undoubtedly the poor. God is deeply concerned to see us meet their needs. His concern does not arise because the poor are inherently better but because they are needy. And from the beginning of creation, He has desired to meet human needs. He wants to meet some of them through you and me.

Again, I'll have much more to say about this in Chapter 12. But we need to see that loving others involves not only our work, but the income from our work as well. Of the five purposes of work, this is probably the one that gets neglected the most.

THROUGH WORK WE LOVE GOD

The final reason God has given us work is so that we can love Him. Does this sound odd to you, the idea of work as a means toward loving God? In fact, is the concept of "loving God" itself fairly nebulous and esoteric to you? I find that it is for most Christians.[4]

Let me suggest that your work makes loving God very practical. An investor I know serves as an excellent illustration. Over lunch one day, he explained to me why he invests in convenience stores and restaurants.

"I like to take a raw piece of land and make it productive," he told me. "The store or restaurant I put up sells food and other items that people need. And it provides an income for the employees I hire. It also gives me a good return on my investment."

Does God want people to have food and other items they need? Yes. Does He want people to have jobs? Yes. Does He want my investor friend to get a fair return on his investment? I think He does. Consequently, we can say that my friend is loving God through his work, because in his work he is doing something God wants done. I also happen to know that his motives for investing are legitimate and godly.

The test of love. That is, after all, what it means to love God: to do what God wants us to do, and to do it out of a sincere desire to please Him. In fact, that is the only way we can love Him.

Let me apply this idea to you and your work. If you want to love God through your work, then you need to determine that what you are doing in your job is something God *wants* done, and that you are doing your job *because* God wants it done.

This may take some thought. Suppose you are a piano tuner. Is that something God wants done? It unquestionably is, because the pianist cannot play on a piano that is out of tune. Furthermore, if you have the ear for it, then you have a God-given means of providing for this need and for your income.

Then are you tuning pianos because God wants you to tune pianos? I'm sure you would have many reasons for working at such a job. But in light of all that we have said so far, I would hope that you go to the job with a belief that in doing that job, you are ultimately serving God as well as man. If you are, then by tuning pianos you are loving God; you are doing something He wants done.

I encourage you as a worker to think through your job on this basis. At first it may be hard to see how your work connects with anything that God wants done. But I advise you to think very broadly about the needs that people have and the work that God has given mankind to do.

Of course, you may evaluate your work and conclude that you are involved in something God does *not* want done. If so, I recommend that you read Chapter 10 on job selection and Chapter 11 on evil in the workplace. That may help you determine what steps you might take.

You might also determine that although your work accomplishes something God wants accomplished, the *way* you work and your *motives* have been far from God-honoring. If so, that calls for a change in your attitudes, your character, and your behavior. As we'll see in Chapter 9, loving God in our work involves not only what we do, but how and why we do it as well.

The Greatest Commandment. In Deuteronomy 6:5, Moses declared the same Great Commandment that Jesus cited in the passage we looked at earlier: "You shall love the LORD your God with all your heart and with all your soul and with all your might."

Everything about you is to be involved in loving God. It makes sense that your work must be involved as well. Just think about how much of your heart, soul, and might go into your work. Imagine, then, as you spend yourself at that task, being able to say, "I'm here to do something God wants done, and I intend to do it because I love Him." The person who can make this statement has turned his work into one of his primary means of obeying the greatest of God's commandments.

CONCLUSION

Loving God. Loving others. Loving ourselves. This is what God has told us to do. This is what He wants us to concentrate on. And our work, far from being opposed to these commands, is actually one of our most important means of fulfilling them. Work matters to God. It has important instrumental value.

I have found that when a person looks at work in this way, it revolutionizes his attitude toward his job. For the first time he sees a connection between what he does all day and what God wants done. And as I mentioned earlier, I think most Christians sincerely want to do God's will. But so often they view His will as something abstract and general. Work makes it very practical and specific—and personal.

This means that you do not have to quit your job and go into the ministry to do something significant for God. Some will undoubtedly need to do that. But God wants most of us to stay where we are and contribute to His work in the everyday tasks of life. This is what He had in mind when He created the world as recorded in Genesis 1 and 2. And this is part of the Great Commandments that Jesus recalled in Matthew 22.

This all sounds wonderful, if not utopian. The unfortunate truth, though, that must be laid alongside these principles is that we live in a fallen world in which sin has dramatically affected work and workers. In the next chapter, I'll examine this sobering reality.

NOTES: 1. For an intriguing Christian discussion of this topic, see H.R. Rookmaaker, *Modern Art and the Death of a Culture* (Downers Grove, Ill.: InterVarsity Press, 1970).
2. Such as stars whose light we will never see, or the amazing micro-life that swarms silently around us.
3. See also Ephesians 4:28 and 1 Thessalonians 4:11-12.
4. This is largely because of Two-Story assumptions like those mentioned in Chapter 3. "Loving God" is usually confined to religious activities such as attending worship services, praying, or singing hymns.

CHAPTER 7

IT'S A JUNGLE OUT THERE!
The Effects of Sin on Work

So far I have made two very positive statements about work. Work has intrinsic value because of the nature of God and because of the way He has designed work and placed workers in His creation. Also, work has instrumental value because it serves at least five broad purposes.

But unfortunately we must add a third statement to this view of work that is negative. The reality is that we live in a fallen world, a world very much estranged from its Creator. Not surprisingly, sin has profoundly affected our work.

I doubt that it will take much to convince you that this is so. Most of us know all too well that the work world can be a jungle. It not only tears at our spiritual and moral fiber, but at our humanity as well. Consequently, many of us hate work. In that case, the message we need to hear is that, despite its limitations, God still finds value in what we do all day.

In this chapter I want to consider the tragic consequences of sin on work. I'll mention three, and then add a note about confronting these situations. But first we need to deal with a common misconception about sin and work.

WORK IS NOT A RESULT OF THE CURSE

As I travel and speak on the dignity of daily work, I'm often asked, "Doug, isn't work a result of the curse?"[1] This idea that God has punished us by chaining us to a job is one of the most debilitating untruths there is. It destroys all motivation for work, for a punishment can have no dignity. If work is a curse, it is impossible to thank God for it.

It may be that this idea finds its root in the Two-Story assumptions I discussed in Chapter 3. Or perhaps it stems from the weariness so many of us feel at the end of a long day or week. Exhausted, bored, or angry at our jobs, it is easy to think of them as an unbearable curse from on high.

At any rate, I'd like to explode this myth by arguing that work is *not* a part of the curse. Instead, work is a gift from God. Let me offer four reasons why we can affirm this.

1. The nature of work is good, not evil.

In Chapter 5 we saw that God is a worker. Furthermore, God created man in His image as His coworker. He placed man in the garden, where he was given the task of "cultivating and keeping" it.

This alone should dispel the idea of work as a curse. If God works, then work itself cannot be intrinsically evil. And if man has been created as a worker in God's image, then man's work cannot be intrinsically evil either. After all, man's work is an extension of God's work.

2. Work was given before the Fall, not after it.

Perhaps the most powerful argument that dispels the idea of work as a curse is the observation that the work God gave man to do was given before the Fall, and hence before the curse. Therefore, work cannot be the result of the curse.

If you've lived with the idea that work is a punishment, you might want to reread Genèsis 1-3. The sequence of events in that account is important for our discussion. First God creates the heavens and the earth. Then He creates mankind in His image. He places Adam and Eve in a garden, called Eden. Their job is to cultivate that garden. They do so, and the picture presented is one of harmony and right relationships among the Creator, the creation, and the two human creatures.

But in the course of time, Adam and Eve sin. Tempted by Satan, who shows up in the guise of a snake, they do what God has instructed them not to do. At that point God pronounces a curse. But presumably Adam and Eve have been faithfully working in the garden long before the curse. So their labor cannot be seen as a consequence of their sin.

3. The nature of the curse itself shows that work is not a result of the curse.

Let's examine the curse to see what it actually says:

And the LORD God said to the serpent,
    "Because you have done this,
    Cursed are you more than all cattle,
    And more than every beast of the field;

On your belly shall you go,
And dust shall you eat
All the days of your life;
And I will put enmity
Between you and the woman,
And between your seed and her seed;
He shall bruise you on the head,
And you shall bruise him on the heel."
To the woman He said,
   "I will greatly multiply
Your pain in childbirth,
In pain you shall bring forth children;
Yet your desire shall be for your husband,
And he shall rule over you."
Then to Adam He said, "Because you have listened to the voice of your wife, and have eaten from the tree about which I commanded you, saying, 'You shall not eat from it';
   "Cursed is the ground because of you;
In toil you shall eat of it
All the days of your life.
Both thorns and thistles it shall grow for you;
And you shall eat the plants of the field;
By the sweat of your face
You shall eat bread,
Till you return to the ground,
Because from it you were taken;
For you are dust,
And to dust you shall return." (Genesis 3:14-19)

From this passage, we observe that God curses Satan (the serpent) and that He imposes the penalty of death on humanity, just as He had said He would (Genesis 2:16-17).

But note very carefully that in reference to work, God curses the ground, but not the task itself of cultivating the ground. This is a subtle but crucial distinction. The curse made work and the work environment much more difficult. But it did not impose work itself as a punishment. Nor did it take away the dignity and value of work. (Genesis 5:29 supports this distinction.)

If God had wanted to punish man through work, the best thing He could have done would have been to take away man's work entirely. This may sound appealing to you! You might envision a life of ease, sipping lemonade by a swimming pool, and being served by several angels!

But a fallen world would never offer such an environment. To be face-tious, the swimming pool (if it ever got built) would soon be filled with algae and scum, and smell foul. No one would clean it! It would be too cold to swim in. No one would heat it! The lemonade would be weak, bitter, and tepid. No one would have cultivated the lemons properly, or have harvested the sugar cane, or have built ice-dispensing refrigerators!

In all seriousness, work is a gift of God's grace. In fact, after pronouncing His devastating curse, God sends man out of the garden to work the land outside the garden (Genesis 3:23). He sends Adam and Eve away in order to prevent a worse fate. For had they eaten from the tree of life, they would have lived forever—but that would have meant living forever in sin, separated from God. There would have been no way for God to have recovered them.

So sending them out of the Garden is a tribute to God's grace. But notice that He sends them back to the work He originally gave them, to their occupation of farming. This is also grace. Thus man remains a coworker with God.

4. *God's perspective on work remains positive after the Fall, not negative.*
As we have seen in Chapters 5 and 6, Scripture presents a remarkably positive view of work, even since Genesis 3. For instance, man's work is placed alongside of God's work in Psalms 8 and 104. In fact, man is presented as a coworker, a partner with God.

Furthermore, God actually enables people to work. In Deuteronomy 8:18, Moses reminded the Israelites that God Himself "is giving you power to make wealth." And as we have seen in Ecclesiastes, work and its benefits are called a gift from God.[2] Furthermore, the New Testament expressly commands us "to lead a quiet life and attend to your own business and work with your hands."[3]

If work were somehow evil or cursed, commands like these would never appear. Not only is work *commanded* after the Fall, but it is *commended* as well. In Ephesians 6, for instance, Paul commands slaves to do their work "as if you were serving the Lord," and offers this motivation: "The Lord will reward everyone for whatever good he does" (Ephesians 6:7-8, NIV). In other words, the work of these Christian slaves will someday be evaluated and commended by Christ.

Despite these passages of Scripture, though, I have occasionally encoun-tered the argument that because mankind is sinful, then whatever comes from mankind is sinful. Thus, since the time of the Fall, mankind's work is a result of sin, no matter what its original purpose might have been.

This sounds compelling. But it overlooks the fact that work is ultimately from God, not from man. We like to say that a businessman "creates" jobs for his employees, or that a given company or sector of the economy "has created thousands of jobs in the past year." Or we may even say that "people have many needs, and these needs create jobs to fill those needs." Such is our human perspective on work.

But Scripture portrays things differently. God created mankind to be needy—at a minimum, in need of a relationship with Him and with each other, in need of food, and in need of a home. God provided for all these needs. He provided a garden, and He required Adam to do the corresponding *work* of cultivation.

Sin only increased mankind's need. After the Fall, Adam and Eve and their descendants needed redemption, clothing, justice, and so forth. Throughout history, God has continued to provide for these needs. But in many cases, He requires that our work meet these needs. The point is that work has always originated from God as His assignment to us. So we cannot say that work is a result of sin, or that it originates from sinful humans.

And yet, sinful humans do work. And thus work can become a vehicle for people to express their sin. This is what happened at Babel, when the people used their skills in construction to thwart God's purposes and to display their pride (Genesis 11:1-9). This is what happens today when any of us approaches his career with selfish ambitions and evil intentions.

In short, sinful people may corrupt God's gift of work, just as they may corrupt sex, poetry, or prayer. Though created in God's image to do God's work, human beings may become workers of wickedness instead. But work itself is not inherently sinful or evil.

THE RESULTS OF SIN ON WORK

What, then, were the results of sin for work? Let me mention three.

1. Sin made work harder.

First, as I have indicated, the Fall made work much more difficult, because the work environment became much less cooperative. The sweat, the toil, and the burdensome aspect of work are products of the Fall.

This may be a hard idea to sell in twentieth-century America, especially when so many of us work in air-conditioned, clean offices, "ergonomically designed" for comfort. But we must remember two facts. First, the vast majority of mankind always has and still does grind out its living through strenuous labor in fields and factories. If we work in easy surroundings by comparison, we must appreciate the fact that this is not the norm.

Furthermore, there are no free lunches! Everything has its price, and what we cannot produce we must pay for. I find it curious that our very affluence results in many of us working the same hours as the peasant—unless, of course, we mortgage our expectations through heavy debt, the ill will of our suppliers, the unjust wages of our laborers, or the future of our children. But sooner or later we must pay the piper.[4]

2. Sin rendered life and its work "futile."
A second consequence is that we cannot escape the effects of the curse in this life. This is the message of the Old Testament book of Ecclesiastes. Ecclesiastes is a strange book to be in the Bible. Even a casual reader picks up a sense of overwhelming pessimism and weariness about life in reading it. This clashes with the positive outlook of the rest of Scripture, particularly the New Testament.

For this reason, scholars have long debated what we are to make of this text. The prevailing opinion seems to be that Ecclesiastes is the ultimate statement of secular man, man without God. In other words, if you leave God out of life, then you'll end up with the perspective of Ecclesiastes.

But there is an alternative view. Ecclesiastes systematically examines life—its pleasures and pains, its goods and evils—and concludes: Life is *hebel*, Hebrew for fleeting, vaporous, futile, enigmatic, profitless. This is life in a fallen world.

This applies to Jew and Gentile alike, to every human at all times and in all cultures. It even applies to the Christian. For every person, life holds an ultimate futility.[5]

But Ecclesiastes goes on to describe the only meaningful response one can make in light of this situation: we should enjoy, if possible, the "stuff" of which life consists—our food, our families, our work. Yet this enjoyment is not hedonism, nor is life's meaning existential in nature. Rather, we should live with a "fear" of God, a perspective that the things we have are gifts from Him and that we will be held accountable for what we do with them.

The New Testament view. By the way, this message is reinforced for the Christian in Romans 8. Paul teaches that "the creation was subjected to futility" by God (Romans 8:20). And it will remain under that curse until God remakes it someday.

In the meantime, we as Christians are to live in obedience to God's Holy Spirit. However, we will still live in a fallen world, which means we, too, will experience something of the gripping futility of life—until we go to be with the Lord.

Futility in work. This all has dramatic implications for work. You might want to read some of the specifics highlighted in Ecclesiastes 2:18-6:9. In general terms, this passage tells us that futility characterizes much of our work. Let me illustrate.

As an Air Force instructor, I flew a plane called the T-38. In its day it was one of the hottest aircraft our country had to offer. In fact, in the early '60s, it set the world's time-to-climb record to 10,000 feet.

The engines of this bird used to be rocket engines. They put two of them on the plane and made quite a sports car out of it! So in 1965, the T-38 was state of the art. We still use it as our advanced jet trainer for pilot training today.

Yet compared with some of the aircraft in the sky today—the F-16, the F-15, the F-14—the T-38 is something of an antique. The avionics, the navigational aids, and other systems on board these newer jets are so much farther along than those of the T-38 that there is as great a gap between them and the T-38 as between the T-38 and some of the planes in World War II.

So how do you suppose the engineer who designed the T-38 feels today? Sure, it was hot in its day, but it's rather outdated now.

The point is that *all* work has a certain futility attached to it. We do the work, but it never lasts. It must be done again and again—if not by us, by someone else. This is even true for the minister's work. In many churches, for instance, the turnover rate is so high that the pastor forever trains lay leaders, only to have them transferred away by their companies. Certainly there is a satisfaction for the pastor in the relationships he builds with these people and in the sense of contribution he makes to someone's life. But many pastors in this situation feel a certain sense of frustration, a feeling of constantly "re-inventing the wheel."

Likewise, the evangelist may spark a major revival, as has happened at several points in American history. This is wonderful. Yet within a few generations, the culture inevitably finds itself in need of even more gospel preaching.

Ecclesiastes and Romans 8 are clear: in a fallen world, *all* of our work is marked by futility. It lasts for a brief, shining, enjoyable moment. And we should celebrate that moment, if we can. But then the work passes. More work must be done. And such is our lot until God restores His creation—and us.

3. Sin affects our coworkers and the system.
One final effect of the Fall on work is that each of us must work alongside sinful humans and participate indirectly in sinful systems and societies. This is inescapable.

I once spoke at a luncheon and related an incident involving a friend of mine in real estate. My friend was a partner with two others in a development project of condominiums. When it came time to apply for the final funding of the project, the partners met at a bank. According to the terms of the bank, they would need contracts written on the final six condominiums in order to secure a loan. However, my friend knew that they did not have those contracts.

While the three partners waited in the loan office lobby, my friend asked how they were going to obtain the loan without those contracts. His two partners smiled and explained that they had written up bogus agreements with relatives and in-laws—agreements that would be torn up as soon as the loan went through. Before my friend could respond, the loan officer arrived and invited the men into his office.

At this point in the story, I asked the luncheon crowd what my friend should have done as a Christian. This led to a lively discussion of ethics and integrity in business dealings.

After the luncheon, however, a gentleman approached me and said my story was absurd. "No one would be so stupid as to get into a partnership with people like that!" he claimed.

I reminded him that the story was true.

"Maybe so," he replied. "And maybe that's how people do business in Texas" (where this incident occurred). "But I've never heard of anything like it."

The conversation ended there. But afterwards I wondered what planet this man worked on! As I interact with business and professional people, I hear incredible "war stories." In fact, the last time I checked, questionable ethics hardly seemed limited to Texas.

> Large sections of the nation's ethical roofing have been sagging badly, from the White House to churches, schools, industries, medical centers, law firms and stock brokerages—pressing down on the institutions and enterprises that make up the body and blood of America.[6]

So comments Ezra Bowen in a 1987 *Time* magazine cover story. And asked to survey America's spiritual landscape, Father Joseph O'Hare, president of Fordham University, concludes that "there don't seem to be any moral landmarks at all."[7]

People lie on résumés and loan applications. People shortchange their clients or the government. People destroy each other in ambitious power plays. Indeed, while street crime drains our country of at least $4 billion a year, white-collar crime costs no less than $40 billion.[8]

In short, one cannot do business in a fallen world without at some point encountering the effects of the Fall in the attitudes and behavior of individual people.

Indirect participation in evil. Nor can we escape at least indirect participation in the evil of collective society. For example, I find much to question in the moral and spiritual climate of this country. Yet I pay taxes, some of which fund activities to which I object and to which I think God objects.

Likewise, I buy goods and services and otherwise participate in our economy, knowing that some of my providers have little or no regard for righteousness, justice, or ethical integrity.

To that extent, at least, I aid and assist a culture that often seems to be headed *away* from God, like the culture at Babel in Genesis 11. This is what it means for me to live and work in a fallen world.

Our own sin. But there is a more sinister result of the Fall. Our own sinfulness many times tempts us to work against God and to pursue wrong ends with wrong motives. As we saw in Chapter 2, we sometimes work with very secular attitudes and leave God out of it. We may even turn work into an idol.

I know that I face a daily struggle: Will I go to work to serve Christ and to meet the needs of people? Or will I do my work out of selfish ambition, for my own pride, using people as steppingstones for my agenda?

This may be your struggle, too. Or it may not. You may sign in at work with the attitude that you'll do only the bare necessities of what it takes to keep the job and collect your paycheck. Or perhaps you are on a fast-track to the money tree, motivated purely by a lust for wealth. Or maybe you work overtime simply to escape the needs and pressures of your family life. Or maybe you're driven by a wounded psyche, perhaps out to prove something to your father or some other significant person in your memory.

There are probably dozens of sinful and unhealthy motives that affect work. But the point is that these have never been God's intentions. They are the ways in which sin has permeated each one of us. And they cause us so often to pervert the gift of work into a vehicle for expressing our sin and unhealthiness.

I suggest that you carefully examine yourself and the attitudes with which you approach your work. You may need to confess sin in this area. You may need emotional healing. But be certain that none of us escapes the tragic effects of sin on his own work.[9]

MADE FOR THE STREET

The outcome, then, is that the work world is a jungle for most of us. Work itself, as we have seen, has great dignity before God. But as Christians we cannot avoid conflict between the absolute values of Scripture and the values vacuum in which our culture floats. Nor can we avoid the effects of sin on our own lives.

How, then, can we adequately respond to such a jungle? First, we can rule out two inadequate responses that seem to be gaining popularity: flight and fight. Some Christians think they can escape evil, either by withdrawing from society, or by attempting to capture the culture and its institutions and reconstruct them along Old Testament lines.

Both of these approaches are foolishness. They overlook a crucial fact: As soon as one has eradicated the evils of a society without Christ, or as soon as he forsakes such a culture, he suddenly discovers at least as much sin in himself and among his Christian associates!

Instead, we need to learn from Jesus' parable of the wheat and the weeds in Matthew 13:

> Jesus told them another parable: "The kingdom of heaven is like a man who sowed good seed in his field. But while everyone was sleeping, his enemy came and sowed weeds among the wheat, and went away. When the wheat sprouted and formed heads, then the weeds also appeared.
>
> "The owner's servants came to him and said, 'Sir, didn't you sow good seed in your field? Where then did the weeds come from?'
>
> "'An enemy did this,' he replied.
>
> "The servants asked him, 'Do you want us to go and pull them up?'
>
> "'No,' he answered, 'because while you are pulling the weeds, you may root up the wheat with them. Let both grow together until the harvest. At that time I will tell the harvesters: First collect the weeds and tie them in bundles to be burned; then gather the wheat and bring it into my barn.'" (Matthew 13:24-30, NIV)

There can be no debate about the interpretation of this parable, inasmuch as Jesus Himself explains its meaning several verses later. He says plainly that at the end of the age, "The Son of Man will send out his angels, and they will weed out of his kingdom everything that causes sin and all who do evil" (Matthew 13:41, NIV).

Thus, the task of eliminating sin from society lies with Christ. The task of eliminating sin from our own lives as individuals lies very much with us and our relationship with Christ.

So neither flight nor fight is adequate. That is because people who opt for these responses react to the wrong enemy. Work is not our enemy. Sin is our enemy. And only Christ is adequate to deal with sin. His strategy for dealing with sin, however, is never to remove us from the jungle, but instead to make us adequate to live in the jungle. In John 17:14-15, Jesus prays to His Father regarding us:

> "I have given them Thy word; and the world has hated them, because they are not of the world, even as I am not of the world. I do not ask Thee to take them out of the world, but to keep them from the evil one."

Christ wants us in the world. Not of it, but in it. He has made us for the street. Without question, the street is hostile to Christlikeness. Yet God uses that very tension to teach us how to walk with Him. He uses the workplace, dominated as it is by sinful people and their sinful systems, to test and build our faith and character.

Sin may make the work world a jungle. But we must never forget that Christ is the Lion of Judah, the King of the jungle! If we want to prevail over the tragic consequences of sin in our work, we need to determine that we serve Christ as the King. Let's consider how this can happen in the next chapter.

NOTES: 1. The "curse" is the point in human history, recorded in Genesis 3, at which mankind first sinned, and God pronounced His judgment on that sin and on sinners. This "fall" represents a fundamental disruption in man's relationship with God.
2. Ecclesiastes 2:24, 3:12-13, 5:18-19.
3. 1 Thessalonians 4:11.
4. Alfred L. Malabre, Jr., argues convincingly and disturbingly that this payment will come due quite soon in his disturbing book, *Beyond Our Means* (New York: Random House, 1987).
5. Part of our difficulty in properly interpreting the message of Ecclesiastes comes from a misunderstanding of the word translated "futile" or "vanity." We tend to read it through our twentieth-century eyes as "meaningless." But that is not exactly the idea. Ecclesiastes is not saying that life is absurd and has no purpose. Rather, life is transitory, passing. The person who seeks to ground the meaning of his life in the pursuits of life itself will find that meaning to be as fleeting and temporary as life is. By contrast, the person who establishes the meaning of his life in God, who is outside the system, can accept and live in this very transient life with a moderate sense of satisfaction and joy.
6. "Looking to Its Roots," *Time* (May 25, 1983), page 26.
7. "Looking to Its Roots," page 26.
8. "Looking to Its Roots," page 23.
9. See Chapter 11 for a discussion of our response to this situation.

CHAPTER 8

NEW WORK OR NEW WORKERS?

How Christ Affects Work

I n Chapter 7 we looked at some of the consequences of sin for work. We saw that the curse of Genesis 3 made the work environment much more rugged and uncooperative, which causes work to be toilsome and marked by many setbacks. We also saw that work, even the work of ministry, is characterized by a certain futility. And finally, we noted that living in a fallen world requires that we work alongside sinful people and their systems, and that we also must deal with our own sinfulness.

And yet, it is just at this point that the central message of Christianity makes a big difference for you as a worker. The central message of Christianity is that Christ dealt with your sin at the Cross. This means that He has conquered your greatest enemy.

In this chapter I want to begin to look at the profound difference this makes for everyday work. Let me state the difference this way: Christ's death does not change work but changes the worker. Let's examine this idea and its implications.

CHRIST'S DEATH DID NOT CHANGE WORK

Since Christ conquered sin when He died on the Cross, one would think that that would have reversed the effects of sin, not only on work, but on the whole of creation. And in a sense it did. But it is important for us to appreciate in what sense it did.

Think back to the final year of World War II. In Germany, the Allied troops eventually fought their way to Berlin and surrounded it. In his bunker, Hitler recognized that all was lost and committed suicide. Was the war over? Yes and no. Yes in the sense that the enemy was defeated. But no in the sense that a certain amount of mopping up had to be done.

Likewise in the Asian theater, the atom bomb was dropped on Hiroshima and Nagasaki. Did that end the war? Again, yes and no. Yes in that Japan realized at that point that the end had come. But no in that a surrender had to be negotiated, and a few troops continued to fight on.

In a similar way, Christ's death dealt a mortal blow to sin and to Satan, sin's champion. That victory has ensured the final outcome—the ultimate triumph of God over evil. If the conflict with sin rages on, it is for the simple reason that each human being who is born into the world becomes a new battlefield on which sin launches a new campaign. That may be why things appear to get worse rather than better. There are simply more people, which is to say more sinners.

What does this mean for work? It means that for now the effects of sin remain in effect, even though Christ has won the decisive victory and has promised to some day lift the curse from creation. This is the message of Romans 8:19-21:

> The anxious longing of the creation waits eagerly for the revealing of the sons of God. For the creation was subjected to futility, not of its own will, but because of Him who subjected it, in hope that the creation itself also will be set free from its slavery to corruption into the freedom of the glory of the children of God.

Much could be said about this amazing passage. But the key thing to note is that the creation is still waiting to be released from its "subjection to futility." This is clear from the "hope" mentioned, and from the future tense of the phrase, "will be set free."

Someday Christ will restore the creation to the way God intended it to be before the Fall. Until then, the effects of sin remain in effect. Consider three such effects.

1. The work environment remains uncooperative.

In practical terms this means, first of all, that the work environment remains less cooperative, which makes your work especially difficult and burdensome.

I am reminded of this whenever someone tells me that his business is not doing well. A broker, for instance, complains that he is doing everything he can to close a deal, and yet the deal won't go through. Why? A thousand factors may account for it, but the broker's frustration and anxiety, and the fact that he must try a thousand strategies to overcome those obstacles only underscore the fact that work remains hard.

In other words, Christ in no way eases the difficulties you must face when you hit the street each day. Nor does He give any particular advantage to the Christian. As He told His disciples, God "causes His sun to rise on the evil and the good, and sends rain on the righteous and the unrighteous" (Matthew 5:45).

So being a Christian doesn't automatically exempt you from losing a sale, from having a shipment lost, from seeing your office or store go up in flames, from losing your top sales agent to a competitor, or from being laid off or fired.

2. Work is still marked by futility.

Furthermore, as we saw in the last chapter, a sense of futility still characterizes every human's work. This does not mean that we should not work but that we should remain realistic about what we can accomplish.

For example, the person who discovers a cure for AIDS will undoubtedly win a Nobel Prize and go down in history beside Louis Pasteur, Jonas Salk, and other pioneers of immunology. And rightfully so. That researcher will have made an invaluable contribution to humanity and to history.

And yet that cure, as profoundly valuable as it will be, will solve only one problem at one point in history. Surely, new diseases will arise in the future, demanding even more research and discovery.

Do you see the point? The nature of the curse is such that there can never be any lasting progress. We live and work amid endless cycles of life. As the writer of Ecclesiastes puts it:

> What advantage does man have in all his work
> Which he does under the sun?
> A generation goes and a generation comes,
> But the earth remains forever . . . .
> That which has been is that which will be,
> And that which has been done is that which will be done.
> (Ecclesiastes 1:3-4,9)

3. People are still sinful.

Finally, Christ's death does not alter the fact that we must work alongside sinful people and their systems. In fact, all the way through the New Testament we are reminded as believers that in the world we will come up against people whose values are very different from ours.[1]

CHRIST'S DEATH CHANGES THE WORKER

In light of all this, we might ask, What difference does Christ's death make for work? It is all well and good that He has promised to *someday* do away with the effects of sin on work. But what difference does He make *right now*?

The answer is that right now Christ's strategy is to change you as a worker, not just your work. We caught a glimpse of this truth in the Romans 8 passage listed above: The creation is waiting for "the freedom of the glory of the children of God" (Romans 8:21). You are one of the "children of God" if you have placed your faith in Christ's death as the payment for your sin. Christ now has you in the process of transformation, a process of making you like Him. There are at least three main aspects to this transformation.

1. Christ puts the worker in right relationship with God.

The whole problem with sin is that it separates us from God. Our relationship with Him is cut off. This has unfortunate consequences for our work, but it has absolutely tragic consequences for us as individuals.

It means, on the one hand, that we are face-to-face with an enemy—sin—that has only one goal: to destroy us. And it means, on the other hand, that we are cut off from the one Person who has power over sin and who would do anything to keep it from destroying us.

Now Christ has done everything possible to reestablish the relationship. The one thing He will not do is force us against our will to be reunited with God. But if we freely choose to accept His offer of reconciliation, then our relationship with God is restored.

This puts us back in touch with someone who can deal with sin in our lives. And as I pointed out in the last chapter, sin is our real enemy as workers, not other people and not our work.

This is why it will do no good for Christ to simply do away with the unfortunate effects of sin on work. As we have seen, He intends to do precisely that someday. But what good will it do for Him to restore the creation to the way things were in Genesis 1 and 2 if He fails to also restore people who are fit to live in that creation?

2. Christ puts your work back in right relation with God.

The change that Christ makes in you as a worker is not without consequence for your work. The effects of sin remain in effect, as we have seen. But as a Christian you have more reason than anyone to view your work as significant. Furthermore, Christ becomes your Boss. Let's examine these two implications.

The Christian's work is Christ's work. If you are a Christian, the New

Testament unequivocally affirms the significance and contribution of your work. The apostle Paul said:

> Slaves, in all things obey those who are your masters on earth, not with external service, as those who merely please men, but with sincerity of heart, fearing the Lord. Whatever you do, do your work heartily, as for the Lord rather than for men; knowing that from the Lord you will receive the reward of the inheritance. It is the Lord Christ whom you serve. (Colossians 3:22-24)

To appreciate the importance of this passage, we must understand how slaves fit into the Colossian culture. Like slaves in any society, these were captive, conquered peoples who were assigned the most menial tasks. The Romans had adopted a lifestyle of leisure for the elite, a freedom from mundane tasks. Slaves provided them with that freedom.

So Paul was addressing the lowest members of that culture. What did he tell them? That they were working for God, not merely for their Roman masters. Paul said this *four times* in this passage!

But *how* were they to serve Christ? *Through their work!* In other words, daily work, menial work, often disgusting work, is considered Christ's work.

Now if the lowest members of that culture were to serve Christ, then we should certainly serve Him as well. We know this because Colossians 4:1 addresses the masters of these slaves:

> Masters, grant to your slaves justice and fairness, knowing that you too have a Master in heaven.

The masters also had a Master! Both slaves and masters were to serve Christ. That's rather inclusive. One historian estimates that easily half the Roman population were slaves, while only fifteen to twenty percent were freemen.[2] So, no matter where you or I fit in the pecking order of the work world, Christ takes a direct interest in our work, which means that He views it as significant.

Christ is your Boss. Furthermore, when you become a Christian, Christ becomes your Boss. He takes an extreme interest in your work itself, no matter what it is. This is shown by a parallel passage in Ephesians 6:7-8:

> With good will render service, as to the Lord, and not to men, knowing that whatever good thing each one does, this he will receive back from the Lord, whether slave or free.

Slave or free, no matter what you do for work, you will be rewarded appropriately by Christ.

By the way, notice that Paul calls work a "good thing" in this passage. Earlier in Ephesians, he says that "we are [God's] workmanship, created in Christ Jesus for good works" (Ephesians 2:10).

But what are these "good works"? They are not just "spiritual" activities. That would be a Two-Story assumption. Instead, the context of Ephesians suggests a much broader understanding. In Ephesians 4:1, Paul exhorts his readers to walk in a manner worthy of "the calling" that he explained earlier in chapters 1-3. He then proceeds to show that this "worthy walk" extends to five categories of life: the personal life, the family, work, the Church, and the community.

In other words, "good works" includes anything we do in life that honors God, that fits the way He created us and intends for us to live.

Your work can be one of those "good works." Ephesians 4:28 says:

Let him who steals steal no longer; but rather let him labor, performing with his own hands what is good, in order that he may have something to share with him who has need.

The Greek word for "good" here is *agathos,* which means "noble" or "intrinsically good." We have already seen that all legitimate work is inherently good because it is Godlike. But as a Christian you should strive with all of your being to make your work a "good work," by doing it "as unto the Lord."

And the Lord is Lord of *all* of life. The New Testament knows no distinction between the "sacred," over which Christ has control, and the "secular," which is up for grabs. Instead, Christ expects us to live all of our lives under His lordship.

That's why Paul writes:

And whatever you do in word or deed, do all in the name of the Lord Jesus, giving thanks through Him to God the Father. (Colossians 3:17)

As a Christian, then, you have more reason than most to view your daily work as profoundly significant. You are a servant of Christ, and He is using you and your work to accomplish His purposes.

The Christian is to serve Christ at work. Every time I read the Ephesians 6 and Colossians 3 passages, I am impressed with Paul's emphasis on the dominance Jesus Christ should have in our work. Notice the following statements:

- "as to Christ"
- "as slaves of Christ"
- "as to the Lord"
- "their Master and yours"
- "fearing the Lord"
- "as for the Lord"
- "it is the Lord Christ whom you serve"
- "you too have a Master in heaven."

Why this preeminence? Because Jesus is God, the Creator, the Lord of all of life, the Work-Giver, the Master, the Boss. You and I are His servants, His employees.

Therefore, *everything* about our jobs should be directed toward Him— our purpose and motives, our profits and their use, our decisions, our problems, our relationships with coworkers and customers, our plans, our goals, our equipment, our financing—*everything*.

I'm not suggesting some pious routine by which we sprinkle our labor with a few mumbled prayers. Instead, we need to return to something much more basic: the notion of accountability.

The Ephesians passage teaches that someday we will get to explain our work life to the One who gave it to us. Perhaps we'll get to explain how difficult it was, how inconsiderate our boss was, how lazy our employees were, how our customers didn't pay their bills, and the other vicissitudes of the marketplace.

But we'll also get to explain the puzzling arithmetic on our tax forms, or what really happened to the shipment we promised our client but that never arrived, or the comments we made about associates behind their backs, or the days we called in sick but weren't, or the movies we watched in our hotel rooms on business trips, and so on.

After we've reviewed it all, both the good and the bad, the Lord will then weigh it out and pronounce an evaluation that is just, merciful, and true.

What will He say of you?

If you think I'm being facetious or dramatic, it is probably because Christian teaching has largely dropped the subject of "the fear of the Lord." But this topic relates directly to our work, because it asks the question: Whose opinion of our work ultimately matters? Our own? Our customers'? Our boss's? Our investors'?

Or our Creator's? If we work with the expectation that we and what we do and how we do it and why we do it will someday all come together before Christ for review, then that will make a profound difference in our attitudes, values, and behavior on the job.

3. Christ wants to transform you as a worker.
In 2 Corinthians 5:17, Paul says:

> Therefore if any man is in Christ, he is a new creature; the old things passed away; behold, new things have come.

The change here is as radical as it sounds. Christ is not content to make us good people or even better people; He intends to make us new people, people who are like Him. In regard to our work, this means that He sets about changing our character, our motives, our attitudes, and our values.

Earlier, for instance, I cited Ephesians 4:28. And in Chapter 6 I used this as an illustration of the radical change that takes place as a person turns from sin and pursues Christlikeness. The change is a change of character. If you were to examine the context of Ephesians 4, you would see that Christ has us in a process of transformation. The picture there is of a person changing clothes, taking off a way of life that is unholy, and putting on a way of life that is Christlike.

So a thief, for example, would change from a person who steals to a person who works at honest labor in order to give generously to someone in need. That's a complete transformation!

A friend of mine, Frank Tanana, is one of the best illustrations I know of a guy who is letting Christ remake him into a new person. Frank will be the first to tell you that he is still far from perfect. But he will also tell you that whatever positive traits are in his life are there because of Christ.

Frank has had a fairly distinguished career as a professional baseball pitcher. He talks about the "Old Frank," and the "New Frank":

> I remember in 1977 things were not going my way in a particular game. I'd given up a couple of runs and the fans hollered and really got on my case. Finally, management came out and pulled me.
>
> Well, as I was about to go into the dugout, I gave the crowd an Italian salute—everybody in the stands! Well, that wasn't a good decision. I embarrassed myself, my team, and my profession. I even blew a $100,000 contract with a clothing manufacturer who wanted me to model their line! You reap what you sow!
>
> But you also learn. In 1982, I was 7 and 18, and really just stunk! But I kept my composure—and my job. In the process, I had opportunities to talk about the Lord to a few people who were impressed by how well I was handling things not going so well. So that was a good move on my part, and I was able to influence others.

I learned a lot about responding to authority in 1982, as well! Doug Rader told me in spring training, "You're not going to pitch for me right now. If we need you, we'll use you."

Well, for the first 20 games they didn't need me or use me! But I learned an entirely different attitude. I decided he's the manager and it's his choice. I'm just a player and I'll go down and stay ready. Quite a contrast there from the Frank Tanana of old to the Frank Tanana depending on the Lord to direct my path in the way I respond to authority.[3]

What you find in Frank, as in other workers, is that when Christ goes to work on the character and values of a person, it can have a profound impact on his work. This could happen for you. I have said all along that Christ's strategy is not to transform your work, but to transform you as a worker. And yet by producing a change in you as a person, Christ actually makes a dramatic difference in your work itself, because you are different.

In what way? What are the practical implications of Christlikeness for your job? I invite you to examine some of these in the rest of this book. You'll find that Christ makes a difference:

- In the overall attitude with which you approach your job (Chapter 9)
- In the choices you make about what you do for work (Chapter 10)
- In the way you confront evil at your workplace (Chapter 11)
- In the way you spend your income and live your lifestyle (Chapter 12)
- In the way you approach leisure and non-work activities (Chapter 13)
- In the way you relate to your church (Chapter 14)
- And in the way you relate to coworkers, both Christian and nonChristian (Chapters 15 and 16).

NOTES: 1. For instance, 1 Corinthians 5:9-10, Philippians 2:15, and 1 Peter 4:3-4.
2. Paul F. Scotchmer, "The Christian Meaning of Work," *New Oxford Review*, 47 (May 1980), page 12.
3. Frank Tanana, "Reaping What You Sow: The Consequences of Our Choices," *Christianity at Work* (April 1986).

PART III
WHAT DIFFERENCE DOES IT MAKE?

CHAPTER 9

WORKING FOR GOD
His Work, His Way, His Results

I n Chapter 8, I said that Christ transforms you as a worker, and that this causes significant changes in how you approach your work. In this chapter, we'll see how this affects your overall attitude and perspective toward your job.

Anyone who has been in the service is familiar with the old cliché: There's the right way, the wrong way, and the Navy way!

That pretty much sums up life in any mammoth institution. If you're a rank-and-file member, you're not paid to think—just do your job.

Things were not much different in the Air Force. From day one, they helped me understand that the system did not exist to serve me; rather, I was there to serve the system. As you can well imagine, this came as something of a shock to me as a seventeen-year-old cadet!

That's why I chuckle sometimes at the popular conception of fighter jocks. Novels, TV, and films convey the idea that the defense of our country rests on twenty-two-year-old kids cowboying across the skies in screaming hunks of techno-exotica fueled by jet-powered libido.

I assure you life in the cockpit is much more disciplined. Much more!

We served an extremely elaborate code of instructions, regulations, and protocol designed to ensure efficiency, safety, order, and, as much as anything, respect. The tolerance for violating this code was as thin as a discharge order.

In short, we were commissioned to do the Air Force's work, the Air Force's way. Why? In order to achieve the Air Force's results. That's why we called our flights "missions." They always had a purpose behind them. We were never simply joy-riding across the skies.

Now this way of life is somewhat similar to the way our work relates to God. I stress "somewhat" because God is not a drill sergeant barking orders from heaven. Nor is His tolerance for our failures so slight.

But I would like to suggest that as humans, we need to view our work as *His work*. We need to do it *His way*. And we need to trust Him for *His results*. Let's unpack these principles.

HIS WORK: OUR MOTIVES

Earlier we saw that God is a Worker and has created you in His image to be His coworker. Consequently, your work is an extension of God's work. Furthermore, your work is a means whereby you can fulfill His Great Commandments: to love Him, to love other people, and to love yourself. So as a Christian, you are to go to work for the same reason you go to church: to worship and serve Christ. Though you obey human bosses and meet the needs of human customers, your ultimate Boss is Jesus Christ.

All of this should have a profound effect on your motives on the job. Imagine as you tie your tie or put on your makeup in the morning asking yourself: How does my work relate to God? Am I going to work as His coworker? Do I see my work as part of His work in the world? And how does my work relate to others and the needs they have? Am I serving them? And am I faithfully providing for my family? Answering questions like these every day could infuse your work with a new enthusiasm and vitality!

How does your work relate to God? So often I meet people who tell me their employment is "just a job." They might as well say that their life is "just a life."

I realize that not every job is thrilling or spectacular. Nor must every job be particularly fulfilling. But what I hear these people saying is that their work is boring and insignificant.

This is tragic because God doesn't view your work as insignificant. As we have seen, He regards your job, and you, with great dignity and value. So should you!

Obviously, employers could do far more to remove some of the boredom of many tasks and to convey meaning and worth to their employees. But as a Christian you need to sign in at work as God's coworker and as an employee of Christ.

A business model. One way to gain this perspective is to ask: As God's coworker, how does my work serve other people and their needs?

Let me suggest a model to illustrate this perspective on work. Imagine a triangle with "customer" at the apex, "employees" at one point of the base, and "employer" at the other point.

These are the three human roles involved in most work world situations in our culture. And God desires that the needs of *each* should be met. The customer obviously has needs that you and your business are there to serve.

But if you are an employer, you also have a responsibility to serve the needs of your employees. They need adequate, appropriate compensation. But they also need proper, fair management; equitable employment policies; a reasonably safe work environment; appropriate tools, supplies, and equipment; regard for their lives outside of work, especially their families; and much more.

If you are an employee, you have a responsibility to serve the needs of your fellow employees and your employer. Your coworkers need you to do your part with excellence, with a spirit of cooperation, with honesty, and so forth. Likewise, your employer needs a dependable worker who is conscientious, puts forth his best effort, is honest, and gives value in exchange for his wages.

Using the model. Let's use this model in a real-life illustration. Suppose, for instance, that you are a single parent who works for the Department of Defense processing CHAMPUS claims. (CHAMPUS is a sort of medical insurance program for dependents of military personnel.) As God's coworker in the CHAMPUS system, how does your work serve the needs of others? I might suggest a few ways; you can think of others.

First, you directly help those who have filed claims. Any insurance program, military or otherwise, creates a monolithic system. The size is an asset in minimizing risk to the company and those it insures. But it sometimes works to the disadvantage of the individual who needs help from the system.

Now obviously, you cannot be responsible for every aspect of every claim that comes your way. Yet to the extent of your ability and responsibility, you can treat the claims that cross your desk as though they were crossing the desk of Christ.

Why? Because some sixteen-year-old mother of a sick infant whose husband is off on a ship somewhere sits at the other end of that claim. The form is her only way of communicating with the system. When it reaches you, is she dealing with an impersonal "system" or with a conscientious worker representing Christ? It all depends on your attitude at work.

So the mother, her child, and her husband need you to do your best work on their behalf. The same is true for every claim that comes your way.

But your coworkers also need you. This may sound laughable in such a huge enterprise, especially if your boss or others act as though "No one is indispensable here! There are plenty of other hires where you came from!"

Yet despite the inherent foolishness of this view, your work contributes to the overall objective of supplying health benefits to people. In your own way, you actually help keep the system running. And since the system provides income for you and your coworkers, you serve the needs of your coworkers.

You also serve the interests of American citizens and their government. Your work is part of what it takes to field a reliable defense. It would be difficult if not impossible to recruit qualified people for the service without providing medical benefits for their families. These dependents need such care, and in some small way you make that care possible.

Thus, your work ultimately has benefit for me and my family, and for anyone who lives and works under the protection of the United States.

Finally, your work obviously provides an income for you and your family. Since, in our illustration, you are a single parent, your child or children probably need daycare. Certainly you need housing, food, clothing, and transportation. Your work helps to provide for these needs.

Can you see how a biblical view of work redefines how you think about your job? As God's coworker, you can enter the workplace with a tremendous sense of God's presence and the conviction that God's power is at work in you to accomplish His work on behalf of other people.

Feel His pleasure! Perhaps you saw the movie, *Chariots of Fire.* You'll recall that the film tells the story of Eric Liddell, an Olympic runner from Scotland in the 1930s.

In the film, his sister questions why he intends to run in the Olympics rather than enter the ministry as a missionary. In a very dramatic moment, he turns to her and says, "Jenny, when I run, I feel God's pleasure."

That's an impressive appreciation of the presence of God. Liddell recognizes the fact that God wants to use him in the arena of running. God wants to do the same with you in your sphere of influence. When you do your work, He wants you to feel His pleasure.

HIS WAY: YOUR "WORKSTYLE"

Your work is an extension of God's work. That is why it has great dignity. But if it is God's work, then it must be done God's way. With dignity comes responsibility.

This means you need to work with a godly "workstyle." By "workstyle" I mean the way you do your work—the attitudes you express, the methods you employ, the strategies you use to achieve your results, and so forth. If the term "lifestyle" refers to how you typically live your life, "workstyle" has to do with how you typically do your work.

What should such a workstyle look like? So far in our study, I've tried to show that you as a layperson have the same dignity in your work as the pastor or missionary. But this implies that you also have the same responsibility to honor God in your work.

Character. Think about what this means for a moment. I am the president of Career Impact Ministries, a nonprofit Christian organization. What kind of behavior would you expect from me because I lead such an organization? How would you expect *me* to relate to my associates? Would you expect me to be selfish, ambitious, and excessively competitive? What would you expect in terms of the quality of the materials we produce? What would you expect of my language and the way I respond to people? How would you expect me to resolve conflicts? No doubt, you have a whole world of expectations for my conduct because of the position I hold.

And yet, I would challenge you that the same standards apply to you. Maybe not according to our culture, but certainly according to the Scriptures. You should pursue healthy relationships with the people you work with, just as I should. You should resolve conflicts with coworkers as peacefully and wisely as possible, just as I should. You should maintain high integrity, just as I should.

After all, you are doing God's work, just as I am. It is not just I who am doing God's work. You, too, are doing His work. And this gives you great dignity. But it also gives you great responsibility to do God's work, God's way.

This responsibility extends to a host of day-to-day work situations. Bill and I have identified at least ninety "critical issues" as we call them, areas in which Christians need to live with ethical distinction. These include matters of integrity, relationships on the job, hiring and firing, the quality of one's work, and many more. In areas like these, you need to distinguish yourself by your character.

Two workstyles. By way of illustration, Bill recalls taking his car to a mechanic for service. He had asked around, and someone had suggested this particular mechanic. "He'll do a good job. He's a Christian," this reference had said.

Bill asked the mechanic to check his brakes, check his carburetor, and change the oil, but not the filter. Yet upon returning, Bill discovered that the shop had given him a complete tune-up, new brakes, and a new oil filter! The total came to more than $400!

Needless to say, Bill disputed both the work and the price. But what struck him most was the slipshod performance and questionable ethics of the shop, run as it was by a believer.

By contrast, Bill took his car on another occasion to a different mechanic, also a Christian. In this case, the fellow wrote down in detail what was to be performed, what the estimated charges would be, and where to contact Bill if additional costs seemed likely.

The work was completed on time and according to the agreed upon charges. In fact, part of the job had included replenishing the freon in the air-conditioning. But once the mechanic had hooked up the gauges and so forth, he had found the level to be fine. He didn't charge for that. "Can't charge for what don't need fixin'," he explained.

This man impressed Bill by his workstyle, and by the quality and honesty of his work. He was doing God's work, God's way. In fact, I submit that in the transaction between Bill and that mechanic, the central question from God's perspective was: Did the mechanic service the car as though Christ Himself were wielding the tools? Remember that in the last chapter we looked at Ephesians 6:7-8, which says that God will someday evaluate the performance and motives of that mechanic.

Authority. Another crucial aspect of workstyle is our attitude toward authority. We've already seen that as a Christ-follower, you work for Jesus; He is your Boss. But He demands that you respect and obey whoever is in authority over you on earth (Ephesians 6:5-6):

> Slaves, be obedient to those who are your masters according to the flesh, with fear and trembling, in the sincerity of your heart, as to Christ; not by way of eyeservice, as men-pleasers, but as slaves of Christ, doing the will of God from the heart.

Or as Peter told his readers (1 Peter 2:18):

> Servants, be submissive to your masters with all respect, not only to those who are good and gentle, but also to those who are unreasonable.

In practical terms, this means abiding by the rules and policies of your company, and carrying out the orders of those above you. It also includes obeying the law. I'm well aware that there are special cases where we might question whether blind obedience is the best policy. And of course rules, policies, and laws sometimes need to be revised or done away with.

But these few exceptions ought never to justify our ignoring authority, even authority we do not respect. No matter how despicable those over us may behave, we must see that standing behind them is Christ Himself. Naturally He takes no pleasure in despotic or dishonest leaders. But neither does He think much of disobedient or devious employees.

The point is that the *way* we do our work says everything about how seriously we take our faith. In fact, Paul claims that when we work with a godly workstyle and live with an ethically distinctive lifestyle, we "adorn the doctrine of God." That is, our character and our work paint a beautiful picture of Christlikeness.[1] This is doing God's work, God's way.

HIS RESULTS: OUR OUTLOOK

But when we do God's work, God's way, we can also trust Him for the results. This is a remarkably liberating concept, both for those who tend toward boredom at work and for those who find work to be extremely stimulating.

Boredom. First of all, the idea that God is using you to accomplish a specific purpose can be a real help if you question the significance of your career.

Three years ago, a dentist studied the same ideas that I have presented in this book. Time and time again ever since, he has told me that these biblical principles of work have revolutionized his feelings about his job.

You may know that dentists have one of the highest suicide rates of any profession. It's a career that has the kind of routine and monotony that make it a high-stress occupation. And this particular individual had been experiencing quite a bit of that.

But as he began to think about his work as being God's work, and as he attempted to do it God's way, he developed a sense of destiny and calling. He perceived that God had called him to contribute to the physical well-being of people, and that his skills as a dentist contributed to the health of the people who came to see him.

In short, he saw his work, dentistry, as a ministry. This has helped him in the midst of his routine, everyday work.

And so it is for all of us. We all find aspects of our job to be very mundane, or perhaps even distasteful. And yet, when we realize that we are in the job because God has placed us there, it lends a sense of dignity, as well as destiny, to our work.

Careerism. But this saw cuts in the other direction, too. Perhaps you are like many in our culture, in that you find work to be fulfilling and exhilarating. This is wonderful—to a point.

Unfortunately, many people place more expectations on their careers than any career can possibly fulfill. If you are one of these, you probably have a very unrealistic view of the product of your labor.

In Chapter 7, I mentioned that Ecclesiastes points to the futility that marks so much of our labor. The book explains that we work amid endless cycles of life, so that whatever we do has pretty much been done before, and will need to be done again after we're gone. Hence, we should never look to the product of our work to give us ultimate meaning and dignity.

That is not to say that the product of our work has no meaning or dignity—only that it need not form the basis of our personal worth and significance.

But unfortunately, this is precisely what work has come to mean for too many of us. The outcome depends on us, and we depend on the outcome. This turns work into an idol, and as we saw in Chapter 2, idols make harsh masters.

By contrast, those who put Christ first in their careers find a refreshing sense of release from the slavery of work. You may have discovered that while hard work satisfies, overwork destroys. Yet overwork is the inevitable slavery that captures the person who believes, "It all depends on me!"

Winning isn't the only thing. A few years ago, a major NFL coach retired. Following the news conference at which he announced his resignation, a reporter pulled him aside. "Coach," he was asked, "how is it that you are retiring from professional football after only three or four years, while men like Tom Landry, the coach of the Dallas Cowboys, has been in the game for twenty or more years?"

The retiree paused for a moment, and then looked the reporter in the eye and said, "Well, as you know, Tom Landry is a Christian. He loves to win about as much as anyone I have ever met. But Tom realizes that the biggest thing in life is not football."

That's a profound comment! And Landry has a profound testimony, in that his faith lends perspective to his work. Over and over the press carry reports about the personal side of Coach Landry. To a man they praise him for pursuing a high level of excellence, for having a high regard for good coaching, and for turning in as professional a performance as he can. And yet they also report that for Landry, there are bigger things to life than just winning.

A man like Landry is able to rest and relax because he knows that his job is to do God's work, God's way, and to trust God with the results. Not that he is excited when he loses; he hates losing. We all do. And yet he realizes that losing a football game is not the ultimate disaster. He avoids that stress because he has a biblical view of the outcome of his work.

Who is in control? God, in His sovereignty, may select you to go through adversity in your career. He would allow that to show a watching world the reality of your faith and how you deal with adversity as His coworker. On the other side, He might shower you with incredible success and achievement, again to show a watching world how you handle it.

Either way, the outcome of your work is largely out of your control. Not totally. You have some measure of control over what happens. You must make decisions, perform as best as you can, monitor your character and ethics.

But so much is beyond your direct control: the overall economy; decisions made by foreign governments; the value of the dollar; the choices of your coworkers. You have no way of controlling these events.

Consequently, you must ultimately trust God for the results of your labor, and do whatever is within your limited sphere of power to promote a God-honoring outcome. But having this perspective can be a tremendous relief from the stress and anxiety that plague our culture.

CONCLUSION

His work. His way. His results. Adopting such a perspective could transform the way you approach your job each day. It could eliminate the chasm between your work and your spiritual life, bringing them back together into a meaningful whole. It could mean working with a sense that you are participating in the highest and noblest thing any man or woman could ever do—God's work.

NOTES: 1. See Titus 2:9-10.

CHAPTER 10

FINDING A JOB YOU CAN LOVE
Job Selection

O
ne of the great puzzles to solve in life is to find a job you can love and
that someone will pay you to do. Notice the two sides to this issue: a
job you love and a job worth doing. The trick is to solve both of these.
For example, you might love to go fishing every day, but who would pay
you to do that? On the other side, you might find a job that pays well, even
extremely well, and yet every morning find yourself hating to get up out of bed
and go do it.

How about you? Do you love your job? Do you think it is a job worth
doing? In this chapter I'll look at the issue of job selection. As you'll discover,
the principles we covered in Part II have much to say to this important topic.

First I'll consider whether God even has a specific "career" in mind for
you. Then I'll discuss two broad areas that seem to confuse many people in this
regard: finding God's will and the idea of calling. Next I'll mention some
practical steps you can take regarding career decisions. And finally I'll look at
two special topics, deciding whether you should pursue vocational ministry
and the question of whether to change careers.

If you are dissatisfied with your career, you are not alone. The Marketing
and Research Corporation of Princeton, New Jersey, reported in 1976 that
"fifty to eighty percent of Americans are in the wrong jobs."[1] In fact, getting a
big paycheck has very little to do with job satisfaction.

Of course, most of us don't care whether one percent or ninety-nine
percent of Americans are satisfied with their jobs. In the end, we're mostly
concerned that *we* find a job we can love and that is worth doing. So how can
we solve this puzzle? Let's see what help the Scriptures give us in job
selection.

131

GOD AND CAREER PLACEMENT

In Part II we said that God is a worker and has created man in His image to be His coworker. But if God has created people to be His coworkers to help Him manage the creation, then it makes sense that He would create people with different abilities to accomplish different tasks. The needs of creation are so diverse and managing it takes so many different skills that a wide variety of workers with different skills would be required.

Vocational variety. And that is exactly what we find. As early as Genesis 4, we can see a variation among workers. Adam and Eve had two sons: "Abel was a keeper of flocks, but Cain was a tiller of the ground" (Genesis 4:2). A shepherd and a farmer. Later in Genesis 6, we find Noah and his sons constructing an ark—a truly astounding project, given that it had not yet rained on the earth! Perhaps this is why it took them almost one hundred years to complete the task.

Of course, after the flood Noah went back to farming. Many generations went by, and in Genesis 11 we find that people had learned the skills of construction and how to manufacture building materials. The point is that from its beginnings, humanity demonstrates a rich variety of skills and abilities, all of which have been given by God.

Your design. This implies that God has made you with a specific design. As one of His creatures, He has given you personal resources—a personality, talent, abilities, interests, and so forth—which can be used vocationally. Evidence that this is so comes from passages such as Psalm 139:13-16:

> For Thou didst form my inward parts;
> Thou didst weave me in my mother's womb.
> I will give thanks to Thee, for I am fearfully and wonderfully made;
> Wonderful are Thy works,
> And my soul knows it very well.
> My frame was not hidden from Thee,
> When I was made in secret,
> And skillfully wrought in the depths of the earth.

It is clear that you are not simply a random collection of molecules thrown together by chance. God has crafted you in a very unique and personal way. In terms of your vocation, this means that you are fit to do certain tasks.

It therefore follows that the "right" job for you is one in which there is a good match between the way God has designed you and a job requiring someone with your abilities. How, then, can you find such a match? This is the career question. Before addressing it, however, we must discuss two issues that surround this discussion: God's will and the idea of calling.

FINDING GOD'S WILL

There can be no question that God has a will. He is a volitional Being, who from eternity chooses in a way that accomplishes His purposes and honors His nature and character. Within His will, we find things that He directly wants, such as the creation of the earth, the creation of individual people, and so forth. Of course, there are also things that God permits but that He may or may not "desire," such as evil and death.

As Christians, then, it is obvious that if we want to please God, we must determine what His will is and we must obey it. This is Paul's point in Ephesians 5:15-17:

> Therefore be careful how you walk, not as unwise men, but as wise, making the most of your time, because the days are evil. So then do not be foolish, but understand what the will of the Lord is.

How can we understand what the will of the Lord is? Let me suggest three principles.

1. Know the Scriptures.

The most direct revelation of God's will is found in the Scriptures. For instance, the Bible reveals that it is God's will that people find salvation in Christ. It says that it is God's will that people find jobs and become self-supporting. It says that God wills that people reject evils such as lying, cheating, immorality, and the like.

This makes it critical that if we wish to do God's will, we must understand the Scriptures. I often hear some Christians complaining that they do not know what God's will is. Yet I find that those same Christians do not know their Bibles. If they did, perhaps they would know more of God's will. In fact, one wise scholar has said that if we spent all of our time obeying what is revealed in Scripture, we would have very little time left to worry about what is not revealed in Scripture!

2. Use wisdom.

And yet, many areas of life are obviously not addressed by the Word. Career and job selection is one of those areas. There are certainly a few broad parameters set forth. For instance, certain kinds of work would be ruled out as being illegal or immoral. But none of us will find a passage telling us directly which job to take.

So, then, how can we find God's will in such a "gray" area? Gary Friesen has written an excellent book that addresses that very question entitled *Decision Making and the Will of God*.[2] He explains that in an area like career choice, in which God has not directly spoken, we have freedom of choice:

> In nonmoral decisions, the goal of the believer is to make wise deci-
> sions on the basis of spiritual expediency. In this statement, some
> definitions are important. "Spiritual" means that the ends in view, as
> well as the means to those ends, are governed by the moral will of
> God. In nonmoral decisions, as in every other aspect of life, the Chris-
> tian's aim is to glorify and please God. In that sense, every goal and
> procedure is to be "spiritual." "Expediency" refers to the quality of
> being suitable or advantageous to the end in view. Put simply, it
> means what works best to get the job done—within God's moral will,
> of course. And finally, Dr. J.I. Packer's definition of "wisdom" is right
> on target: "Wisdom is the power to see, and the inclination to choose,
> the best and highest goal, together with the surest means of obtaining
> it." Wisdom is the ability to figure out what is spiritually expedient in
> a given situation.[3]

3. Examine God's design.
I agree with Friesen's point of view. However, I would also point out that God has in fact revealed His will to a great extent in the way He has designed creation, including you. For instance, it is God's will that the earth has four seasons. It is God's will that different parts of the world have various climates. It is God's will that salmon swim upstream to spawn, and that bees and other insects pollinate flowers.

Likewise, at an individual level, it is God's will that you and I are living in this day and age, and in this culture. And it is God's will that you have various talents and abilities and skills, some of which you have already demonstrated, and some of which you have perhaps not yet demonstrated.

The point is that if you want to find God's will for a career, you should start by assessing what equipment He has sovereignly designed into you. That equipment is part of His will. For example, if you have a large, muscular frame and enjoy working with your hands, that is obviously God's will, in that He has designed you that way. Likewise, if you have a brilliant mind and the ability to think abstractly, that is God's will.

Yet, I find this to be one of the *last* places some Christians look to find

God's will. This is unfortunate, because while self-assessment is not the only means of determining God's will, it is certainly a major one.

Design reveals the designer's will. How major? Let me illustrate. Suppose I built an airplane, and then asked you, "How are we going to use it?" You might suggest a variety of uses for the plane: perhaps as an air taxi, perhaps as a commercial jetliner, perhaps as an air-cargo plane, perhaps as an intelligence reconnaissance craft, perhaps as a fighter for defense purposes, perhaps as a bomber, or perhaps as a test aircraft.

There could be a dozen or so uses for that plane. But the main thing to notice is that no matter what purpose the plane is put to, that purpose will likely involve flying. As the designer, I have designed into the plane the capacity for flight. So it wouldn't make sense to use the plane for anything besides flying.

Of course, people are far more complicated than planes. But you see the point. God has designed you with certain abilities, so it makes sense to say that He wills you to pursue a certain type of work that utilizes those abilities.

In fact, we might take this illustration a step further. While the plane is obviously capable of flight, I as the designer have no doubt foreseen that it should be made suitable for a special type of flight.

For instance, suppose I built it with radically swept wings, a honeycomb structure, extremely light but durable skin, ultra-advanced avionics, and engines built for speed. That would predispose the craft to a certain type of mission. I would not want to use it merely as a sightseeing plane, though it certainly could serve that purpose. Nor would I want to load it up with cargo, because it probably could not hold very much, and it would be hard to load and unload. No, I would likely recommend it for flight involving supersonic speed, such as reconnaissance or intercept.

In a similar way, God has not only designed you in general terms, but with many refined specifics as well. Those specifics fit you for a particular type of work. So if you want to determine God's will for your work, then I suggest you start with self-assessment.[4]

CALLING

Another issue often raised in regard to career selection is the concept of calling. The idea is that God somehow has a special plan or purpose for some workers, and that He indicates it via a "call." Normally, we think of this call in connection with a call to some ministry.

For that reason, many workers feel that while it is easy to see how a missionary or a preacher might be called, it is much less certain whether God's call extends to a plumber, a doctor, or a salesperson.

Of course, this has unfortunate implications for the dignity of everyday work and workers. For if only clergy are called, that implies that "secular" workers are not called—that somehow they did not make God's "first team." A related idea is that all believers are called, but that clergy have a "special calling" or "higher calling." The result is the same.

The New Testament evidence. What do we find in the New Testament regarding calling? The first thing that leaps out at us is that all believers are "called."[5] The idea is that God has summoned us from a condition of sin to share in the benefits of His salvation in Christ. This is a general call, which does not seem to have reference to vocation.

Are there any vocational "calls"? Yes, there is *one*: the apostle Paul. Gary Friesen explains:

> In the New Testament, there are three instances of this kind of call:
> (1) God's call of Paul to be an apostle (Romans 1:1; 1 Corinthians 1:1);
> (2) God's call of Barnabus and Saul to be the Church's first mission-
> aries (Acts 13:2); and (3) God's call to Paul and his companions to take
> the gospel to Macedonia (Acts 16:9-10). However, careful examination
> of these examples along with the rest of the New Testament reveals
> that they are the exception rather than the rule.[6]

Friesen goes on to build a plausible case for why a vocational "call" like Paul's is not normative, either for the New Testament Christian or for Christians today.

Vocational implications. However, let me suggest one improvement on Friesen's view, which may clarify this issue of calling. I think a more accurate way to describe Paul's "call" is to say that, like every believer, he was called first to be God's person, but that that call had significant implications for his career. In fact, given the nature of his career, Paul's call had spectacular implications. But it had implications for far more than just his career. It involved the whole of his life.

But the same could be said for *any* of us. Each of us is called, and our calling has implications for our careers, as well as for the whole of our lives.

The evidence that Paul saw his call as nothing fundamentally different from that of other Christians is found in Romans 1:1,6:

> Paul, a bond-servant of Christ Jesus, called as an apostle, set apart for
> the gospel of God . . . among whom you also are the called of Jesus
> Christ.

The word "also" indicates that the call in verse 6 is the same call as verse 1. This does not mean that Paul saw every believer as an apostle, but that Paul saw himself, as well as every believer, as being "called of Jesus Christ." The reason why Paul so often speaks of himself as being "called as an apostle" is because he saw his calling inextricably wrapped up with his life's work. (See Galatians 1:11-17 in this regard.)

Similarly, evidence that calling has implications for our work and the rest of our lives comes from Ephesians 4:1:

> I, therefore, the prisoner of the Lord, entreat you to walk in a manner worthy of the calling with which you have been called.

In Ephesians 1-3, Paul has described this "calling with which you have been called." In Ephesians 4-6, Paul describes the "worthy walk" that should characterize those who have been called. As I mentioned earlier, this walk involves broad categories of life: our personal and spiritual life, our home, our work, our church, and our community.

In short, *all* believers, including Paul, are on an equal footing in terms of calling. God has called us—that is, summoned us, set us apart; as we would say in business, has "tapped" us—to be His people. And He expects us to be His people in the five areas mentioned.

But what are the specific implications of this "call" for career?

THE CAREER QUESTION

Let me answer this question by asking another: What is the common ground for Paul and every other believer in terms of *what* we should do vocationally? I think the answer to this question is: *In our work we should strive to make the greatest contribution we can to people in light of the resources and responsibilities God has given us.* Let's unpack this statement.

1. Resources and responsibilities

How can we know what vocation will enable us to make the greatest contribution? The place to begin, as I suggested before, is with self-assessment: What work has God designed us to do? What personal resources has He equipped us with?

For Paul, this was easy to determine. He was gifted by God as an apostle. In fact, Paul tells us in Galatians 1 that God gave him extremely clear directions as to what He wanted him to do vocationally. However, as we have said, this is the exception rather than the norm.

Of course, some people find their vocational bent fairly early. Mozart, for example, was a child prodigy, who knew from an early age that he would spend his life in music. Likewise, Einstein knew as a youth that he would contribute his greatest work in the area of physics. In a similar way, I've met a number of people, both in business and in the ministry, who have known all of their lives that they belonged in the career they are in.

An assessment tool. However, for most of us, career direction is not so evident. Fortunately, the technology exists to help us discern our God-given design. It is a simple and natural tool that is now widely used to help people in career decisions.

This tool was unnecessary a hundred or more years ago since few people then had a choice about their careers. But today, most people in our culture, and certainly most college-educated workers, have extremely wide latitude in determining their careers. In fact, this freedom of choice actually proves to be something of a problem. So we are fortunate to have a resource that helps us perceive how God has wired us before we start looking for a job.

The tool I am referring to no doubt goes under different names. But I am most familiar with it as the System for Identifying Motivated Abilities (SIMA). I was introduced to this resource by Ralph Mattson of People Management, Inc.[7] He and his partner, Arthur Miller, describe this tool and some of the theory behind it in their fine paperback, *Finding a Job You Can Love*[8] (from which the title to this chapter is borrowed).

To briefly summarize the SIMA process, the assessment asks you to look back on your whole life and answer three questions: What have I enjoyed doing? What have I done well (as *you* define "well")? And what have I done that accomplished something? You must list as many incidents that fit these criteria as possible—not just things that you have done in a job, but accomplishments and situations from childhood and youth as well.

Usually an individual can list about thirty or so situations that fit these criteria. The process then asks you to go back and detail eight of them in terms of the specifics of what you did, how you did it, and what you found fulfilling about it.

The motivated abilities pattern. Then, as you or some specialist sift through those details of personal accomplishments, etc., and analyze them, a *pattern* emerges that tells you a great deal about what motivates you and what you are able to do. Specifically, the pattern presents a central motivational thrust that is the main end toward which all of your activity is driven; the abilities you are motivated to use in accomplishing that central motivation; the subject matter with which you do your best work; the recurring circumstances and environment in which you do your best work; and the nature of your operating relationships, especially in relation to authority.

Mattson and Miller refer to this as your *motivated abilities pattern* (MAP). Unlike most skills and aptitude tests, the SIMA process tells you not only what abilities you have demonstrated, but which ones you are motivated to use. This process is based on the premise that we learn more about ourselves from our successes than from our failures. If we can identify not only *what* we have done well but *why*, then we have enormous clues as to what we are likely to do well in the future and why.

Follow your map. One of the values in knowing your MAP is that it redefines the way you think about yourself and your career. You no longer think of yourself as simply "a lawyer." Instead, your MAP might say you are "someone who is motivated to prevail in a cause that he believes is right." You just happen to express that motivation through law. But if you were ever to leave law, or needed to leave law, your career would change, but your MAP would not. You would simply use it in another career.

In short, I believe that the SIMA process puts you far more in touch with the way God has designed you than any other current means of assessment or analysis. Knowing that design will take you a long way toward knowing how you can make your greatest contribution vocationally.

2. Your greatest contribution

But of course, knowing what you are fitted to do is only the first step in the career question. You must go on to consider what work you should do, given your design.

Once again, for Paul this was not a problem. God gave him a specific vocation and sometimes even gave him specific projects within that vocation. So Paul had little choice in terms of his career.

He really was much like Christians who were slaves in the New Testament, who likewise had little if any choice about being slaves. They were stuck in their situations and had to live out God's will and make their vocational contributions as slaves.[9]

By contrast, so many of us today have wide latitude in our career options, as I mentioned earlier. So for us, the question of where we could make our best contribution vocationally is problematic.

Unfortunately, too many Christians try to solve this problem by putting on the Two-Story glasses I mentioned in Chapter 3. Looking at the career question through those lenses, one will inevitably conclude that the ministry makes the greatest contribution, because it deals with the eternal, the sacred, and the souls of men.

But may I suggest an alternative model for evaluation. Let's consider a career option three ways: according to its contribution to people, its value to God, and how you as a worker in that career will be rewarded by God.

Contribution to people. First, we all recognize that different careers make differing levels of contribution to people. But we run into trouble when we start comparing careers in order to determine those levels. Sometimes the difference seems obvious: The brain surgeon clearly makes a greater contribution to mankind than the guy who sells firecrackers. Likewise, the evangelist who leads hundreds to Christ makes a greater contribution than the acrobat who entertains hundreds.

But more often, the level of contribution is extremely difficult, if not impossible, to determine by mere comparisons. Who makes a greater contribution, the brain surgeon or the evangelist? I submit that the question is nonsense. Both can make outstanding contributions, but their contributions are of *two different kinds.* So comparing careers probably won't help you to determine in which career you could make your greatest contribution.

Of course, you could try to show that one kind of contribution (the evangelist's) is more significant than the other (the surgeon's). But that's putting on Two-Story glasses! I prefer to leave them off. The two careers make important but different contributions, and I'm content to leave it at that.

Value to God. But secondly we must ask: How does God value these different careers? Remember that it is God who gives each person the abilities and opportunities he has. So when He evaluates each worker, He is able to avoid comparing him to others. Instead, He measures each person as an individual and asks, "How faithful was this person with the resources and responsibilities I gave to him?"

Thus, the careers of the firecracker salesman and the acrobat can have great value to God, if these workers are faithful to be all that God made them to be. Likewise, the brain surgeon and the evangelist could be great disappointments to God if they squander or abuse their great gifts.

Reward. Needless to say, God will reward each worker on his own merits, and not in comparison to others. You might want to review the Parable of the Talents in Matthew 25. You'll recall that one slave doubled his five talents, while a second slave doubled his two talents. Different contributions, humanly speaking. But both were praised by the master, and since both had been as faithful as possible, given their capacities, both received the same reward.

3. The importance of service.

I'll discuss more about deciding for the ministry in a moment. But first, let me mention that many people in our culture are now basing their career decisions not on whether those careers contribute to other people but on whether they contribute to themselves. They look for the best-paying jobs, or ones that will provide them with the most comfort. Of course, there is nothing wrong with good pay or a comfortable job. Yet to make these the main criteria for job selection is opposed to a godly view of work.

You'll recall that in Part II I said that one of the purposes of work is to serve the needs of people. This flows out of the Great Command to love our neighbor as ourselves.

This does not mean that the only significant work is work that is directly involved with people, but rather that our work should in some way *serve* the needs of people.

As we consider careers, we need to think about far more than just our comfort. Recall the business model I presented in the last chapter, where I said that work is a triangle of relationships between yourself, your employer or employees, and your customers. Biblically you are responsible to contribute to the needs of *all three*. If you are only concerned about your own comfort, then you will not be able to contribute responsibly to your customers or your coworkers.

YOU MAKE THE CALL!

In the end, of course, you must make a decision regarding your career. Hopefully, you have carefully examined yourself and the resources God has given you. And hopefully you have evaluated your different options in terms of the questions raised earlier. But how can you then decide which direction to go?

The answer is, Choose! No one, not even God, can make the choice for you. To a large extent you must decide how you will answer the question, How can I make the greatest contribution to people in light of the resources and responsibilities God has given me? In our culture, this is a freedom you have, but it is also a responsibility you have before God, as well as a privilege.

In making that choice, you will find that the decision is largely subjective. Sure, you may have many objective factors to weigh: your past accomplishments, your educational credentials, various job offers, the locations of those offers, different salary packages, different family needs, etc.

But in the end, you will find that nothing makes the choice for you. You must decide, and for most of us, that decision has a largely subjective or intuitive dimension to it. Consequently, many of us feel a sense of uncertainty about whether we are embarking upon the "right" career. This is normal.

Many Christians deal with this subjective element by praying for a "peace" from God about the "right" decision. I find nothing wrong with asking God for peace, for a confidence that He is with you in the decision. In fact, we should ask God for His wisdom, which James describes as "peaceable."[10]

But I certainly would advise against basing a career decision on the notion that God has somehow committed Himself to giving a mystical, inner prompting one way or another. While inner impressions and feelings are valid and normal, it is impossible to define with certainty either their source or their meaning. Consequently, we must not invest these subjective impressions with divine authority.[11]

DECIDING FOR THE MINISTRY

In light of these principles, I am often asked, "Doug, I agree that my work should honor Christ and meet the needs of people, and that I should pursue a career for which I am fit, and that I have great latitude in terms of my career choice. But what about the ministry? How do I know whether God wants me to go into the ministry?"

The answer is, How does *anyone* determine what career to go into? As I have suggested, he looks at his God-given resources (his design, his experience, his background, whatever training he's had); he looks at his options and opportunities; he looks at his own feelings, desires, and motivations; he prays; and then he chooses.

The red herring of significance. Just make sure that you don't base your decision on the idea that going into the ministry will bring you greater significance. In fact, if that is your motivation, I suggest that you actually have worldly motives. You would be no different than the person who goes into business purely out of a desire to become filthy rich. You would be doing what James and John did when they asked Jesus to give them positions of prominence in His Kingdom.[12] You would be pursuing a certain career out of a faulty belief that it could somehow earn you more value, standing, or importance with God.

When I was in seminary, I was the president of my class for a year. This position gave me the opportunity to counsel many of my classmates. Unfortunately, it seemed that so many of them had arrived at seminary via the same logic: "I wanted my life to be significant, to really count. So I looked around to determine who the significant people are in the cause of Christ. And then I asked where they went to school, and so many of them went here. So here I am."

It was a logic focusing on significance. A perverse logic, though. The idea that going into the ministry will make you significant is sub-biblical. Likewise, the idea that you will become significant by going to a particular school, where some of your heroes attended, is absurd.

The fallacy of "special calling." Of course, a related perception is the notion of ministry as a "higher calling." I have tried to debunk this myth in Chapter 3. The ministry is not a higher calling, but rather an important calling for which God has designed some people. Those in ministry are not of higher value to God than other professionals, though they can make an outstanding contribution to the glory of God and to the lives of people.

Questions to consider. The real question, though, is, How has God designed you? Have you ever demonstrated any facility in teaching spiritual things? Have people responded positively and obediently when you have taught? Have you seen many friends and acquaintances respond in faith to your presentations of the gospel? Have you demonstrated an ability to lead people? Do people follow you? Do they look to you for perspective and insight and direction in spiritual matters? Do you have any desire or conviction or motivation to do vocational ministry "full-time"? Do you fulfill the criteria for church leaders listed in 1 Timothy 3?

Unless you answer "yes" to most of these questions, I question whether God has designed you for the ministry. Especially if you have proven abilities in other areas.

But don't fret if you are not "cut out" for a full-time career in the ministry! Your design is God's sovereign choice and you should rejoice in who you are—as He does! He has designed you to be His coworker in a given career, and He regards you as neither more nor less valuable than any preacher, evangelist, or missionary.

On the fence. You will make your greatest contribution when you work in a career that corresponds to the way God has designed you. But suppose you are someone who could go either way—either into the ministry or into a secular field. I, for instance, was quite satisfied as a flight instructor before I left the Air Force to train for the work I'm doing now. Likewise, Bill was pursuing a career in media production and consulting before he joined me in our partnership. How did we decide to do "ministry" instead of flying jets or shooting videos?

The answer is that we looked at ourselves, we looked at our options and opportunities, and we looked at how we felt. We prayed and we made choices. We believe we are in God's will. But just because we are using our design in a ministry right now, and just because we feel confident that we are doing God's will in that ministry, doesn't mean that down the road we couldn't utilize the same design in a "secular" career. The issue comes back to determining where we believe we can make our greatest contribution as God's people.

CHANGING CAREERS

Having read this far, you may feel that you are not in a job where you are making your greatest contribution. In fact, you may be very dissatisfied with your vocation, and feel that it is time to change jobs or even to change careers. Is this permissible for a Christian?

Again, you need to determine whether the job you have fits with the person you are. Jobs can change. You change. And so you may discover that you no longer have a good match.

For instance, a person might start out as the administrator of a young but growing company. Then one day he realizes that the organization has grown to the point where most of the responsibilities and authority he once had have been assumed by other people. This causes him to be frustrated, but it is simply a case of the job no longer matching who he is. Perhaps he needs to always work for a young, aggressive company. Perhaps that is where he will do his best work.

In that case, he may need to start looking for a change. That is a freedom we have in America: We can change jobs. In many cultures, one cannot.

Of course, this raises an important point. The bulk of mankind has never had "career options." People have generally been tied from birth to the vocation they would likely pursue throughout life. And so the idea of finding a job that fits with the person you are is a fairly recent development. Indeed, it would sound silly if not self-indulgent to someone not raised in a "culturally mobile" society.

I think the question we must consider, if we do have options, is not which job will give us personal comfort and convenience but which one will enable us to be most effective for God. Job dissatisfaction *alone* is not grounds for a job change, inasmuch as any of a variety of factors might account for the difficulties. Indeed, the spirit of the New Testament seems to be one of endurance, patience, and contentment.[13]

But on the other hand, the reality of living in America is that most of us *must* choose a job. Consequently, we confront a situation uncommon to most of mankind throughout history. What, then, should be our criteria for job selection? As I have suggested before, we should evaluate the abilities and motivations God has given us, and then ask where we can best apply them as His people.

Free to choose. This seems to be a freedom we have as Christians. In 1 Corinthians 7, Paul's discussion of slaves and their calling suggests that as opportunity permits, we have freedom to change jobs. However, let me point out some things in that passage:

Let each man remain in that condition in which he was called. Were you called while a slave? Do not worry about it; but if you are able also to become free, rather do that. For he who was called in the Lord while a slave, is the Lord's freedman; likewise he who was called while free, is Christ's slave. (1 Corinthians 7:20-22)

A study of the context here will reveal that as people were coming to faith in Corinth, they had questions about how their new walk with Christ affected their marriages and their vocations. Paul's point is that becoming a Christian does not automatically mean that one should change jobs, or change marriages.

Slaves, for instance, wondered whether being a Christian required that they seek to terminate their service to an unbelieving master. Paul clearly says that they should probably remain as slaves. There was nothing inherent in becoming believers that necessitated their leaving their masters. And yet, if the opportunity were to come along so that they could become free, then Paul says that they had the freedom to choose that.

The implication for us is that becoming a Christian does not necessarily mean one should seek to change jobs. And yet, if we can find a job that more closely aligns itself with the way God has designed us, then we have freedom in the Lord to take that job.

CONCLUSION

Some people act as if choosing a career is like a game show. Is God's will behind Door #1, Door #2, or Door #3? You only get one choice, and if you miss it, well, you'll have to settle for a consolation prize—maybe a nice office, or a swell partner, plus a video of your performance (in heaven)! But otherwise, God puts you on the shelf.

Yet reality says that the average American will change careers—not just jobs—four times or more in his life! This is due to the volatile nature of our economy, the world economy, the impact of mergers and technology, and a host of other factors.

So the idea of one career per life is out of date. God knows this. He has designed you with a set of skills and motivations to do His work in the world today. But His work may take many different forms in the course of your working years.

The main thing in your search for the right job is to deepen your understanding of how God has put you together and how you can make your greatest contribution. Then pray and ask God to open and close doors so that you will have opportunities to use what He has given you.

In any case, you should regard the job you have as important but not all-important. It should honor Christ and serve others. But keep in mind the limitations to work. No job can provide total and/or ultimate fulfillment. But if you find a sense of contentment in your work, rejoice! It is a gift from God.

NOTES: 1. See Mattson and Miller, *Finding a Job You Can Love* (Nashville: Thomas Nelson Publishers, 1982), page 55.
2. Gary Friesen, *Decision Making and the Will of God* (Portland, Oreg.: Multnomah Press, 1980).
3. Friesen, *Decision Making*, pages 187-188.
4. One tool that might help you do that is the *Career Kit*, available from Intercristo. See the section called "For More Information" at the back of this book.
5. For example, 1 Corinthians 1:26; 1 Timothy 1:9; Ephesians 1:18, 4:1; Hebrews 3:1.
6. Friesen, *Decision Making*, page 313.
7. See "For More Information."
8. Mattson and Miller, *Finding a Job You Can Love.*
9. That is why Paul gives Christian slaves specific instructions in passages like Ephesians 6 and Colossians 3.
10. James 1:17.
11. See Gary Friesen's discussion of this in *Decision Making and the Will of God*, pages 128-144.
12. Matthew 20:20-24.
13. See, for example, 1 Timothy 6:6, Hebrews 12:1-13, and 2 Peter 2:18-21.

CHAPTER 11

WHAT CAN ONE PERSON DO?
Evil in the Workplace

In Chapter 7 I showed that even though work itself is an inherently good gift from God, it nevertheless suffers, along with the rest of creation, from the impact of sin. From top to bottom, the workplace bristles with evil.

On the grandest of scales, it shows up in our national economy and its major institutions. In themselves, these institutions are not evil. But often they promote, fall victim to, or otherwise contain evil.

White-collar crime, for instance, saps an estimated forty billion dollars annually from corporations and governments.[1] And the evil of AIDS is quickly transforming the workplace into a legal, medical, political, and moral battleground.

Institutionalized evil is complex, often subtle, and difficult to comprehend. However, all of us confront evil at eye-level when we enter our particular workplace each day. Each of us can recall instances of injustice in the politics of our company, or of shady dealings with customers, or of sloppy procedures, or of sheer incompetence. We all have seen the terrible results at work of someone whose personal choices and habits have brought down other people and even entire businesses.

And finally, we must face the evil in ourselves that we bring to work. It might be greed, one-upmanship, deception, sexual lust, negligence, laziness, power plays, insensitivity, impatience, or any of a hundred other sins. But each of us struggles with at least some of these, and we are always capable of all of them.

Faced, then, with working in a world seemingly saturated with evil, the tendency for many of us is to throw up our hands and throw in the towel. "There's nothing we can do!" we lament. "Why fight it? It's a dog-eat-dog

147

world, so you just have to go in and look out for yourself and do the best you can. After all, what can one person do?"

It is to this last question that I want to devote this chapter. For, in fact, I believe that there is a great deal any follower of Christ can do to appropriately confront the evil he finds in the workplace and in himself. But first I want to make four observations that should inform any discussion of this subject.

1. Expect evil.

First, we need to expect that when we enter the marketplace, we will confront evil and experience conflict. This may sound obvious, but I find that too many Christians act surprised by the moral flaws and failures of people at work, and bothered by the inevitable conflict that arises with the system. Yet that is what it means to live and work in a fallen world. We must not be naive about what happens in that world:

> If you see oppression of the poor and denial of justice and righteousness in the province, do not be shocked at the sight, for one official watches over another official, and there are higher officials over them. (Ecclesiastes 5:8)

"Do not be shocked." Those are exceedingly sad words, but they point to the sad condition of our humanity. Jesus echoes them when He cautions us to be "shrewd as serpents, and innocent as doves."[2] Paul goes so far as to say that we live among "a crooked and perverse generation,"[3] a generation that, like Noah's, is headed away from God. Such people, Peter points out, are actually surprised when we *do not* participate with them in evil.[4] And Jesus explains why:

> "If the world hates you, you know that it has hated Me before it hated you. If you were of the world, the world would love its own; but because you are not of the world, but I chose you out of the world, therefore the world hates you." (John 15:18-19)

So as Christians, we can just anticipate conflict in the world. We serve a different Lord than most of our associates.

This also means that on this side of heaven we will always have to live with tensions we don't like. In other words, we cannot have the ideal. We may eliminate some evils, as happened with slavery. But others will soon take their place, such as racism and discrimination. And many evils will probably never be eliminated.

So we must accept living in a very imperfect world. This includes learning to live with casualties, because in such a world, people all around us are going to go down. Some will lie in beds of their own making. Others will find themselves victims of someone else's sin. This calls for both sober-mindedness and compassion.

2. God is sovereign.

A second observation is that in many cases there is little, if anything, we can do to stem evil. Sometimes we arrive too late. Sometimes we have no control over a situation. Sometimes our hands are tied and we must stand by and watch people destroy themselves and others.

However, we must also keep in mind that although a situation may be out of our control, it is never out of God's control. I do not have room here to present a complete discussion of evil and how God deals with it.[5] But we must keep in mind two aspects of God's character. First, He is all-loving, so He cares that people suffer from evil in the world. In fact, His love demands that He deal appropriately with evil. Second, He is all-powerful, so He is able to deal with it. Indeed, the Scriptures indicate that someday He will finally do away with it.

In the meantime, when we often feel helpless and it seems we can do nothing, there is always one thing we can do: we can pray. We have the authority as believers to approach the One who has what it takes to conquer evil. For this reason Jesus has encouraged us to pray at all times and not lose heart.[6]

3. God expects us to act.

Though at times there may be nothing we can do, God never gives us the option of throwing up our hands in despair. Instead, He expects us to take what action we can to appropriately deal with evil.

This is the thrust of Romans 12:9-21. As in other New Testament passages, Paul gives us two assignments (verse 9), one negative and one positive. The negative is, "Abhor what is evil." The positive is, "Cleave to what is good." These are obviously two sides of the same coin.

In other words, when we see evil we should hate it, and in response we should do whatever we can to promote good. Paul lists quite a number of positive steps we might take in different circumstances. But he climaxes the passage with a restatement of the principle (verse 21): "Do not be overcome by evil, but overcome evil with good."

This does not mean we are to be moral policemen. We are not to fastidiously point out all of the sins and faults of people. In the first place, unbelievers have not experienced the transforming work in their hearts that only Christ can do. Furthermore, the emphasis in the New Testament seems to focus on holiness in the believer and the Church. If we faithfully concentrate on that, we may find ourselves having more of an impact on a nonChristian world.

To "overcome evil with good" relates directly to the principles of work presented in Part II. As God's people, our job in the workplace is to serve Him and to serve the legitimate needs of people through our vocations. Indeed, great evils will result if we fail to do that. If teachers don't teach, we will have illiteracy. If farmers don't farm, we will have starvation. If pharmaceutical chemists don't carry out research, we will continue to die of diseases. And if government officials don't govern, we will have social and legal confusion.

Of course, even if we do our jobs, we will still find evil somewhere, if only because someone else is failing to do his or her job. The teacher may try to teach reading, but if the citizens don't provide adequate funding, if the school board doesn't allocate sufficient resources, if the principal doesn't maintain an appropriate environment, if the parents don't make sure homework is done, and if the student doesn't discipline himself and make sufficient effort to learn to read, then the intended outcome of the teacher's work will be thwarted.

Yet even here we must avoid a very strong temptation: to point the finger at others' problems as an excuse for not doing our jobs. I believe God holds us accountable for faithfulness to do our part. If the failures of others torpedo the success of our efforts, that may be a great evil and very frustrating—but it does not excuse us from doing God's work.

4. God uses evil.
A final point worth noting is that God uses the evil of the workplace to build our character. As James puts it:

> Consider it all joy, my brethren, when you encounter various trials; knowing that the testing of your faith produces endurance. And let endurance have its perfect result, that you may be perfect and complete, lacking in nothing. (James 1:2-4)

Occasionally I meet a person like the one James describes. He is usually older, has been through the wars of the workplace, and has emerged scarred, to be sure, yet proven, seasoned. Such a person did not survive the jungle because he was such a good person. Rather, he became a better person as he learned to overcome the pitfalls of the jungle.

And it is a jungle out there! Let's discuss how you can cut a path of righteousness through it, how you can "overcome evil with good."

EVIL IN SOCIETY AND INSTITUTIONS

When we consider evil at the level of societies and institutions, the complexities of defining the problems are often exceeded only by the difficulties of adequately dealing with them. This is particularly problematic for lawmakers and government officials, and for those who head major commercial and educational institutions. For with them so often lies the responsibility of leadership in working through these problems and their results.

And yet even if we are not in a position to "solve" problems, we are likely in the position of having to live with them. So one way or the other, each of us must learn to deal with evil on a larger scale.

In confronting such evil, especially as it pertains to work, I find it helpful to make two distinctions.

1. Legitimate versus questionable work

The first is the distinction between legitimate as opposed to questionable work. In Chapter 5, I said that illegal work is an obvious corruption of God's intention in that it fails to serve people in a God-honoring way. But there are some jobs that, while legal, are still questionable in terms of their contribution to the needs of people.

For instance, if you work in the tobacco industry, I believe you have to wonder whether you are contributing or detracting from God's work. Certainly, you are meeting legitimate survival needs for yourself and your family, and perhaps providing jobs for others.

And yet, you are also providing or promoting a known carcinogen, nicotine, which destroys the health of people, escalates health and insurance costs, and (at least for now) depletes tax dollars through subsidies from the government. Is this what God would have you do?

Other kinds of work are even more difficult to evaluate. Some question whether they should participate in the production of nuclear weapons. Others question whether they should be involved with any device or substance used in warfare, or even whether they should serve in the armed forces.

Or how about the manufacture of radar detectors? Is this helping people obey the law? Or the sale to the general public of Uzzi machine guns, M-1 rifles, or Bowie knives? Do these serve any legitimate human needs, or are they merely pandering to survivalist paranoia and unbridled machismo?

Each generation faces gray areas like these. Luther believed that three vocations a Christian could not legitimately pursue were the priesthood, prostitution, and banking—the priesthood because of his strong views on the universal priesthood of all believers, prostitution for obvious reasons, and banking because of scriptural prohibitions against usury.

But we must not be too hard and fast in either advocating or condemning various careers. There are complex issues involved that each individual must evaluate and decide according to his own conscience. We must avoid legalistic, uninformed pronouncements. Instead, each of us should ask, Is my current work enabling me to make my best contribution as a coworker with God?

2. Direct versus indirect participation in evil

A second distinction worth making is between direct and indirect participation in evil. In this life we will inevitably participate, at least indirectly, in evil. If that sounds less than ideal, remember that we live in a less than ideal world, thanks to the presence of sin.

For example, I occasionally work with professional athletes, helping them think through how their faith applies on the playing field. In many sports, huge sums of money are bet, and much of this betting is controlled by organized crime. Hence, these athletes participate indirectly in evil, in that their sport and their performance is a known opportunity for illegal, destructive gambling.

Likewise, you may be a grocer whose store sells food to people who, on the strength of the food you sell them, go out and commit crimes. In fact, some of the money from these crimes pays you for the food you sell!

Again, you may be an executive in a company that employs people who are involved in adultery, drugs, weird cults, and so on. And your work makes that company viable, and hence provides an income for these people. So you actually contribute to their well-being, even though you deplore their sinful behavior.

How can we operate as God's coworkers in such a world? Here we must distinguish between direct and indirect participation in evil. The three examples above demonstrate indirect participation.

I do not believe the Scriptures regard this indirect participation as wrong, but merely inevitable. The key is to recognize who is doing the wrong. The criminal and the adulterer clearly are, but the athlete, the grocer, and the executive are not. They are simply doing their work, hopefully to the glory of God. Indeed, if God were to fault them, He would have to fault Himself, because "He causes His sun to rise on the evil and the good, and sends rain on the righteous and the unrighteous."[7]

Another aspect of indirect participation in evil is the misuse of products. Take airplane glue, for instance. It is a useful product for constructing models and repairing broken ceramics. It should be made and used for such purposes.

But the manufacturer of that glue probably knows that some teens will purchase his product in order to sniff it and get high. Is he contributing to that evil? Only indirectly. He cannot be held morally accountable for what someone does with his product after buying it. Of course, he and his distributors should take whatever steps they can to prevent abuse. But they can only do so much.

However, you have a definite problem when your career calls for direct participation in what you know to be wrong. You now have not just a tension with evil but an outright conflict with it.

In Chapter 2, I mentioned the manufacturer of baby food that was putting sugar water in bottles instead of pure apple juice. Suppose you were an executive in that company? How should you respond as a Christian?

This brings us to two major questions in dealing with institutionalized evil. God commands us to "overcome evil with good." But *when* should you act? And *what* should you do? I find the answer to these questions in studying the life of Daniel.

THE EXAMPLE OF DANIEL

Daniel's remarkable story is told in the Old Testament. He and a number of other Hebrew youths were taken captive by the Babylonians in about 605 BC. Through the sovereignty of God, he eventually ended up as the virtual prime minister of the empire. Nevertheless, he is remembered for his unswerving integrity and his allegiance to YHWH, the God of Israel.

To appreciate the significance of this man's example, let's put it in modern perspective. Suppose, through some flaw in our national policies, America came under the domination of the Soviet Union. In fact, suppose that some of our best young students were forced to fly to Moscow and undergo a rigorous training period in Soviet doctrine and customs.

Among these students is a Christian. Despite his faith, he is conscripted into this program. And as the program progresses, he distinguishes himself by his wisdom, his faith, and his integrity.

Now the Soviets are not fools. They have no use for Christian faith. But wisdom and integrity are prized commodities in any culture. So, despite the objections of some, the authorities place this young Christian in a position of responsibility. They figure that in time he'll jettison his religion as a childhood triviality. And in the unlikely event that it proves troublesome, they can always ship him off to Siberia.

Time passes. And in situation after situation, this young man excels in his performance. Indeed, as the old guard of Soviet leaders die off, he rises higher and higher in the bureaucracy. Yet he never compromises his Christian convictions. Then one day he faces a showdown with the elite of the Politburo. In a flash of brilliance, he not only beats them at their own game, but exposes them as frauds and incompetents.

The reward for this victory is an appointment as the number-two man in the Soviet Union. In effect, a Christ-follower winds up at the top of a totalitarian government that is admittedly atheistic.

This is essentially what happened to Daniel. Somehow he not only survived in such an evil system, but actually accomplished his work to the glory of God. Consequently, I think we can learn much from his extraordinary example about how we can deal with institutionalized evil.

Let me suggest some of these lessons. They won't cover every contingency. But as starting points, they may prove helpful in answering two questions about confronting evil: When should we act? And what should we do?

WHEN TO ACT

I can think of at least four circumstances that should trigger some response from you as a Christian.

1. You must definitely act when you are called upon to do what is wrong.
In other words, the believer is to avoid direct participation in evil.

In Daniel 3, we find an excellent illustration of this. Daniel had three friends who shared his faith and went with him into captivity. These three men were confronted with a direct order to bow down to an idol, something expressly prohibited in the Old Testament Law.[8] They simply refused to obey the order, because to do so would have violated God's unequivocal commandment.

The same principle applies to us as Christians today. To lie to a customer, to cheat the government, to steal from our employer or a vendor, or to ignore the laws that govern our industry is to directly oppose the express teaching of Scripture.[9] We'll discuss how to avoid such evil in a moment. But we must begin with the understanding that the Bible clearly rules out any direct involvement in what we know is wrong.[10]

2. You should act when your own conscience is violated.
Most of us can easily discern that falsifying tax records or pilfering supplies is wrong. But so many issues of integrity in the workplace are gray areas, in which the line between right and wrong is blurred.

Is it altogether right, for example, to enthusiastically recommend someone for employment when you know of serious questions regarding that person's competence? Is it right to use your influence as a corporate executive to bump someone else off an over-booked flight and take his place yourself? Is it legitimate to flirt with a potential customer of the opposite sex in order to promote a sale? Is it right to choose Las Vegas as the site of a national convention, knowing that nearby casinos and brothels will attract a better turn-out than if it were held in Denver?

Questions like these are matters of conscience. That means that there are no explicit biblical instructions one way or the other, and there are no legal statutes involved. Instead, you must answer them for yourself. Some people will see them one way, some another.

We can well imagine that Daniel must have faced countless instances of this situation in Babylon. We find one such instance in Daniel 1. He and his three friends were offered a diet that they found unacceptable on religious grounds.

We don't know the exact details. It may be that some of the food was in the category of unclean foods proscribed by the Law of Moses (see Leviticus 2 or Deuteronomy 14:3-20). In that case, eating it would have been a direct participation in evil.

But it may be that the food was perfectly acceptable under the Law. Nevertheless, Daniel determined not to eat it, because he did not want to "defile" himself, according to the text (Daniel 1:8). So apparently he found something evil connected with it.

The evil may have been that the food had been offered first to idols. In that case, Daniel may have felt that eating it would have violated his conscience. Eating it would have more or less acknowledged pagan deities as legitimate gods. This he would not do, and so he took the matter up with his superior.

The lesson to learn from Daniel is not that we opt out of certain activities just because we don't "like" them or because they bother us. Rather, we do so because we have developed a biblically informed conscience, one that has been trained to discern good and evil in situations where they are hard to distinguish.

Many situations in the workplace should trigger our conscience. Once aroused, we should look for clear scriptural grounds for our uneasiness, and then take appropriate steps to avoid evil and promote good.

3. You should act when it is in your power to end or to avoid evil.
I sometimes hear people sigh that there is nothing they can do about societal evil. And yet God has given each of us a limited sphere of control. That sphere may extend no further than our desk or work station. But as long as we have

responsibility for what goes on there, we can claim that territory for God, even if it seems like an island in a sea of evil.

We find an interesting illustration of this principle in Daniel 2. Apparently the king spent one too many sleepless nights, troubled by various nightmares. He longed for an explanation, yet distrusted his counselors, knowing that they usually told him only what he wanted to hear.

So the king gave them the impossible task, not simply of interpreting the dreams, but of actually recounting them without having heard them from the king! Exposed as frauds, the counselors received a death sentence, and the king's executioners began rounding them up, along with their families.

However, when Daniel heard of the matter, he immediately sprang into action. The text suggests that he was high enough up in the system to be included in the roundup, and also to speak directly to the authorities. In fact, he apparently was able to get in to see the king. Daniel persuaded him to stay the executions until he and his friends could have a shot at declaring and explaining the dreams, which they eventually did.

As I consider this incident, I am struck by the fact that Daniel used his influence to spare the lives of his associates. One wonders why he would do so. These were men totally opposed to God, who worshiped idols and participated in the evil practices of a pagan empire. Furthermore, they were deceptive, self-seeking advisors, and probably did more harm to the king than good. Indeed, Daniel might have tried to use this as an opportunity to advance himself as God's man in the palace. Yet, as a tribute to his integrity, he saw the evil in the king's decree, and purposed to use his position to thwart it.

Today, we as Christians in this culture probably occupy positions of greater influence and authority than any other Christians in history. We have people who call Christ their Lord from the top to the bottom of our society: in its governments, corporations, military, educational institutions, and media.

Like Daniel, we should use our authority to "overcome evil with good." As Proverbs 3:27 puts it, "Do not withhold good from those to whom it is due, when it is in your power to do it." Or, as Paul says, "While [or as] we have opportunity, let us do good to all men."[11]

My point is that whatever power we currently have has been entrusted to us as a responsibility by God. Like Daniel, we should use it to promote good—good for all people, not just Christians. And if God chooses to increase our influence, we should use that as a greater opportunity for good.[12]

4. We should act when innocent people stand to be affected by evil.

In a sense, innocent people are always affected by evil. But what I have in mind is circumstances in which you can see a direct threat or impact of evil on someone who has no ability to protect himself—cases of danger and injustice, for example.

Daniel does not provide any clear illustrations of this, though I suppose his intervention on behalf of the fraudulent counselors and especially their families might serve as an example. But other examples in today's workplace abound. For instance, if you are an airline pilot or a construction worker, and you know of coworkers who abuse drugs or alcohol, you should step in if their behavior endangers others.

Or suppose you are a financial planner, and a client requests that you set him up in a fairly volatile but potentially lucrative investment. However, you know that the person's finances will suffer severely if the investment goes bad. In that case, I believe you have a responsibility to fully apprise him of all the risks, and perhaps even advise him against the investment. After all, his family will suffer, too, if his investment turns sour.

The point is that God does not want His people to stand idly by while innocent people suffer. We may not be able to prevent their suffering; in fact, we may scarcely be able to alleviate it. But we must not ignore it. And to the extent that we can, we should circumvent it by doing good today, before evil even arrives.

WHAT TO DO

In confronting evil, deciding that you must do something is relatively easy to do. But deciding what to do and doing it may be much more difficult. In light of everything I have said so far, here are a few suggestions. I suggest that you see these as a constellation of strategies rather than single actions.

1. Go to the source, if possible.
Quite often, the source of evil may also be the party most in a position to do something about it. For instance, earlier I mentioned the baby food company that was putting sugar water in bottles and selling it as pure apple juice. Suppose you were an executive in that company, and you found out about this practice. Dealing with the situation would first call for determining who at your company has made this decision.

Where is the problem? Let's say it is a certain vice president. If you could arrange a conversation with him, you might be able to clarify the facts and, if necessary, challenge him to reconsider his decision. It is possible that there is a reasonable explanation, or that not all the facts have been brought out. It is also possible that the vice president needs someone to challenge him to do what is right.

By the way, if the person is an unbeliever, then I doubt you will get very far by quoting Scripture to him. I've known Christians who have done this. Almost always they have found that the person has no regard for the Bible, certainly not as an authority for how he should live.

A better approach, I believe, is to appeal to him along the lines of broad categories of morality and justice. While few nonChristians accept the authority of the Bible, most do hold to a general sense of what is human and decent.

I am not so naive as to overlook the political implications to such a conversation. Indeed, my suggestion to confront a powerful corporate vice president may sound laughable and hopelessly idealistic to some. But perhaps too many Christians have become enslaved to corporate politics, and thus have lost the courage of their convictions. I'll say more on this in a moment.

Where is the power? Sometimes, though, it is impossible to determine a "source," or else the source is not a human but simply a process or a condition. In that case, consider going to the person who seems most likely to be in a position to do something about ending the evil. I suggest that you take with you some possible suggestions about what this person might do.

Again, I know that you may risk getting the runaround, as many of those who actually are in a position of doing something fold their hands and plead impotence. Sometimes they are impotent: They may be strapped for resources or may even be prevented legally from stepping in. But sometimes authorities simply need to be made aware of a bad situation, or else need a challenge to act.

You must act. I'm not suggesting that we push all responsibility off on authorities, though. So often, we ourselves need to confront coworkers and others about things they do or fail to do that are harmful or unethical.

Of course, so often in situations such as the one with the food company, the evil itself is rather ambiguous: It is not really sugar water in the bottles, but a mixture of sugar water and apple concentrate—enough to satisfy the consumer and most FDA regulations, but perhaps borderline to some aggressive consumer advocacy group.

In that case, is this really a question of evil? This is where we as Christians need to be "shrewd as serpents, and innocent as doves." I am not interested in turning us all into corporate moralists, into Don Quixotes, out to right every possible wrong in the marketplace.

But I am suggesting that when we see even the potential for evil, we not stand idly by. We need to ask questions, bring out important facts, challenge people to do what is right, and at least raise issues about the ethics and integrity of what is done. And it only makes sense that we do this with people who are in a position to do something about the situation.

2. Join the battle where you feel you can be most effective.
This ties in with what I said earlier about using your authority to avoid evil and promote good. Not everyone is in a position of considerable influence, or even has access to those who do. But each of us has been given abilities, a personality, resources, and relationships, among other things. These can become tools for good in God's hands, if we let them.

Stronger than steel. Wayne Alderson makes an interesting case study in this regard. One would imagine that as vice president in charge of operations at Pittron, a steel company, he would have had considerable influence over the conduct of that enterprise. Certainly he did.

But in 1972, the United Steel Workers initiated a bitter strike at the company. It lasted for months, and negotiations between management and labor reached a stalemate.

In this situation, God used Alderson to accomplish a breakthrough. Yet the key was not his position so much as his person. Alderson had been a grunt in World War II. He knew firsthand the experience of killing and nearly being killed when a grenade exploded in his face. He had been raised in Canonburg, Pennsylvania, the son of a coal miner, in fact the fourth generation of coal miners.

In other words, his background was much like the men in the union. This gave him an entree with certain union representatives. At a tense, surreptitious meeting, Alderson managed to negotiate an end to the strike.

I'm sure many factors accounted for this settlement. And this did not solve all the problems at Pittron. But what impresses me is that Alderson put himself, not just his position, in God's hands as an agent of reconciliation.

Apparently God felt that what it would take to end that strike was a man who instinctively understood the plight of the steelworkers, yet who had earned the respect of management; a man who could speak the right language in the situation; a man with the courage of a combat veteran to win the respect of the union leaders; a man of unimpeachable integrity who could be trusted.[13]

God can use you. Like Alderson, each of us has a background, a style of dealing with people, a reputation, and so forth. And though God may not use us to settle a strike, He might desire to use us to settle an argument. To say something no one else has the guts to say. To say something no one else knows how to say. To suggest an idea that may prevent injustice. To stand by someone who faces a critical but difficult decision. To pay for something when the funds cannot be found elsewhere. To fire someone who jeopardizes the rights and safety of everyone else. To write a letter of support to someone who is trying to do what's right. To stick up for an associate who has been unjustly accused.

There are a thousand opportunities in your workplace in a given day in which God desires good to triumph over evil. As a front-line soldier in that battle, you need to jump in where you feel you can be most effective.

3. Seek limited, measurable gains.
Earlier I said that on this side of heaven we can't have the ideal. Nevertheless, I believe we can score limited and sometimes even impressive victories for what is right and good.

But doing so requires that we first evaluate the situation that confronts us. We must not only define the problem, but also discern which aspects of it are likely to be changed and which are not, and also what possible action might be taken.

For example, some pharmaceutical companies export drugs to Third World countries that our own government has classified as unacceptable for American consumers. Some of these drugs are considered unsafe, perhaps because of age or because they have not passed federal tests. If you were an executive in one of these companies, you might have pangs of conscience about the ethics of this practice. Dumping substandard medicine overseas may provide a profitable aftermarket, but it certainly might endanger innocent people.

Be realistic. If you felt compelled to act, what could you do? First, notice what you cannot do. You cannot by yourself change the practices of an entire industry. You cannot change the attitudes and motives of all the governments and businesspeople overseas who buy the drugs. You cannot change the competitive nature of the marketplace, which demands that your company seek out ways to remain profitable. And you may not even be able to convince your associates at your own company that the practice is even questionable.

Be creative. Does this mean there is nothing you can do? Too often I'm afraid we conclude there is not, and throw up our hands. But this is not confronting evil; it is capitulating to it.

Surely you can use your creativity (or someone else's) to think up some alternatives. And alternatives are a key weapon in the fight for good in the workplace. In a world that often works by the rules of negotiation and compromise, creating shrewd alternatives will often make the difference between some gain and no gain at all.

This was Daniel's creative strategy in the incident with the king's food that was offered to him. Recall that he objected to the food on religious grounds, apparently. His superior thought he was laying down a black-and-white ultimatum of a refusal to eat, and he pointed out the dire consequences if Daniel and his friends ended up looking like skeletons: "Then you would make me forfeit my head to the king" (Daniel 1:10).

Things might have come to an impasse. But Daniel suggested an alternative. He described a substitute menu that he and his friends would eat for ten days. Then the superior could run a side-by-side comparison of them with the others in the program, and decide the next step from there.

God performed something of a miracle in those ten days, and Daniel's plan prevailed. But the point is that he was wise enough to suggest an alternative rather than press for unrealistic gains.

Brainstorm for options. In a similar way, in the case of the pharmaceutical firm, there are perhaps many alternatives that could be considered. Perhaps not all the drugs are potentially harmful, but only some of them. It could be worth fighting to remove this portion from the shipments.

Or perhaps there is some simple, inexpensive way to increase the shelf-life of the drugs, so that even though the expiration date for sale in American stores passes, they are still viable and would pose no major risk overseas. Again, maybe the purchasing patterns of druggists could be evaluated, so that they do not become so heavily overstocked with products; this might not eliminate the overseas sales, but it could reduce the volume of expired drugs available to that market.

These are only possibilities that occur to me, who knows nothing of this field. If you actually worked in the pharmaceuticals industry, I suspect you could think of a number of realistic, practical ways to do something about this problem.

But the point in suggesting alternatives is that since we can rarely eliminate an evil completely, we should press instead for solutions that will reduce it at least partially. Certainly we'd like to have it all. We'd like to score touchdowns on every play. But often I think we need to be satisfied with just advancing the ball a few yards, and occasionally managing a first down. There is no shame in this. Even a little good is preferable to no good at all.

4. Expect positive results, but also expect some negative consequences.

Earlier I said that there are often political risks involved in taking a stand against evil. Given those risks, it makes sense that if you plan to work toward some specific outcome that promotes good, you should expect results from your efforts. In other words, even if you are only playing for a limited victory, play to win.

Perhaps this merely reflects my personality, but I can't imagine putting forth effort and risking negative consequences unless you intend to w̲ Again, my Air Force training instilled in me the idea that in matters and in matters of ethical integrity, losing is not an option.

However, while we need to expect positive results, we also need to expect some negative consequences. And those consequences can be severe.

Count the cost. Whistle-blowers, for example, are treated very poorly in our culture. Major villains can go to court, maybe even go to jail, and yet emerge to write their stories in exchange for six-figure advances, ride the talk-show circuit, and otherwise enjoy celebrity status. But the people who expose them typically find it very hard to function normally afterwards. They may not be able to find employment. They may suffer terrible psychological wounds. And the stress of their plight may take its toll on their families and marriages.

Likewise, people who stand up for right can find themselves staring down the barrel of a political shotgun held by someone who doesn't want to be reminded of what is right. Firing is not the only possible fate. One could conceivably find himself both fired and blacklisted, unable to continue in his industry.

One may also remain in his job, but find a sudden loss of power, or a loss of friendships. Or a loss of opportunity—in other words, imprisonment in one's current position. This is an especially terrifying prospect to some who aggressively and ambitiously aspire to a vice presidency or higher. To them, a career in middle management may seem like the corporate equivalent of Siberia.

All of these are potential costs. And you would be wise to weigh them and determine whether you can afford them. What you must weigh is the issue involved against the risk involved.

If the risk is too great. For instance, I once heard from a man who worked for a state agency. His supervisor, a younger man, kept harassing and abusing this man and making his life miserable. Part of it was an age gap. This civil servant was three years from retirement and his pension. In addition, the supervisor had a friend he could hire in this man's place if he quit.

So he asked me what he should do. We discussed filing grievances with the appropriate authorities. But the man pointed out that not too many years before, his work had not been above reproach, and his supervisor might conceivably trump up new charges that could result in his firing.

It became apparent to me that for this man to risk his entire pension just to get an immature supervisor off his back seemed too great a risk. I advised him to endure for the remainder of his career; indeed, to love his enemy and allow the experience to build his character.

If the issue is too important. However, there are cases when the issues involved so far outweigh any risks or consequences that we should be prepared to pay any price to do what is right. I mentioned Daniel's three friends in this

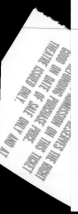

regard earlier. They refused to bow down to the idol, and so the king prepared a death chamber, a furnace.

Standing before the furnace, the king gave them one last chance. But they essentially replied, "No way! God is certainly capable of delivering us from the flames. But whether or not He does, we're not bowing down!" So the king had them thrown in.[14]

We need more people like that today, for there are certainly enough people like the king, who think nothing of blowing away those whom they perceive as moral crusaders. But we need believers who, if necessary, will defy what is wrong and take the consequences, because greater than their commitment to their job, or their reputation, or their comfort, or even their friendships is their commitment to doing what is right before God.

As Christians we need to be salt and light in the culture. But we also need to realize that many will want to wash off the salt and blow out the light. This is why, in connection with calling us salt and light, Jesus said:

> "Blessed are those who have been persecuted for the sake of right-eousness, for theirs is the kingdom of heaven. Blessed are you when men revile you, and persecute you, and say all kinds of evil against you falsely, on account of Me. Rejoice, and be glad, for your reward in heaven is great, for so they persecuted the prophets who were before you." (Matthew 5:10-12)

5. If necessary, leave.
Some circumstances become so impossible to deal with that your only real choice is to quit. However, before discussing those situations, I want to stress that this should be the last resort for the follower of Christ.

God values endurance. Unfortunately, I find far too many Christians who bail out of their job simply because they are uncomfortable around unbelievers and a "secular" environment. They complain about the language, the dirty jokes, the gossip, the politics, and the cigarette smoke, plus all of the things that occur off the job—adultery and immorality, drugs, wild parties, and so forth.

By contrast, they imagine some Christian environment where Bible studies are held each morning, where people pray before every meeting, where no one gets angry, where no one gets fired, where everyone has a stable family life, where everyone goes to church, where politics never enter into personnel decisions, and where no one smokes.

Two problems with this. First, such a Christian "ideal" doesn't exist. It won't even help to go to work for a church or Christian ministry, because those who do will tell you the problems are really the same. In some cases, sadly, they are worse, especially if issues get spiritualized and never dealt with honestly.[15]

But secondly, even if the ideal did exist, we still would have no biblical grounds to leave our current job and go into it. In other words, Christ has explicitly sent us into the culture, into the workplace. Distaste for what we find there is not grounds for trying to find a way out.

As Christians we must go to work in the marketplace like sheep among wolves.[16] And when we encounter opposing values and behaviors, and even when we find hostility to our beliefs and convictions, the New Testament tells us we should endure, not quit.[17]

God values integrity. And yet, there are times when it is best to leave. I cannot easily define the breaking point. That depends on many factors—the situation, your prospects for the future, your personality, the impact on your family, your financial situation, and so on.

But one situation that probably calls for a break is when you know that remaining would be a direct participation in evil. For instance, if you discover that your company is engaged in fraudulent activity, you should do all you can to change the situation for the better. But if, after having taken as many steps as you can, fraud is still the main business of the company, I would suggest you leave.

Sometimes it comes to that. But you must be willing to pay that price to do what you know is right. For as Chuck Swindoll says, if you have to do wrong to be on the team, then you're on the wrong team.

6. Use a strategy of prayer.

Rarely is this suggestion put forth as a serious strategy for dealing with evil, especially evil in the workplace. Yet this really should be our starting point in confronting any kind of evil. Paul writes:

> I urge that entreaties and prayers, petitions and thanksgivings, be made on behalf of all men, for kings and all who are in authority, in order that we may lead a tranquil and quiet life in all godliness and dignity. (1 Timothy 2:1-2)

Paul's point is that we should pray for people who have the authority to change our culture and our workplaces for the better, as well as for the worse. In fact, even if employers or others in authority make life miserable for us, Jesus still instructs us to pray for them.[18]

How might such a strategy work? I suggest finding one or two others to meet with, perhaps once a week, or more often, depending on the intensity of the circumstances. Don't meet for lunch, or to talk, but to pray. Briefly review the situation at hand and remind yourselves of who God is. Then pray.

First, focus on the character and the person of God. Thank Him, for example, for His power, His ability to deal with human problems and with evil. Thank Him for His holiness, His Word, His compassion, His patience. Perhaps you'll want to "remind" Him of statements He has made in Scripture.

Then move into the situation itself. Be ready to confess any wrongdoing you have done, or any failures on your part in dealing with the issue. Pray for the people involved, especially for those who are in a position of doing something about the problem, that they would be moved to action. Pray also for those who are affected by the problem, that God would use the circumstances in some way to bring about good, even though evil seems so present.

If you have specific plans or desires that you want to see accomplished, ask God to fulfill those. If not, ask Him to work the situation out as He sees fit. Then thank Him for His concern and for what He will do.

Then go away and act if you need to act, endure if you need to endure, or wait if you need to wait. But rest in the confidence that the resources of an infinite God are at work to "overcome evil with good."

7. Start with yourself.

I place this suggestion last because it is often the last thing we think of when confronting evil. Yet personal holiness is really the bedrock from which all of our efforts must spring.

Furthermore, we may be unable to change much in the world around us. We may see many of our associates and friends fall prey to the solicitations of evil and to compromises of integrity. Yet no matter how crooked or corrupt the system becomes, we still have a responsibility before God to live pure lives above reproach.

We have to marvel at a man like Daniel. I have already likened his situation to a Christian serving as a high-profile official in the Kremlin. Yet even so, I doubt that we can comprehend the issues he must have faced. He no doubt faced many pressures from legalized immorality, let alone opportunities for things that were illegal.

Yet even late in his life, when his enemies plotted against him, they checked his files for any possible wrongdoing on which they could hang him. Yet the text says:

> They could find no ground of accusation or evidence of corruption, inasmuch as he was faithful, and no negligence or corruption was to be found in him. (Daniel 6:4)

What an incredible statement! After all those years in the Babylonian hierarchy, working alongside and with and through idolaters, frauds, murderers, and other kinds of wicked people, he was still clean. In fact, those who plotted against him concluded that the only way they could get him would be through his religious practices and convictions.

That's the sort of purity I would want for myself—integrity such that if you decided to accuse me, you'd have to resort to using my walk with God against me.

I hope the same is true for you. I can't think of anything the workplace today needs more than people whose character and integrity are so unique and so distinctive that coworkers wonder why. If you make that your ambition, then you will already be well on your way to "overcoming evil with good."

DEALING WITH EVIL IN OURSELVES

I would be remiss, however, if I ended the chapter here. For the reality is that while we all would like to have the unimpeachable character of Daniel, most of us quite frankly do not. Instead, we find ourselves struggling to overcome, not just the corruption of the systems and people around us, but the sin in ourselves. How can we deal with this?

Take sin to the Cross. First, we need to be realistic. Although Christ has paid the penalty for our sin, we still sin, and it will be a long process overcoming these sins. In fact, some areas of evil we will probably never get rid of completely in this life.

But the thing that should rescue us from despair is God's grace. This means that while God hates our sin, He nevertheless loves us, even in the midst of our sin. It also means that after we have failed, and after we have come to see the folly and the wrong of our ways—after we have returned to our spiritual senses, as it were—God is still there ready to receive us back, ready to move us on toward Christlikeness.

Pursue holiness. This takes nothing away from the emphasis in the New Testament on personal holiness. In fact, it is that very emphasis that makes us aware of how unholy we so often are.

So our task, even if we often fail at it, is to keep picking ourselves back up and pursuing Christlikeness. In Chapter 14, I'll suggest some steps you can take toward personal holiness.

Make restitution. But one thing I would stress here is the importance of restitution in overcoming evil with good. This is particularly relevant to the workplace. If you have lied or if you have stolen, you have a responsibility first to deal with this sin before God, and then to deal with it before those you have wronged, making appropriate amends.

So for instance, suppose you lied to a customer, telling him the manufacturer's warranty would last three years when you knew it would last only ninety days. I believe you should contact that customer and admit that you lied, admit that you were wrong, apologize, and offer to cover any repairs yourself for the three years you sold him.

Or suppose you "stole" a first-class airline ticket from your company, even though policy clearly states that all corporate travel should be booked in coach. I believe you should contact the appropriate person and present him with a check for the difference, admitting that you were wrong.

I suppose that to some people these suggestions will sound naive and picayune. Why bother with what's in the past? And besides, what are these minor infractions compared with the big-time rip-offs of multinational corporations and defense contractors?

But that kind of thinking is already poisoned by the subtle spirit of moral compromise. If we're going to take Christ seriously, then we need to start not with the major evils but with the minor ones. For unless we learn to deal with those, we'll never learn to tackle the big ones.

CONCLUSION

It should be clear by now that God uses everything in the workplace to train our character. He uses the evils we face, the people we can't stand, the circumstances of tension and pressure, the tedium of long afternoons, the solicitations to compromise, the irritations of angry customers, the interruptions, the financial reversals, the deals that fall through, even the traffic on the way home—He uses all of it to make us like Jesus.

Obedience to God is learned through a process that is no fun at the time.[19] Hebrews 12:11 says:

All discipline for the moment seems not to be joyful, but sorrowful; yet to those who have been trained by it, afterwards it yields the peaceful fruit of righteousness.

I challenge you to endure the disciplines of the workplace long enough to see the fruit of righteousness in your life. Such fruit will not sprout in the quicksand of moral compromise.

What can one person do? I once saw a cartoon I will never forget. The cartoonist had drawn an absolute sea of people, extending into the distance, all of them walking about with their heads down. And over every single one of them was a "thought cloud" with the question, "What can one person do?" Do you see that picture in your mind? It is very much like Christians in the workplace today. We are all wandering about, fretting over the deteriorating condition of American life, but throwing up our hands and saying, "What can one person do?"

In comparison to the massive problems and evils around us, one person cannot do much—though, as I've tried to show in this chapter, any believer can probably do far more than he realizes. But if every one of us would concentrate on pursuing Christlikeness on the job, we would together put a great deal of evil on the run.

At least we might. Even if we did not, even if evil actually increased, I doubt that God would hold us responsible for it. Ultimately He Himself must do away with evil. But what He will hold us accountable for is whether we have obediently and diligently done all that we can to become like Christ.

NOTES: 1. "Having It All, Then Throwing It All Away," *Time* (May 25, 1987), page 23.
 2. Matthew 10:16.
 3. Philippians 2:15.
 4. Genesis 6:5, 1 Peter 4:3-4.
 5. See C.S. Lewis, *The Problem of Pain* (New York: Macmillan Publishing Co., Inc, 1962).
 6. Luke 18:1-8.
 7. Matthew 5:45.
 8. Exodus 20:3-5.
 9. See Romans 12:1-2, Ephesians 4:28, Colossians 3:9, and 1 Peter 2:13-15.
 10. Romans 12:2, Ephesians 5.
 11. Galatians 6:10. See also Romans 13:8-10.
     By the way, "doing good to all men" is not the same as trying to accomplish a Christian political or social agenda. I sometimes hear Christians talking as though, if we could just get the right person elected as President, if we could just get the right laws voted through Congress, if we could just get the right decisions coming out of the Supreme Court—*then* we'd be on the road to godliness in our country.
     But have we considered the alternative? Suppose we don't put a Christian in the White House; suppose we put an agnostic there instead, who repudiates Judeo-Christian values. Suppose we don't get the laws we'd like; instead Congress mandates abortions, starts taxing churches, and removes the words "under God" from the Pledge of Allegiance. Suppose the Supreme Court doesn't make the decisions we want; suppose instead it interprets the so-called "separation clause" as an exclusion clause, and effectively banishes all explicitly religious language from public life and discourse.
     To my mind, these are not impossible, unthinkable scenarios. In that case, what is our plan for godly living? I know that some Christians would advocate civil disobedience and perhaps even violence under such conditions. But will that accomplish the righteousness of God? Is that what Daniel did? Or Joseph? Or Jesus? Or the apostles? (I am indebted to Bob Hendricks of Search Ministries for raising this intriguing question.)
 12. On the other hand, we should always hold power with a light touch. If God chooses to decrease our influence, to remove us from positions of power, then our primary goal should not be to try and regain control. As always, our first responsibility is to love God and to faithfully obey Him and serve Him, and to serve the needs of people. When we stand before Him, I doubt that He'll be especially interested in whether we succeeded in getting the vote out. I think He'll be far more interested in whether we honored Him with the limited authority He chose to place in our control.
 13. Alderson's remarkable and inspiring story is told by R.C. Sproul in *Stronger Than Steel: The*

Wayne Alderson Story (San Francisco: Harper & Row, 1980).
14. See Daniel 3:13-23.
15. I should qualify this by saying that not all ministries are like this. I know of many outstanding organizations where the work environment is about as good as one can reasonably expect. Of course, I could mention many businesses, too.
16. Matthew 10:16.
17. 1 Peter 2:18-20.
18. Matthew 6:44.
19. Hebrews 5:8.

CHAPTER 12

THE PROBLEM OF GAIN
Income and Lifestyle

I n this chapter I want to explore the implications of a biblical view of work for the problem of income and lifestyle. Of course I'm tipping my hand by calling this issue a problem. But that is what it is for so many Christians I know who live far above a survival level.

I find that most discussions along these lines center on the subject of money. But in my view, the issue we need to confront is not our income, but our lifestyle. Call it quality of life, standard of living, whatever; lifestyle has to do with the expectations we have about our lives and our ability to fulfill those expectations. In our culture, money is obviously a key factor for most of us in determining lifestyle. And work is the means of obtaining that money.

So what starts out as an issue of money ends up as an issue of lifestyle. And this issue is a major source of tension for most people, especially for most Christians. If it isn't, it ought to be. I call it the problem of gain.

In the pages that follow, I want to first point out why lifestyle is such a problem. Then I'll mention some of the answers to this problem offered by current Christian teaching. Finally, I'll suggest several principles that you can use to think through your own lifestyle and make responsible decisions that honor God.

THE PROBLEM OF LIFESTYLE

Lifestyle is a problem—or ought to be for the sensitive Christian—because it is a fault line where several tensions come together. First we have our own needs to think about, and those of our families. Not just luxuries, but legitimate needs, such as new shoes for our toddler, dental care for our adolescent,

171

heating and electricity bills, and taxes.

Then, of course, we also feel a tension about how much we should fulfill our desires for nonessential items. It may be a certain dress from a certain store, some high-tech gadget from the Sharper Image catalog, or a question of whether or not to include the "power package" on a new car we want to buy. Of course, for so many of us the tension in these situations is not whether we should afford these things, but whether we can.

And this brings us to a further tension, the Scripture's explicit warnings about the dangers of money. Greed and covetousness are always temptations, no matter how much or how little we make. And even if we believe, mistakenly, that we are immune from such temptations, we are certainly not immune from the appeals of advertising or from the pressures of our associates and of the larger society.

Finally, we have at least two other tensions pulling on us, the poor and the Church. The poor cannot be ignored, and for the believer they must not be ignored. So this forces us to ask what we are doing to help the poor, as well as whether our lifestyles may in fact hurt the poor. And as Christians we have a responsibility to underwrite the cause of Christ, not just in our local churches, but also around the world through missions and similar ministries.

This is the problem of gain, the problem of lifestyle. So many tensions to balance, so many factors to weigh, so many demands to answer. And the greater our income, the greater our problem.

SUGGESTED ANSWERS TO THE PROBLEM

Yet I find most of the answers to this problem coming from Christian authors and teachers to be far from satisfactory. If you were to visit a religious bookstore and peruse the resources offered in this area, you would find at least four types of literature available.[1]

1. Prosperity Theology

The first set of books represents what is called "prosperity theology." Its basic message is that God wants you to be healthy and wealthy. Various verses are wrenched out of context to "prove" not simply that you can have prosperity, but that as a Christian you should *expect* to have it.

The teachers of this theology are extremely slick. It is not what they actually say that is problematic, but what they imply. One, for instance, writes:

> After much time spent studying and meditating on God's Word, I have come to this profound, yet simple, conclusion: The Bible is God's Book

of Success. The Bible is the greatest success book that has ever been written. Read and study and meditate on God's Word. Then, by applying those truths in our own lives, we can become the success that God designed us to be.[2]

What does this mean? It means whatever this teacher needs it to mean, depending on who is asking. Suppose I challenge him and say that he is distorting the Word, that he is reading a materialistic notion of success back into the Scriptures. He can reply that there are plenty of Scriptures that speak about success and prosperity, and he would be right. (Never mind the principles of interpretation used.)

Yet he knows that the majority of the people paying attention to statements like his are not skeptics like me, but people who want to believe that God's ultimate goal is their comfort and happiness. When they read such statements, they see something altogether different. Becoming "the success that God designed us to be" can mean just about anything they want to imagine—becoming a millionaire or a movie star, capturing (or stealing) the affections of a man or woman one wants, being rid of lumbago, recovering from terminal cancer, winning "Wheel of Fortune"—the Bible becomes God's Book of Fantasy.

Again, Prosperity Theology is especially devious in its ability to lead a person out on a limb of truth, and then let him cut himself off with the saw of his own imagination. The tragedy, of course, is that on his way down the individual is usually foolish enough to fund the rascal who put him there in the first place!

To return to the statement cited, immediately following it the author tells the story of how he came to a metropolitan area in a trailer and started a church with zero money. Now the church and its related "ministries" are worth ten million dollars, has 8,000 members, is one of the most prominent churches, etc. What would you likely conclude from the juxtaposition of the statement cited with this story? Especially since the author says the same sort of thing could happen for you? Suppose you lived in a rented trailer?

In my view, the teaching that God has promised to make us healthy and wealthy is an insidious heresy tailor-made for our success-driven culture. I cannot refute it in detail here. But it is enough to say that God expressly commands us not to seek to be rich (Luke 12:15)[3]:

He said to them, "Beware, and be on your guard against every form of greed; for not even when one has an abundance does his life consist of his possessions."

Greed, of course, is precisely the outcome of this prosperity teaching. Furthermore, it tempts God by constantly appealing to Him for more.[4] In short, books of this sort are no help at all in dealing with the problem of lifestyle. They simply muddy the waters. Indeed, they pollute them with error.

2. The Franciscan Response

A second genre of resources is available that is more difficult to classify. I call it "the Franciscan response" because it responds to the problem of lifestyle in a way that recalls Francis of Assisi. Like Francis, those who promote this view display a passion for the poor, and in the area of lifestyle they propose that God wants us to live more simply so that others might simply live.

The "response" in this movement is a response in light of the poor. It is a response in light of the ever-widening gap between the haves and the have-nots. It is a response in light of the *billion* people in this world who live—and die—with constant hunger. It is a response in light of the tens of thousands of homeless who wander urban streets in this country, and the millions more abroad. And it is a response in light of the disease, crime, civil strife, and other evils that inevitably overtake these destitute, hopeless people.

In short, the Franciscan response observes this desperate situation and asks: What would God have us do—we who are Christ-followers, and who have so much? In my opinion, given the sobering tragedy of world poverty, this is certainly the appropriate question to ask. This movement responds, first of all, by warning us that we cannot simply ignore the poor. Scripture makes it plain that God abhors poverty and its causes. He wants His people to do what they can to prevent it and relieve it, if not eliminate it.

Consequently, books in this category do a superb job of acquainting us with the plight of the poor, both in America and especially in the developing countries. They have been of enormous benefit in raising the consciousness of American Christians about poverty and injustice and related issues.

Furthermore, these resources have put forth some remarkably creative and helpful suggestions. They have shown how Christians in America can put a check on their lifestyles and avoid allowing them to slip into wanton affluence. They have also put forth practical ways for us to put faith into action by helping the poor.

In my opinion, this tradition has become the major influence on Christian thinking regarding lifestyle in the past ten or fifteen years. Through seminars and conferences, through newsletters and magazines, through an extensive network of agencies and action groups, and as much as anything, through personal involvement in strategies for change, this movement has emerged as the dominant alternative for Christians who want to avoid the spiritual dangers of materialism in our culture.

However, the Franciscan response is not without its problems. First, its critics charge that despite its deep sincerity, noble ideals, and enviable ability to mobilize supporters, it fails in its analysis of the world's problems. It correctly observes the presence and evil of poverty; but its analysis of the causes of that poverty and its suggestions for ending it strike many as too simplistic.

For example, we are told that the wealthy nations of the Northern Hemisphere are the cause of continuing poverty among the developing countries of the South.[5] This is because the rich have a disproportionate share of the best land, advanced technological knowledge, skilled workers, and an efficient use of land. They use these resources to produce goods for sale in the international marketplace, where they earn vast sums that they can then use to buy more goods and resources.

The poor nations, by contrast, lack resources and therefore produce very little. Consequently, they have almost no means of deriving income. Their plight is made the worse by trade barriers and policies that favor the wealthy countries, and by the practices of multinational corporations headquartered in the North. This international socio-economic-political order results in the rich getting richer and the poor poorer.

It is this sort of analysis that strikes some as a very simplistic way of looking at the world. It may appear to explain some cases, but it fails to explain them all. Robert Novak specifically confronts head-on the notion that "the poverty of the poor is explained by the wealth of the wealthy":

> For this there is not a shred of evidence. What causes wealth is intelligent economic activity. Societies can become wealthy through the blessings of nature, which the Creator distributed unequally. Yet richly endowed nations, like the Middle Eastern oil sheikdoms, can remain in poverty for millennia without awareness of the wealth awaiting their awakening. Societies may lack resources and, nevertheless, become wealthy, like Hong Kong and Japan. Societies may be colonies or former colonies, like the United States. Others, like some in Latin America, blessed with climates that make subsistence relatively easy, can languish without significant development for generations. Theories of wealth which try to ignore cultural factors miss the central point. Theories which overlook the importance of a system of liberty miss a crucial lesson of economic history.[6]

As for putting an end to poverty, the Franciscan response suggests that since the problem is inherent in the system, it is the system that must be dealt with. This means, first of all, that wealthy Christians should refuse to cooperate with and assist the system: They may need to quit their jobs at IBM and Exxon, adopt a much simpler lifestyle, and give away their surplus income to agencies that work directly with the poor. Furthermore, it means bringing pressure for change to bear on the system itself.

As I said earlier, some of the suggestions along these lines are creative and worth adopting. Others, however, come off as hopelessly naive. For example, in 1982 it was proposed that American Christians adopt lifestyles that could be sustained on about $1800 per year per person. Yet three years earlier, the U.S. Bureau of the Census had set the poverty level at $7412 for a non-farm family of four. So adopting the $1800 suggestion would put an American family into deep poverty. It is inconceivable that many Christians would accept that. Most would question whether such a move would be responsible, let alone realistic. They would also question how their poverty would enrich anyone else.

To summarize, the Franciscan response is at its best when it raises questions, the central question being: What would God have us do in light of the poor? This is a question that bears directly on lifestyle (though it is by no means the only one). In answering that question, however, this movement is less reliable. It claims to offer a "biblical" view of justice. Yet one could in many cases arrive at the same position by merely reading the editorial page of the *Washington Post*.

3. The Capitalist Defenders

Not being an economist, I leave further critique of the Franciscan response to Novak and others. In fact, these others form the third set of resources generally available on lifestyle. They are distinguished by their attack on the ideology of the simple-living movement and their defense of the capitalist system.

On the positive side, these books build a strong case for a healthy free enterprise system. To my mind, this is positive, first of all because of late there have been more than enough detractors, such that the faults of capitalism have been magnified to the exclusion of whatever positive things it has to offer. One need not close his eyes to the excesses and injustices that occur as a result of our capitalist economy. But he should at least be able to hear about the positive along with the negative. The capitalist defenders point out the positive.

This could be helpful as we think through questions of lifestyle, because, for better or worse, we in this country must discern a godly lifestyle while living in a capitalist economy. Therefore, it helps to know which aspects of the system work to our advantage and which to our disadvantage, morally speaking.

Unfortunately, however, these writings will have little impact on the lifestyle of believers for at least three reasons. First, many of them tend to blur the distinction between Christ and capitalism. They play into the hands of those who link God's will with American economic prosperity. But Christ cannot be the CEO of the American system, which, in order to function, must remain pluralistic. "Christianity has helped to shape the *ethos* of democratic capitalism, but this ethos forbids Christians (or any others) from attempting to *command* this system."[7]

Secondly, these writings fail to address exactly what our response should be to the poor. As the Franciscan response points out, poverty demands a *response*, quite apart from the *reasons* for poverty. The capitalist defenders may reject the notion of wealthy nations exploiting poor ones. They may even suggest alternative causes of poverty (such as the dubious theory that poor people are poor because they lack the ability to think beyond the present[8]). But such explanations do *nothing* to alleviate or eliminate poverty, no matter how accurate or inaccurate they may be. In fact, if we stop merely at explanations, we actually perpetuate poverty.

Yet this is where most of the capitalist defenders stop. Consequently, they tend to come off as insensitive and even arrogant toward the poor. And unless they can articulate realistic answers to the question of what we must do in response to poverty, they are not likely to affect the lifestyles of biblically sensitive Christians.

This brings us to the third deficiency of this camp: it lacks organization and an action plan. Relative to the Franciscan response, the capitalist defenders have all the organization of a junior high marching band. I'm unaware of any congresses on "Christian Capitalist Alternatives to Poverty and Injustice," or "Social Responsibility in the Free Enterprise System." They do not publish books that outline strategies for how the poor might become un-poor, that is productive and self-sufficient. Nor do they have a network of nonprofit groups united in a vision of ensuring justice and economic viability from a Christian (and capitalist) perspective.

As a consequence, Franciscan thinking, even with its limitations, will continue to dominate the discussion of how Christians should handle economics and lifestyle, at least for the foreseeable future.

4. Practical Workbooks
One final group of resources worth mentioning are the growing number of practical helps in the area of finances. These materials tend to be workbooks that guide Christians in thinking through budgets, insurance policies, wills, and other practical matters.

Some present various "biblical principles for finances." But usually there is little or no critique of the overall system in which these principles must be lived out. Consequently, while these resources are on the whole helpful, they lack a comprehensive approach. Thus, they may not provide a stout enough challenge in the area of lifestyle.

NEEDED: A PRACTICAL THEOLOGY OF LIFESTYLE

These are some of the answers Christians have put forth in response to the question of lifestyle. Perhaps you find them more helpful than I do. But I believe we as Christians need resources that are far more savvy about theology, about economics, and about human nature and behavior.

Perhaps the place to begin is to formulate the right question. The right question is not which economic system would be the closest to a biblical ideal. That's an interesting question, but is really a problem of economic theory. Economics enters into this discussion, but economics deals with problems as they exist in an overall system, whereas most of us are trying to deal with problems at our own individual levels, in our own lifestyles. Economics bears on our situation, but what we need is a practical approach to lifestyle.

Consequently, the question I think we need to ask is: How can each of us live and work as a Christ-follower in *this* economy, a democratic capitalist economy of relative prosperity in a world of varying economies linked together in a global economy? How can we and our families live lifestyles that please God?

I certainly cannot answer such a question in full in this book. I am not an economist and I am not prepared to present any sophisticated theory of Christian economics. I think others more qualified than I should tackle that task. But I do believe there are several principles that flow out of the ideas presented in Part II, principles that should feature prominently in any discussion of lifestyle. I'll mention five. The first two are more theoretical; the rest are very practical.

1. God has given us the means to provide for our needs.

In the beginning, after God had created Adam and Eve, He explained to them that they were to rule over the creation. This was a position of responsibility and authority. But it was not without its perks:

> Then God said, "Behold, I have given you every plant yielding seed that is on the surface of all the earth, and every tree which has fruit yielding seed; it shall be food for you; and to every beast of the earth

and to every bird of the sky and to every thing that moves on the earth which has life, I have given every green plant for food"; and it was so. (Genesis 1:29-30)

In other words, God designed into the creation the means to feed these first humans, and presumably their descendants as well. The same idea is repeated in Genesis 2:15-16, only there the importance of work in providing for human needs is emphasized.

Later, after Adam and Eve sinned, God cursed the ground, which, as we saw in Chapter 7, increased the toil involved in work. But even in this fallen world, God intended for the creation to supply mankind's food. Actually, we find it supplying considerably more than food. But the principle throughout Scripture is that God has provided the creation as the primary resource to meet our basic needs.[9]

The problem of starvation. However, this raises the question of why people starve. The answer ultimately lies in the problem of evil. While a fallen creation can still provide our food, the presence of evil often undermines this arrangement. These "thorns and thistles" may be natural forces such as drought or swarms of locusts. Or they may involve the evils that people create: civil wars that displace farmers, disrupt cultivation of crops, and interrupt transportation (consider Ethiopia or Cambodia); political policies that discriminate or that impede the flow of resources (some international trade policies); or sheer incompetence (such as unrealistic planning and quotas in Stalinist Russia, or the disaster at Chernobyl).

But the fact that people sometimes do not have adequate food does not alter the fact that in the creation God has given us adequate resources to feed ourselves.

The creation provides more than survival. Of course, the creation supplies us with considerably more than food. This is evident despite the view of some that the vast majority of mankind throughout history has subsisted in a state of abject poverty. That is one way to look at history, and if it is true, it only underscores the extent of evil in the world. But we must be careful about how we assess standards of living in other times and places against conditions now prevailing in North America.

An equally plausible view is that the mass of mankind throughout history has enjoyed a bit more, and in some cases quite a bit more, than mere survival. Indeed, the rise and longevity of the great civilizations of the world are testimony to the generosity of God and to the abundance of His creation.

However, I am reluctant to say just how far above survival we should expect the earth to support us. This is another way of saying that while we have every indication that God intends to give us what we need, we must avoid presuming on God for much beyond our basic necessities.

For example, God has given us sheep, so it seems legitimate to think about sweaters and coats. It seems less reasonable, however, to think about drawers stocked with dozens of sweaters and closets lined with dozens of coats. After all, we only *need* to wear one good sweater or coat at a time!

Need. This brings us to the concept of need. I find this to be a fairly complicated idea. At the very minimum, humans have basic survival needs: food, water, clothing, shelter. Without adequate supply of these, life is not sustainable.

But are these all that the Scriptures have in mind when they declare that "God shall supply all your needs"?[10] I think not. The Bible presents God as One committed to seeing humans raised above grinding poverty. He appears as a generous Giver, and His earth is pictured as a realm of abundance. And in fact, as I mentioned above, history shows that people and civilizations have enjoyed considerably more than the basics.

It is interesting to observe, though, that as a culture advances and grows more sophisticated, its level of needs rises. In our own society, for example, it is virtually impossible to function without a car. Sure, there are hundreds of thousands of people in places like Manhattan or Boston who get along quite well without a car, but only because of mass transit, which is also an advanced technology far above basic survival. Take this transportation system away, and life as we know it would cease.

Or consider how critical electricity is to our society. Obviously a person could get along without it, but not without disengaging from what has become a normal life. The famous blackouts in the Northeast in the '60s and '70s demonstrate how completely electricity runs through American culture. But generating and delivering it requires a somewhat sophisticated level of technology.

So the point is that after a culture meets its basic survival needs and begins to develop, it starts solving problems at a higher level. Some of these we might regard as "needs" and some as "wants." Either way, once they are satisfied, the means of satisfying them become necessities because the satisfying of them becomes a way of life.

Furthermore, many needs in our culture have little if anything to do with physical survival and yet have a great deal to do with intellectual, moral, and spiritual survival. We could obviously "get along" without novels, sculpture, music, philosophical treatises, and creeds. Yet a good bit of our humanity would remain impoverished without them. To that extent they are necessary.

In short, some things that start out as luxuries often become necessities.

But how does this relate to the idea of God supplying our needs? It seems reasonable to expect Him to provide food, clothing, and shelter. But can we find a Mazda RX7, a Hotpoint rangetop, and an IBM PC in Genesis 1:29-30? How about Michelangelo's *David*, Handel's *Messiah*, or Solzhenitsyn's *Gulag Archipelago*?

I don't think there is any easy answer to these questions. But it might help to think of needs and wants in a hierarchy beginning with survival needs, moving up to necessities, and ultimately up to luxuries.[11]

God obviously allows cultures and people to "rise," to move up that scale. How far up is impossible to say. American culture seems pretty far up in some ways, especially compared to the incredible poverty of so many others in the world. And yet, it is conceivable that a future society could be as far above us as we are above the Stone Age. Of course God also allows cultures to "decline." Sometimes He even allows them to die out altogether.

What is critical, I think, is that we never put claims on God by which we demand to move higher, by which we tell Him He is somehow obligated to advance us. Instead, we need to accept every good thing as a gift from His hand.[12] And we need to hold everything with a light touch. I'll soon say more about the practical implications of this for lifestyle.

2. Every worker should benefit from the fruit of his labor.

In Chapters 5 and 6, we looked at some reasons why God has given us work. This view implied that God has delegated a great deal of responsibility (work) to us. As we have seen in Genesis, He has commissioned us to manage the creation. But along with this responsibility comes the right to benefit from the resources of creation when we fulfill our work. In practical terms, this means that you have a right to a paycheck.

Scriptural evidence. This may seem self-evident to you. But let me mention a number of Scriptures in order to emphasize the validity of this idea. We find it stated in the creation mandate of Genesis 1:29-30. God tells Adam and Eve that the food mentioned is "for you" (verse 29). Again, in Genesis 2:16 God says, "You may eat freely." And even in the curse of Genesis 3:17-23, God says three times, "You shall eat" from the earth's produce.

Later, the writer of Ecclesiastes affirms the legitimacy of income, and even describes it as a reward and a gift from God:

> Here is what I have seen to be good and fitting: to eat, to drink and enjoy oneself in all one's labor in which he toils under the sun during the few years of his life which God has given him; for this is his reward. Furthermore, as for every man to whom God has given riches

and wealth, He has also empowered him to eat from them and to receive his reward and rejoice in his labor; this is the gift of God. (Ecclesiastes 5:18-19)

In the New Testament we find this same connection between work and pay. As we saw in Chapter 6, for instance, Paul exhorts lazy and undisciplined Christians to work in 2 Thessalonians 3:6-15. He says that anyone who will not work should not eat. On the other hand, people who work in a quiet fashion should "eat their own bread" (verse 12).

Earning pay for labor is legitimate. Indeed, James cries out against withholding it from those who have worked for it:

Behold, the pay of the laborers who mowed your fields, and which has been withheld by you, cries out against you; and the outcry of those who did the harvesting has reached the ears of the Lord of Sabaoth. (James 5:4)

Pay for work is disparaged. I stress this point about the legitimacy of earning a livelihood because on the one hand, it is taken for granted in our culture and therefore overlooked; and on the other hand, because I find here and there among many Christians that it is subtly disparaged. To be more precise, some Christians object to the self-interest inherent in the work world, a self-interest that expresses itself most visibly in the paycheck.

The Two-Story view mentioned in Chapter 3, for instance, would likely argue that most people go to work out of "secular" motives, that their main concern is just in making money. Likewise, I think many Christians who adopt a Mainstream view (Chapter 4) do so because they feel queasy about income as a powerful motivation for going to work. It just doesn't seem "spiritual" enough. So they latch onto the idea of evangelism as a more noble motive for participating in the marketplace.

In both cases, the feeling is that Christians shouldn't be in business to make money. In fact, I have actually seen cases in which Christians who were customers of other Christians expected to purchase goods or services at cost, or even to have them for free, based on this rationale!

And then there are those who believe that business is more or less based on greed. The idea is that the customer makes his purchases because he craves the goods of the merchant. Likewise, the merchant sells because he craves the money of the customer. In this view, such self-seeking transactions explain why the customer always feels like the price is too high, while the merchant always feels it is too low.

Others would say that selfishness is not inherent in all business transactions, but only in those of a capitalist economy. In other words, greed runs Wall Street. Consequently, "lifestyle" is a problem only in a materialistic empire of multinational corporations. It is an obscenity in a world of poverty and starvation.

So to some Christians, self-interest is the worst feature of the workplace, and should be eliminated if possible.

Self-interest is inherent in work. But I argue that eliminating self-interest is not possible. In fact, it is not even desirable. I'll suggest two reasons. But first, we need to distinguish between self-interest and selfishness. Without question, far too many workers (and customers) work from self-seeking, greedy motives. They cheat, they steal, they lie, they over-charge, they defraud, they rig the system.

But these are sins of people, not flaws inherent in work. Instead, work as God has designed it anticipates a legitimate self-interest present in every worker. This is one reason why eliminating self-interest is neither possible nor desirable. To do so would contradict the nature of our humanity.

Suppose I were to ask you why you go to work. No doubt you would offer me a variety of reasons. But two would likely feature most prominently: "I work to support my family," and "It's what I know how to do, or want to do." These both reflect legitimate self-interest, and they act as extremely powerful motives for working.

Furthermore, the nature of our partnership with God assumes a degree of self-interest. We are not slaves to God, in which we do all the work but He derives all the benefit and doles out only what is necessary to keep us working. Rather we are noble coworkers with Him, and He allows us to share in the product of our labor. When we eat, we do not eat for His benefit, but for ours.

I happen to think He takes a certain joy in seeing us work and meet our needs, in seeing us enjoy His creation.[13] Indeed, one of the ways we can bring glory to God is by diligently working to provide for our needs, and then lifting thankful hearts to Him when those needs are satisfied. As Moses told Israel:

"When you have eaten and are satisfied, you shall bless the LORD your God for the good land which He has given you." (Deuteronomy 8:10)

Confusion about profits. By the way, I think much of the disparagement of self-interest in work comes from the widespread confusion over the role of profits in our economy. Unfortunately, too many people, and especially too many businesspeople, define a business as "an organization to make a profit." And people speak of businesses and their owners and managers as being driven by a "profit motive" in which the goal of the enterprise is the "maximization of profits." But as Peter Drucker points out, this is not only erroneous, it is exceedingly harmful.[14]

Drucker is not an economist, but his perceptive discussion of profit is essential reading if you run a business or if you want to better understand the American marketplace. For our purposes, though, it is enough to note that profits need not be a self-seeking motivation for business, nor even the goal of business, but rather the *test* of whether a business has managed to achieve its goals, regardless of its motives. Furthermore, profits are a condition of survival; they pay for the cost of the future, the cost of staying in business.[15]

This means that profit has, or should have, nothing to do with self-interest. As I showed before, the reasons why you go to work have a great deal to do with your own concerns, whether they be to provide for your family, to satisfy your vocational bent, or even to make a pile of money. But in Drucker's view, whether or not you continue to have work to go to will be determined by the profit your work produces.

Sure, you can go to work *only* to make money. But to make it demands that you create something of value for which someone is willing to pay. If you *only* concentrate on "making money," you won't create value, so you won't get paid. And businesses that are *only* out to make money don't stay in business for long. So profit remains the condition, not the objective, of staying in business, no matter how noble or despicable your motives may be.[16]

Of course, God wants us to work from the purest of motives. That means working as an employee of Christ. It means working to genuinely meet the needs of people—your employer, your coworkers, your customers. And it also means working to meet your own needs, and those of your family. Love God. Love your neighbor. And yes, love yourself!

3. Develop an attitude of contentment, not covetousness.

Let's turn now to consider some practical implications of all of this for lifestyle. How can we solve "the problem of gain"?

It all begins with our attitudes. Here the Scriptures tell us we can go in one of two directions. We can either be content with what we have, or we can long for more, an attitude described as covetousness. Which one we adopt all depends on the extent to which we depend on God for our welfare. In Hebrews 13:5 we read:

> Let your way of life be free from the love of money, being content with what you have; for He Himself has said, "I will never desert you, nor will I ever forsake you."

This verse pulls together everything we have said so far about lifestyle. God has given us the means to provide for our needs, and gives us the right to benefit from honest labor. Consequently, we have a basis for being content, for being satisfied, for resting in the conviction that God intends to meet our needs.

Covetousness. And yet what torpedoes this arrangement is (1) when we look at what God has given us, and we look at what He has not given us, and we say, "I don't have enough!" and (2) when we start longing for money as the way to get "enough," instead of longing for God as the Provider of "enough."

We could discuss many aspects of these attitudes as we find them among the poor and the starving. But what I want to draw our attention to is how prevalent they are among those of us who are far above poverty and starvation levels.

The materialistic nature of our culture and of many Christians in it is so well-documented that condemning it has become a cliché. I hardly need to restate the obvious, especially since my generation—a privileged group of people, if ever there was one—made the case so forcefully in the late '60s, along with vows to return to spiritual rather than material values. Yet a decade or two later this same generation has managed to outdo its parents in upping the ante of affluence.

This suggests that greed and covetousness are not so easily conquered. In fact, the protests of the '60s failed to even diagnose the disease properly. For the root of covetousness lies in neither the absence nor the abundance of wealth, but in the attitude one holds toward God.

The first step toward covetousness is to buy into either of two ideas: God doesn't care, or God doesn't matter. Obviously these are related.

God doesn't care. The idea that God doesn't care suggests itself when times are lean: when you are out of work, when your bills mount up, when your sales are off, when the economy is down. In periods like these, it is natural to see money as the solution to your problems. And it is natural to blame God as the cause of them: If God cared, He would bring in money. But money isn't coming in, so God must not care. Therefore, I'll have to look out for myself. Such logic draws one away from God to a dependence on oneself and money.

God doesn't matter. In a related way, the idea that God doesn't matter suggests itself in times of plenty: when you get a raise or a promotion, when you make a major and prestigious purchase, when your business is booming, when the Dow is skyrocketing. Then it is quite easy to forget God and to focus instead on your own abilities or business savvy, and on the power of money.

Moses warned Israel about this very tendency: "Beware lest you forget the LORD your God," he told them as they were about to enter the Promised Land, a land with widely acclaimed abundance. They would forget God, he said, if ever they said to themselves, "My power and the strength of my hand made me this wealth." Instead, they needed to "remember the LORD your God, for it is He who is giving you power to make wealth."[17]

How about you: do you believe that God really cares about seeing your needs met? Do you see Him as the ultimate source of all that you have?

Contentment. The test for answering these questions is not only the absence of covetousness, but the presence of contentment. In many ways that is a subjective measure. Only you can know whether you are satisfied with God and with what He allows you to have.

However, I can suggest a few strategies that might help you pursue contentment and avoid covetousness. In mentioning these, however, I want to warn against an all-too-common danger of trying to bargain with God. Many Christians set up a "deal" in which they agree to do everything they can to live a life that pleases God. In exchange, they expect Him to prosper them spiritually and materially.

But this amounts to God paying them to be good![18] God doesn't work that way. In a slightly different context, Paul explains that godliness is not a means toward financial gain:

> Godliness actually is a means of great gain, when accompanied by con-
> tentment. For we have brought nothing into the world, so we cannot
> take anything out of it either. And if we have food and covering, with
> these we shall be content. (1 Timothy 6:6-8)

So we do prosper from our walk with God, but it is not a "deal" in which God pays us for doing what He wants. If we are serving God out of an expectation that He will reward us materially, then we are serving money, not God. For this reason, Paul goes on to say:

> But those who want to get rich fall into temptation and a snare and
> many foolish and harmful desires which plunge men into ruin and de-
> struction. For the love of money is a root of all sorts of evil, and some
> by longing for it have wandered away from the faith, and pierced
> themselves with many a pang. (1 Timothy 6:9-10)

How, then, can we pursue contentment? Here are several ideas.

1. Thank God for what you have. When you pray before your meals (I assume you do; if not, this is an excellent habit to form) thank God not only for the food, but for all the many provisions He has supplied and for the many means He has used to supply them. You might even want to mention some of these specifically—your house, your car, a treasured piece of furniture, or intangible gifts such as vacations, music, or a good book. This keeps the source of these good things in mind. It also keeps us thankful.

2. *Take care of what you have.* I often see people abuse their car or their property with the excuse that "it's a piece of junk anyway." But surely this suggests a certain loss of contentment. On the contrary, faithfully maintaining what you have, no matter how humble, demonstrates a quiet gratitude for the provision of God.

3. *Consider how much God has given you.* One of the best ways to acquire contentment may be to look carefully at what many people *do not* have in comparison to what you do have. For instance, people who visit areas of poverty in Third World nations almost always come away with a deep sense of appreciation for how richly they have been blessed. I suggest that you arrange for such a trip, perhaps through your church or a mission agency.

Of course, the point is not to come home feeling guilty, though that may happen, but to grow content with what you have. Likewise, such a trip should never result in an attitude of superiority. The idea is that so often we lose our contentment by comparing ourselves to those who to us seem rich. We might regain our perspective by instead noting how much we have when we consider the poor.

4. *Call coveting sin, and confess it.* When we do find ourselves coveting— longing after something, having our mind controlled by the fantasy of having it, or perhaps being angry with God for "denying" us a certain thing—when we recognize this attitude, we need to call it covetousness, which is a sin. This calls for confession, for admitting that such an attitude is wrong and must be done away with. Such confession needs to be spoken to ourself, to God, and probably to someone else who knows us and will stand with us to overcome this attitude.

5. *Be aware of the signs of covetousness.* Two warning signs that covetousness rather than contentment may be controlling us are excessive work and excessive debt. Excessive work may be a signal that we are relying on ourselves, not on God, to meet our needs. Likewise, excessive debt is a good indication that we have grown discontent with what we have and are determined to gain more.

6. *Just say "No!"* A final strategy as a check on covetousness is to simply say, "No!" I'm thinking particularly about impulse purchases, which are usually fairly small. Strolling through a shopping mall—a dangerous environment in which to control covetousness and remain content—it is inevitable that you will see a "little something" you want: a cookie, a scarf, a tie, a

knick-knack. Can you afford it? Probably. But to deny yourself this item may help; you learn to live without, to not always satisfy the impulse for having more and still more.

A similar strategy that works well with larger purchases is the commitment to wait before buying. Waiting rarely hurts. It allows you to get past the initial flush of excitement over some new thing, and thus puts you in closer touch with your true motives and values. You may change your mind. You may decide that you can be content with what you already have.

This brings us to the issue of limits in our lifestyle, and to the ways we can act on an attitude of contentment.

4. Pursue a lifestyle of limits, not luxury.

Contentment is a noble attitude, but it won't do us much good unless we translate it into a lifestyle. Now this is a real challenge, because as I mentioned earlier, lifestyle requires that we balance a number of competing tensions. This guarantees that there can be no simple answers, no easy decisions. Yet decisions we must make. And I believe there are a number of principles that can help us please God in our lifestyle.

The first thing to say is that none of the discussion that follows will mean much to you unless you are captivated by the cause of Christ. By "the cause of Christ," I mean the over-arching plan and purpose of God in history. Unless you perceive that this world involves infinitely more than your comfort, there is no point in discussing your lifestyle.

But if you want to honor God by how you live, then the place to begin is to ask: How can I use my income as a responsible manager before God, given the culture in which I live? Let me suggest that money is an important means by which you can love God, love others, and love yourself. Let's begin with yourself.

As I mentioned in Chapter 6, one of our primary responsibilities is to take care of our own needs and those of our families. But in our culture, most of us can easily pay for survival needs of simple food, clothing, and shelter. In fact, I suspect that if you have the means to buy this book, you probably have quite a bit more income than it takes merely to survive.

In that case, we must begin to decide at what lifestyle level we will live. Unfortunately, too many of us don't make this choice. We let the culture make this choice for us. And inevitably, the choice is for more, more, and still more.

Without question, it takes more to survive and function in our modern Western culture than it does in more primitive agrarian, non-technologically oriented societies. And I refuse to debate whether or not this should be so. It is so, and I believe we have almost no control over it. But what we have much more control over is our personal choices about money in the midst of such a culture.

Levels of luxury. For so many of us, however, what happens is that we work our way up to an income that not only covers our needs as dictated by survival in this economy, but goes beyond those needs to "discretionary income." Faced with such a surplus, we so easily spend it on various "luxuries"—items we don't necessarily need, but which we want.

Right here I would again point out the danger of covetousness. While desiring something we don't absolutely need is hardly sin, it does create an opportunity for covetousness. And as I showed above, the Scriptures strongly admonish us not to get carried away by our desires.

How do we know when we're carried away? When we desire the thing itself more than we desire God. In other words, when we lose our contentment. If we find ourselves angry with God because we feel that He is "depriving" us of something we want, then we have lost our contentment and have been carried away into covetousness.

At any rate, whether motivated by covetousness or by honest desire, purchasing such wants raises our lifestyle to a higher level—what I'll call a luxury level. In time however, luxuries become necessities, and new wants replace old ones. If our income rises, we again spend the surplus on the new wants, and thus raise our luxury level a notch higher.

And so we become "upwardly mobile," stair-stepping our way from luxury level to luxury level, ascending to the limits of our income—and maybe considerably beyond! It is worth asking yourself, at what point will *you* refuse to climb to the next level?

Limits to luxury. The issue here is responsible management of God-given resources. When I was in the service, I visited Germany. While there, I rode on the Autobahn, a superhighway on which there are no speed limits. Instead, every few miles are signs that simply read "Genug!" ("Enough!") with a picture of a speedometer pointing to "100 kph." The idea is, once you get up to 100, 110, 120 kilometers per hour, do you really need to go faster? "Enough!"

We need the same principle in our decisions about lifestyle. Many of us are so blessed with so much that we reach a point well beyond saturation. We need to say, "Enough!"

So, I'd like to suggest a concept called *the limited lifestyle*. A limited lifestyle means that as your income increases and your basic needs are met, you decide before God at what level you intend to live. Then whatever you make beyond that level, you purpose to invest in something outside of yourself. In essence, you give the excess away.

Sacrifice and discipline. The operating principles of a limited lifestyle are sacrifice and discipline. The New Testament encourages us to practice such values. In Matthew 16, Jesus explains that following Him has a cost to it:

> Then Jesus said to His disciples, "If any one wishes to come after Me, let him deny himself, and take up his cross, and follow Me. For whoever wishes to save his life shall lose it; but whoever loses his life for My sake shall find it. For what will a man be profited, if he gains the whole world, and forfeits his soul? Or what will a man give in exchange for his soul?" (Matthew 16:24-26)

We must guard against lavishing our riches on ourselves, which is a lifestyle that attempts to "save ourselves," that turns us away from God. Christ must be the Lord of our possessions. He has placed us as His managers over the money we have. Are we managing that money responsibly before Him? Or is the money managing us? If it is, then we are no longer serving Christ, but money.[19]

Functional economy. What will this limited lifestyle mean in practical terms? Should we all take vows of poverty? Should all of us live at some subsistence level, in rented quarters, driving used cars (if we even own cars), wearing secondhand clothes? Or should we perhaps find out what the median income is and use that as the standard?

I'd like to suggest an alternative called *functional economy.* Functional economy says that when I make a purchase, I buy the least expensive item that will get the job done. Of course, the thing that will get the job done won't always be the least expensive item.

To illustrate, a friend of mine sells real estate. Most of his customers are fairly well-heeled and have certain expectations, not only about what properties they will buy, but about who they will buy from. So my friend drives these potential buyers around in his Oldsmobile. It happens to be the top-of-the-line Olds. It is not the most expensive car, obviously, especially for people in real estate. But he felt for several reasons that he ought not to buy a Cadillac or a BMW. At the same time, he needed to respond appropriately to the expectations involved in the job. He felt the Oldsmobile would be a good choice. It was the least expensive item that would get the job done. This is functional economy.

Now immediately I hear a chorus of contrarians who would argue, "He doesn't need a top-of-the-line Oldsmobile! He could get by with a medium-priced Ford, or even a Yugo. He's just into an image, driving a gas-belching piece of prestige sheet metal that deprives Third World people of precious resources."

Two things strike me about such objections. First, I think they point out the need for my friend to think carefully about the car he drives. For him, a car is more than transportation. It is an image, a communication strategy. He uses it to tell his customers something about himself and his business. So, functional economy says that if the Oldsmobile is the least expensive means of achieving this objective, then he should use the Oldsmobile. But if a less expensive car would do just as well, he should buy that instead.

The problem is, that is a very subjective determination. Which brings me to a second point: As an outsider, I have no right to judge my friend's decision about his car. I don't know the issues and tensions and requirements of his world. For me, a top-of-the-line Oldsmobile might be extravagant. But he is not me! So I must not judge him. He must answer to the Lord for the car he drives.

Likewise, each of us must answer to the Lord for how we use the money he has entrusted to us. This will require careful and sober thinking, and some disciplined decision-making. There are no simple answers. Functional economy, though, acts as a brake on an ever-escalating lifestyle.

By the way, one area in which this is especially critical is our houses. Too many Americans take the attitude that a family should buy the biggest or most prestigious house it can afford. But this easily plays into the hands of covetousness and an escalating lifestyle.

Instead, when we consider our homes we need to ask, "Does my present house basically meet my needs?" (keeping in mind all that I have said about "needs"). If so, then there is really no reason to move. Of course, needs can change—children come, an aged relative comes to live with us, etc. In that case, a change is worth considering. But selling a house that adequately meets our needs in order to buy a larger, more expensive one is leaning toward luxury, not responsible limits.

I'm not suggesting that we should never "splurge" and buy something somewhat beyond our usual limits. It may be a certain kind of ice cream, an article of clothing, a special vacation, or some other luxury. There is a healthy joy and spontaneity in occasionally exceeding the normal boundaries. But if splurging is a way of life, such that all of our purchases are nothing but excesses in prestige and affluence, then I suggest we may be ensnared in the love of money warned of earlier.

5. Cultivate habits of generosity, not greed.
Earlier I said that money is an important means by which you can love God, love others, and love yourself. We've looked at how you might love yourself, by using your money to meet the legitimate needs of yourself and your family.

We've also seen how spending more and more on yourself is not really loving yourself, but hurting yourself, by subtly drawing you away from God. Instead, you need to practice limits in regard to your lifestyle, limits that you set.

But aside from loving ourselves, money is a primary means God gives us with which to love Him and love others. Now in this regard, Christians have come up with various suggestions over the years. One extreme advocates giving all our money away. Others argue for a less drastic amount: a "tithe," by which ten percent of your income should go to "the Lord's work." Others say that while the tithe does not apply to the New Testament Christian, it is a good benchmark, and should represent the *least* amount you should give. A related concept is the "graduated tithe." Others point out that "God loves a cheerful giver," so just give as you feel led. Still others point to the crying needs of various ministries and people, and urge us to give sacrificially "until it hurts."

We could debate these suggestions forever. But one fact that should be mentioned is that despite them all, most American Christians opt to give very little if any of their money away: only 2.5 percent, according to one source.[20]

Whose money is it? What troubles me about this statistic is not its size, but the underlying assumption to which I think it points. As I talk with Christians about their money, they speak about it with a sense of ownership: "This is *my* money; *I* worked hard for it; I'll use it the way *I* want."

But this is all wrong! All of our money belongs to God. He has given us the earth to supply our needs. Thus, the money we make is really a gift from Him. It is actually a trust over which He has set us as trustees or managers. We have a right to benefit from our work, but we must never forget that God is the ultimate Provider of what we have.

God intends us to give money away. Furthermore, as we saw in Chapter 6, one of the purposes of work is that we earn enough to support those who have financial needs. On that basis I argue that every Christian, no matter what his income, should invest part of his money in the material needs of others.

These needs fall into two broad categories. First, there are poor people who cannot pay for all of their needs. We have a responsibility as Christians to assist them.[21] Secondly, we should also support Christian ministries and those whose vocation it is to preach and teach the gospel.[22]

Obviously there is great latitude and opportunity in both of these categories. Whom you give to and how much are decisions you must make before God. Again, the question to ask is, "Where can I invest my money wisely for God?"

However, asking that particular question in today's world is a bit like standing in a huge shopping mall with a $20 bill in your pocket, asking, "What could I spend my $20 on?" There are literally tens of thousands of ministries and good causes that could use your dollars, to say nothing of churches and needy individuals you may know.

For that reason, let me offer some suggestions, first in regard to assisting the poor, and then in regard to ministries.

Assisting the poor. I am far from prepared to suggest any ways to "solve" the problem of poverty. I sometimes wonder whether solutions are even possible. Yet there is no way that a Christian can read his Bible and call Christ "Lord" and yet ignore the poor. John writes:

> Whoever has the world's goods, and beholds his brother in need and closes his heart against him, how does the love of God abide in him? Little children, let us not love with word or with tongue, but in deed and truth. (1 John 3:17-18)

So God calls us to action. Yet the problem is exceedingly complex, and anyone who says, "No, the problem is simple; it's just a simple matter of greed on the part of rich Christians," is blind to reality.

On the other hand, we must not be blind to the reality of poor people. I'm impressed that when Paul received the right hand of fellowship from the early Church leaders, they specifically asked him to remember the poor. He writes that this was the very thing he was eager to do.[23] Do we *remember* the poor? Are we *eager* to assist them? I think the Franciscan response mentioned earlier is right on target when it asks: In light of the staggering reality of the poor, what would God have us do—we who are Christ-followers, and who have so much? What will be our response?

I could offer many ideas. But I want to highlight just one strategy in particular. It proves instructive because I think it demonstrates a realistic model for assisting the poor in this economy. The model is Mendenhall Ministries.

Mendenhall Ministries is an outgrowth of Mendenhall Bible Church in Mendenhall, Mississippi, a small town about thirty miles south of Jackson. The church has perhaps one hundred members.

Pastor Artis Fletcher and the leaders in that church surveyed the situation confronting their people and their community. They observed the tragic cycle of poverty that still afflicts so many rural black communities in the south. But they purposed, as the people of God, to do what they could to obey the Scriptures and work out their faith in service to the community.

They chose to channel these efforts through Mendenhall Ministries, a nonprofit organization established alongside the church. A young man who had grown up in Mendenhall, Dolphus Weary, assumed the leadership of that ministry.

For the most part without government aid, and utilizing a mix of volunteers from the church and a handful of outside workers, Mendenhall Ministries has grown into a model of rural community development from a Christian base. Today it operates a grade school, a legal assistance clinic, a health clinic, a cooperative thrift store, a farm, a housing rehabilitation ministry, a vocational skills program, a youth program, and related programs that serve the surrounding community.

By any measure, what has happened in Mendenhall is remarkable. And yet Artis Fletcher, Dolphus Weary, and the others there see it as the natural outcome of a church acting on the truth of God's Word to address the needs of the poor around them.

Obviously they have required some outside funds for some projects. But one of the keys to their impressive ministry is the idea that people need to achieve economic self-sufficiency. Not that everyone can obtain this goal. But they've seen that unless a person can provide for himself and his family, he inevitably falls into the quicksand of poverty, with all its tragic consequences.[24]

You and your church may or may not be positioned to give to the poor in quite the way Mendenhall Bible Church has. And yet there are many churches, organizations, and individuals who are directly involved in similar efforts. You should look for ways to underwrite their efforts financially. You should also make your resources and skills available to them, for use as they see fit.

As I say, this will not eliminate all poverty. But I'm not sure that that should be your goal. Rather, you can assist a handful of people by sharing with them out of the abundance God has given you.

Supporting ministries. In Galatians 6:6, Paul writes:

Let the one who is taught the word share all good things with him who teaches.

Likewise in 1 Corinthians 9:14 we read:

So also the Lord directed those who proclaim the gospel to get their living from the gospel.

Such is some of the New Testament basis for supporting ministries and the people who work in them. I wish that in bringing up this subject we could remain at the level of pristine integrity that passages like these assume. However, to do so would be unrealistic in light of recent history in the financing of so-called Christian ministries.

I am not thinking only of the much-publicized scandals that have made

Christianity a laughingstock among unbelievers. I am thinking of the increasing commercialization of the gospel. As an acquaintance of mine put it, Christianity began in Palestine as a relationship; it spread throughout the Roman Empire as a movement; across Europe and Northern Africa it became a culture; today in the West it has become an enterprise.

One wonders at times when donating to a ministry whether he is underwriting God or Mammon. As a consequence, many people are now giving much less, and some have stopped giving altogether.

Yet is this responsible? Is this what God would have us do? I think not. The Church has always had to contend with those who abuse and prostitute the gospel as a means of gain.[25] Consequently, the issue is not whether we should give, but how much and to whom we should give.

Evaluating ministries. Determining the legitimacy of someone to whom you donate is perhaps not as difficult as it may appear. Three key questions to answer are: Is the ministry doctrinally sound? Is it effective? Is it financially wise and honest?

A ministry's doctrinal position is easily reviewed by examining its statement of faith and any materials it publishes or distributes.

Its effectiveness may be slightly harder to discern. Newsletters usually broadcast the successes and leave out the failures and the problems. Even so, I suggest evaluating everything you are told against the organization's statement of purpose. You might also ask individual personnel to report on programs, progress, and problems. If possible, you might talk directly to those who are participants in the ministry's programs.

Financial fitness and integrity also require reading between the lines. If you can, review a financial statement of the ministry. At the least you should be told what the annual budget is and how it is spent. It is also instructive to determine how much money it takes to achieve the organization's purpose, and to examine the ratio between money spent directly on ministry objectives and money spent for administrative and auxiliary purposes.[26]

So much for sorting out the wheat from the chaff among the many Christian ministries appealing for your dollars. It remains for you to decide exactly who you will choose to fund.

Get the big picture. First evaluate some of the broad categories of things God seems to be doing in our day. For instance, experts in missions say that the cutting edge of missionary efforts right now lies in reaching unreached people groups—cultures that have not yet been exposed to the gospel.

A similar vanguard is a movement of people toward cities. Consequently, urban strategies must be developed. Likewise, a movement is afoot among laypeople, who need training and help in doing their work of ministry.

By cooperating with these broad streams of activity, your dollar can go much further. If you are like me, you want your contribution to be as effective as possible. You want to "leverage" your donation, so that it accomplishes great things all out of proportion to its size. So I'd encourage you to ask, "What is God doing in my day, and how can I participate financially?"

Give in the area of your interest. Ultimately, of course, you will likely give to areas that minister to you directly or areas in which you take a special interest. And this is appropriate. For instance, your church deserves your generous support if your pastor faithfully ministers the Word to you week after week, if it instructs your children in spiritual things, and if it otherwise serves many of your spiritual needs.

Similarly, a ministry from which you benefit—perhaps a radio Bible teacher, or a youth organization that helps your teenager, or a discipling ministry—deserves your support. You should underwrite those who meet your personal and spiritual needs.

Likewise, you may be drawn to a particular cause because of personal interest or conviction. For example, I know a man who has benefited greatly from the education God has enabled him to have. As a result, he contributes to seminaries and schools because he believes in their mission. Likewise, another man I know feels strongly that families today need support, so he donates heavily to a cause that counsels troubled families.

The point is, evaluate the needs that are out there, and decide where you feel your contribution could make the greatest impact. This will require research, reflection, and prayer on your part.

Giving is for everyone. But don't think this applies only to the wealthy individual. No matter what your income, you have some responsibility to consider the needs of others. Remember the widow in Mark 12:41-44:

> He sat down opposite the treasury, and began observing how the multitude were putting money into the treasury; and many rich people were putting in large sums. And a poor widow came and put in two small copper coins, which amount to a cent. And calling His disciples to Him, He said to them, "Truly I say to you, this poor widow put in more than all the contributors to the treasury; for they all put in out of their surplus, but she, out of her poverty, put in all she owned, all she had to live on."

This woman received high praise from the Lord because of her obedient, faithful, and sacrificial donation. The cause of Christ today needs far more donors like this widow!

CONCLUSION

Before leaving this subject of lifestyle, I want to emphasize how crucial it is that you take action in this area. Money is a major source of tension for most of us. The reality is that family incomes are highly volatile, and a rapid rise or drop in living standards is closer to the rule than the exception. In fact, in any ten-year period, one-third of Americans will see their standard of living drop by fifty percent or more.[27]

Such a statistic only heightens the importance of Paul's warning to us not to fix our hopes "on the uncertainty of riches, but on God, who richly supplies us with all things to enjoy."[28]

Paul knew what he was talking about. His own lifestyle apparently lurched its way through booms and busts:

I know how to get along with humble means, and I also know how to live in prosperity; in any and every circumstance I have learned the secret of being filled and going hungry, both of having abundance and suffering need. (Philippians 4:12)

What is this "secret" that Paul had discovered? It was Christ. Earlier he had written:

Whatever things were gain to me, those things I have counted as loss for the sake of Christ. More than that, I count all things to be loss in view of the surpassing value of knowing Christ Jesus my Lord, for whom I have suffered the loss of all things, and count them but rubbish in order that I may gain Christ. (Philippians 3:7-8)

God may give you an abundance or He may take away everything you own. What matters is that no matter how much or how little you have, you have Christ and He has you. That is the secret to solving the problem of gain.

NOTES: 1. After writing this review, I chanced upon a similar survey, which is excellent, by Randy Petersen, "Modern Voices: The Christian and Money," *Christian History*, 6:2 (1987), pages 28-29.
2. Robert Tilton, *God's Laws of Success* (Tulsa, Okla.: Harrison House, 1983), page 10.
3. See also 1 Timothy 6:6-10.
4. See 1 Corinthians 10:9.
5. See Donald Hay, "The International Socio-Economic-Political Order and Our Lifestyle," in *Lifestyle in the Eighties: An Evangelical Commitment to Simple Lifestyle*, edited by Ronald J. Sider, (Exeter, Devon, England: The Paternoster Press, 1982).
6. Robert Novak, *The Spirit of Democratic Capitalism* (New York: Touchstone, 1982), page 285. Novak later castigates as uninformed those who promote ideas such as those cited: "It is, therefore, a sad commentary on the sociology of knowledge in the Christian churches that so few theologians or religious leaders understand economics, industry, manufacturing, trade, and

finance. Many seem trapped in pre-capitalist modes of thought. Few understand the laws of development, growth, and production. Many swiftly reduce all morality to the morality of distribution. They demand jobs without comprehending how jobs are created. They demand the distribution of the world's goods without insight into how the store of the world's goods may be expanded. They desire ends without critical knowledge about means. They claim to be leaders without having mastered the techniques of human progress. Their ignorance deprives them of authority. Their good intentions would be more easily honored if supported by evidence of diligent intelligence in economics" (page 336).
7. Novak, *The Spirit of Democratic Capitalism*, pages 68-69. All of these writers could take a lesson from Novak, who shows that it is possible as a Christian to defend democratic capitalism as an economic system: (1) without confusing it with Christianity; (2) without trying to show that it is the only possible "Christian" economic system; (3) without needing to "Christianize" it in order to function in it; (4) without excusing or ignoring its sins, flaws, and failures; and (5) without compromising one's allegiance to Christian theology and practice.
8. See Ronald Nash, *Poverty and Wealth: The Christian Debate Over Capitalism* (Westchester, Ill.: Crossway Books, 1986), pages 173f. Nash is citing a theory put forth by Edward Banfield.
9. See also Psalm 104:14-17 and Matthew 6:31-32.
10. Philippians 4:19.
11. This is in no way related to Maslow's "hierarchy of needs," which I reject.
12. See James 1:17-18.
13. See Psalms 104:14-15, 128:1-4.
14. "It is a major cause for the misunderstanding of the nature of profit in our society and for the deep-seated hostility to profit which are among the most dangerous diseases of an industrial society. It is largely responsible for the worst mistakes of public policy—in this country as well as in Western Europe—which are squarely based on the failure to understand the nature, function, and purpose of business enterprise. And it is in large part responsible for the prevailing belief that there is an inherent contradiction between profit and a company's ability to make a social contribution. Actually, a company can make a social contribution only if it is highly profitable. To put it crudely, a bankrupt company is not likely to be a good company to work for, or likely to be a good neighbor and a desirable member of the community—no matter what some sociologists of today seem to believe to the contrary." Peter F. Drucker, *Management: Tasks, Responsibilities, Practices* (New York: Harper & Row, 1973), pages 60-61.
15. Drucker, *Management*, page 114.
16. Some will object that this naively overlooks the profiteering with which too many corporations and their executives conduct business. They rape the environment, abuse and exploit people, and bend or violate the law in a greedy quest for ever-higher revenues. They appear to be wholly motivated by a lust for money and the power to make more money. And they need to be stopped. I agree. I view their motivation as unbridled greed, and I think they should be exposed and thwarted. However, (1) their greed does not alter the appropriate role of profit; (2) we must be careful not to characterize all business in a capitalist economy this way, which would be grossly unfair and misleading; and (3) the best strategy for stopping this greed and for promoting justice is a topic worth discussing at length elsewhere.
17. Deuteronomy 8:11,17-18.
18. This, in fact, was Satan's accusation of God in regard to Job: "You're buying him off! No wonder Job is so righteous!" See Job 1:10-11.
19. See Matthew 6:24.
20. See David L. McKenna, "Financing the Great Commission," *Christianity Today* (May 15, 1987), pages 26-31.
21. See Acts 2:44-45, 4:32-35; Galatians 2:10; James 1:27, 2:14-17; and 1 John 3:17-18.
22. See 1 Corinthians 9:14, Galatians 6:16, and 1 Timothy 5:17-18.
23. Galatians 2:10.
24. For more information about Mendenhall Ministries, or about how you could initiate a similar effort in your area, contact them at 309 Center Street, Mendenhall, MS 39114.
25. See 2 Corinthians 11:12-15, 1 Timothy 6:3-5, Titus 1:10-11, and 2 Peter 2:1-3.
26. For additional information on how to evaluate the finances of a ministry, contact the Evangelical Council for Fiscal Accountability, 2915 Hunter Mill Road, Suite 17, P.O. Box 659, Oakton, VA 22124, (703) 938-6006, or (800) BE-WISE.
27. See Greg J. Duncan, "On the Slippery Scope," *American Demographics* (May 1987), pages 30f.
28. 1 Timothy 6:17.

CHAPTER 13

LIVING FOR THE WEEKEND
Leisure and Non-Work Activities

O
ne of the most helpful benefits of a biblical view of work is its impact on non-work areas. This is because such a view puts work in its proper perspective with the rest of life. This can be especially liberating for the person whose career keeps gobbling up increasing amounts of time and energy.

In this chapter I want to lay a biblical foundation for leisure, which is really the flip side of work. I'll introduce a model you can use for planning, a tool that goes beyond most time management resources by putting work in its proper perspective. I'll also offer some practical suggestions for achieving and maintaining a balance between work and leisure.

But first, let's examine two common problems that warn us when we have gotten work out of balance. These symptoms are busyness and boredom.

CHRONIC BUSYNESS

Earlier I suggested that work is quickly becoming the new religion of our generation. When you talk about work, you have your hand wrapped around the aorta of life in our times. But if work is a new religion, then surely its Bible is the date book. It turns the careerist into a person obsessed with time. As columnist Molly Ivins observes:

> In New York, the world capital of busyness, everyone carries a little date book around with him. In Manhattan you cannot call a friend at 4 p.m. on Friday to ask, "What say we knock off work early and go get a beer?" In New York you don't just make appointments weeks in

advance to meet your friends for a beer and write the date down in your book, you make appointments to call your friends to see when you can schedule a beer. "All right, I'll give you a call at 3 p.m. Tuesday at your office, and we'll find a date that's free for both of us for lunch." One of the few cries of distress that will elicit immediate sympathy from strangers in New York is the wail, "Oh no! I've lost my Book!"[1]

Down the road in Washington, D.C., things are no different. An acquaintance of mine at the State Department described to me once how extremely difficult it is for anyone in that town to maintain focus. There are simply too many intriguing opportunities and ideas, and never enough time. As a result, people ride the laser lane from project to project, appointment to appointment, relationship to relationship, diversion to diversion. Never time to concentrate. Never time to reflect. And for goodness' sake, never time to stop.

However, busyness is raised to a virtue when it characterizes someone in the ministry. How would you feel if you approached your pastor and asked, "What are you doing next Tuesday?" and he replied, "Nothing, you wanna go fishing?" No, you'd want him to get a pained expression on his face and sigh, "Gee, Tuesday's tight. In fact, I don't have a free moment until the twenty-eighth of next month. Can we schedule something then?"

The idea is that someone that busy must really be accomplishing something for God. In other words, the fact that he doesn't have time for you is an indication of how much God is using him. Busyness is next to godliness.

CRUSHING BOREDOM

But this is only half the story. While some people may be too busy to think, many others are too bored to care:

If the daily job is no longer the most time-consuming aspect of human existence, it has nonetheless for countless thousands become life's most time-oppressive factor. Today the hours "on the job" are like a grievous, unending plague. Even with the shortened work week—from forty-eight to forty-four to forty hours—perhaps even more conspicuously where workers propagandize for thirty-five—men remain restive and disgruntled under the crushing weight of time. Hours seem like interminable days, days like unending weeks. . . .

Much as he may grumble about punching the tyrannical time clock on the job, the modern man sports his self-winding, shock and

waterproof calendar wrist watch that by the minute, even by the
second, relentlessly mirrors the predicament of his unmotivated life.
This zooming from one split second to another (whatever blessings
modern conveniences may have brought) discloses an unwitting modern paradox of our day: we dread its barrenness, yet enslave ourselves
to the crowding of time.[2]

Arthur Miller, the playright, has called boredom "the hallmark of society
as a whole," a society in which people merely exist, and move among "a string
of near-experiences marked off by periods of stupefying spiritual and psychological stasis, and the good life is basically an amazed one."[3]

THE ROOT PROBLEM

Busyness and boredom: They appear to be opposites, but they are really
symptoms of the same disease. Those of us who suffer from either of them display a tragic lack of purpose, a lack of a reason not only for being but for doing.
     Another way to say this is that either condition reveals that we have
gotten work out of perspective, that we are no longer relating our work to God.
The overworked careerist tries desperately to derive meaning and value from
the work itself. But he forgets that only God can infuse not just work but the
whole of our lives with dignity and purpose. Likewise, the bored worker
watching the clock has lost all sense that his work matters to God, that it is
anything other than an excuse for a paycheck. He has really lost the dignity of
himself, at least of himself as a worker. Work is a pointless but necessary evil.
     Perhaps the greatest tragedy in all of this is how it impacts life outside of
work. For even if work were an enslaving evil—which I don't believe it is—at
least we could look forward to the freedom of life after hours. But if we lack a
sense of purpose as people, then not only will work suffer but our leisure will
suffer as well.
     All work and no play. This is precisely what has happened for many of us.
On the one hand, some of us who look to our careers to define life seem almost
afraid of non-work, of unstructured time. Descriptions of the classic work-
aholic are commonplace.
     But how many others of us leave work, yet work never leaves us? We never
"punch out" emotionally. We are like sports cars, cruising along at ninety,
with one foot mashing the clutch and the other stomping the accelerator. Yes,
we are physically disengaged from the job, but our engine keeps racing.
Consequently, as Tim Hansel puts it, "When we relax we feel guilty."
     TGIF. On the other hand, others of us attempt to find the meaning in

leisure that we cannot find in work. We're "living for the weekend." Yet do we really find in the evenings and on the weekends the purpose that eludes us on the job?

I realize that not all jobs and not all aspects of all jobs are particularly challenging or interesting. I also realize that when it comes to a sense of meaning, many people place very slight expectations on their jobs. But as I evaluate where so many people spend so much of their leisure—watching television, reading novels, watching ball games, going to shopping malls—I wonder how much life purpose these diversions offer.

Indeed, I question whether they are even diversions from the work world. Take television, for instance. The biggest deception ever foisted on a mass of otherwise intelligent people lies hidden in the words, "Brought to you by . . . ." For it is sheer fantasy that any program is "brought to you by" an advertiser. The reality is that you and I and millions of other viewers-as-potential-customers are brought to the advertiser by the program.

In other words, television is entertainment, but in our society entertainment is business. Every time you turn on your TV set, you invite someone into your living room or den or bedroom to sell you something. Later, your purchases in the marketplace ultimately fund the entire system.

Don't worry. I manage to watch more than enough television. But my point is that this exercise is not necessarily a break from work but a continuation of it. Television is how we talk to each other in this society. And the real conversation of television revolves around the same topic as the workplace: buying and selling. In many ways television tells us what to buy, while work enables us to pay for it. Can this arrangement provide freedom from work?

In short, whether we are compulsively busy, chronically bored, or somewhere in-between, we are empty, without meaning, if we lack the sense of purpose that can ultimately come only from our relationship to God. For such "hollow men," leisure is a liability. As one thinker puts it, "All the evils in the B-zone—burden, boredom, barrenness, bane—descend on people swamped with free time if they don't know who they are, whose they are, and why they are in this world."[4]

A PROPER VIEW OF LEISURE

Obviously what we need is an appropriate and biblical view of leisure. In fact, this must go hand-in-hand with a biblical view of work.

Much could be said in this regard. But the main point for our discussion is that we can obtain great meaning and freedom and rest from the belief that our day-to-day work is an extension of God's work.

God gives us purpose. I can't think of any greater source of purpose than the truth that God has personally crafted you to fulfill a unique destiny. He has fashioned you with a specific design. He has given you certain abilities, interests, motivations, and aspirations. He provides you with appropriate responsibilities and opportunities. He even enables you to feel a unique sense of accomplishment and "rightness" whenever you fulfill your design.

The extent to which work expresses that design will vary from person to person. And the same is true for non-work activities. But the meaning of your life derives neither from work nor from non-work activities, but from God. Therefore, your greatest need is to relate every aspect of yourself to Him, to determine how it fits with who He has made you to be and what He wants you to do.

God gives us rest. Furthermore, all of this provides a basis for rest. Because our work is God's work, and because He is ultimately responsible for the results, He gives us the freedom to leave it, to trust Him with it, and to enjoy the rest of life.

This pertains especially to the person who works too much, who is chronically busy, or who feels guilty when he relaxes. However, I find such persons to be unusually resistant to the suggestion that they have gotten work out of perspective. And even if they admit that they have, they are even more resistant to changing their perspective.

Why? This is a complex problem. But I believe the roots of it ultimately lie deep in the relationship between the overworker and his God. This person has various emotions and needs: an anxiety about providing for his family; a fear of falling behind in the rat race of the culture; a desire to feel important, liked, in control, or successful; a need to feel significant, that his life matters. There are no doubt many others.

But the knot of the problem lies in (1) the fact that *ultimately* God must provide for this person's needs; (2) the deep conviction he holds that God either cannot or will not provide for these needs; and (3) the conclusion that he must therefore provide for his own needs, mostly through his work.[5]

No one can rest, holding such a belief. No one can enjoy peace or freedom in the presence of such a conviction. This is the anxiety that comes from serving Mammon, or riches, from serving the belief that work and its reward, money, will be the salvation or the provision of one's needs rather than God.[6]

Working for God. The only way out for such a person is to stop working for himself and to start working for God:

> "Come to Me, all who are weary and heavy laden, and I will give you rest. Take My yoke upon you, and learn from Me, for I am gentle and

humble in heart; and you shall find rest for your souls. For My yoke is easy, and My load is light." (Matthew 11:28-30)

The "rest" that Jesus describes here is a rest in our spirit, a rest or confidence in the promises and provisions of God for our deepest, most private, and most gripping needs. This means that leisure, freedom from work, actually begins at work. It begins when we stop relying on the job and start trusting Jesus to supply our needs.[7]

How can we do this? How can we keep work in its proper perspective? This is not easy to do in our culture. And there are so many aspects to the problem. But I propose that we need a realistic model for life to use for evaluation and planning. I'll suggest such a model, and then offer a number of practical strategies that you can use on a day-to-day basis.

THE PENTATHLON

If you've been around Christian teaching in our culture for very long, you've undoubtedly heard reference to a hierarchy of priorities. This hierarchy says that in your life you should put Christ first, your marriage and family second, your church third, people fourth, and so on. The priorities become far less specific and ordered after number two or three, but you get the basic idea. God and family are up at the top. Work is never higher than number three or four.

While this hierarchy has some value, let me suggest that it is both unbiblical and inadequate as a model for life. Its value lies in its usefulness for tradeoffs. For example, if your choice is between achieving a major career success but losing your family in the process, then biblically you would need to sacrifice your career success and give preference to maintaining a healthy family. Thus the hierarchy is somewhat useful.

Does the New Testament teach a hierarchy? Although the hierarchy seems somewhat useful, as we examine the New Testament, we don't find the hierarchy taught. Not exactly. In the first place, the Scriptures present Christ not as the first in a series of priorities but as the Lord of all of life.

This may seem to you to be splitting hairs. But the point is that Jesus must be brought in on everything we do—our family lives, our jobs, our friendships with neighbors, our play, our hobbies, our sex lives, our conflicts, our politics, our financial decisions—everything! He is not simply the first of many demands to be satisfied. He is a Person who intends to walk through life with us.

When I say He must be "brought in," I'm not thinking of mumbling a few pious prayers, or of trying to squeeze a presentation of the gospel into our activities, or of wearing a lapel pin. Instead, I mean that we need to live every aspect of our lives purposefully, with an eye toward how it might be affected by something He has said, and how it will please or displease Him. We need not be neurotic about this, but simply reflective and intent on carrying out what He wants.

So if we're going to have a list, then Christ shouldn't even be on the list. He should be the Lord over everything on the list.

Does the New Testament propose lists? However, even the list itself is questionable. I think we as Americans tend toward pragmatism and expediency. We want to reduce everything to the lowest common denominator, to the minimum recommended daily allowance. With so much to do, we only want to do the minimum required and then move on to the next expectation.

But a New Testament view of life is considerably more full-orbed and, in my view, considerably healthier. The picture that emerges from the Scriptures is not a segmented life of minimal requirements, but a wholistic, comprehensive view of life in which everything affects everything else.

Such a view is more true to life than any hierarchy. Think about it. A man is not a father one minute, then a salesman the next, a church member the next, and a husband the next. No, he is a father-salesman-church member-husband-consumer-golfer-commuter-voter-neighbor *all at the same time.* The focus of his attention will vary throughout his day. But he himself remains a whole person. All of his roles and commitments affect each other.

The pentathlon. What, then, is this comprehensive New Testament view of life that I have mentioned? I've heard people describe it in different ways. I find it helpful to liken it to the pentathlon.

In Europe, the pentathlon is the most prestigious and demanding sporting contest there is. It is similar to our decathlon, only it has five events instead of ten: running, swimming, horseback riding, pistol shooting, and fencing.

Five very diverse events. And to succeed in the pentathlon, an athlete must do well in all five areas. This demands that he train for all five. He cannot run at the expense of fencing. For if he wins in running but does poorly in fencing, he loses the pentathlon.

I find this to be a useful metaphor for planning and evaluating life, for two reasons. First, it promotes the idea of a comprehensive approach to life. What you do in one area affects everything else. For instance, choices you make in your business often have a profound impact at home. Likewise, things at home may bear directly on your attitude and performance at work.

A New Testament view of life. But second, and even more important, is that the New Testament addresses life in terms of five major categories. These five categories are especially evident in the "applicational" sections of the major Pauline letters: Romans 12-14, Galatians 5-6, Ephesians 4-6, and Colossians 3-4. Naturally, they are addressed elsewhere as well.

The five areas are: (1) your personal life, including your relationship with God, your emotions, and any other private, individual areas; (2) your family, including your marriage, your children, and your relationship to your own parents and any dependents; (3) your church life, including both your local church as well as your involvement with all Christians everywhere; (4) your work, including what you do, how you do it, how you relate to employers, coworkers, and customers, and the products and results of your labor; and (5) your community life, including your responsibilities toward governments, and your relationships in the broader society, especially with nonChristians.

Five diverse categories. I call them the pentathlon. God says we need to honor Him in all five. And because they all impact each other, we cannot arrange them into a hierarchy. The New Testament does not do that, and if we do it, it will actually hinder us from being faithful in all five areas. Instead, we need to strike a realistic balance among these areas, each of which presents many demands that compete for our time.

Beyond time management. In a moment I'll offer some practical suggestions for how to do this. But first, can you see why time management strategies rarely help us pull life together? Not that there is anything wrong with time management. But most of us apply such resources with the assumption that doing so will put our lives in order.

Yet most time management books and seminars either supply a sophisticated shoehorn that enables us to cram more into our schedules (greater efficiency), or else a machete that enables us to lop off dead weight (greater effectiveness).

What usually goes unaddressed, though, is the larger question of how work fits into perspective with the rest of life. I maintain that unless we see work as only one of five areas in which God wants us to be faithful, we will merely excel at work and fall down in most of the other areas.

KEEPING WORK IN PERSPECTIVE

How, then, can we balance these five areas? How can we keep work in its proper perspective? I've listed a number of strategies below. You can doubtless think of others. But in applying these suggestions, keep in mind that life is a whole, and that what you do in one area affects other areas. The ideas here are especially slanted toward work, since that is our concern in this book. But much more could be said about the other four areas.

1. Organize your prayer life around the pentathlon.

People have all kinds of ways to remind themselves of things they need to pray for. Yet far too many of us don't even know where to begin in praying about our lives. I suggest that in our prayers we think through each of the five areas of the pentathlon. This does two things. First, it ensures that we remain conscious of our responsibilities in all five. Second, it keeps work in tension with the other areas, so that it doesn't become our sole focus.

2. Determine how much time you need to spend at work.

This suggestion is especially for people who find that work expands until it eats up all of their time, who inevitably put in 50-, 60-, and 70-hour weeks.

How much is too much? Let me begin by saying that there is nothing sacred about a 40-hour work week. I sometimes hear teaching that suggests that if a person, particularly a parent and especially a father, puts in more than 40 hours, he is virtually sinning, because he is overworking.

But this is insupportable biblically. About the only work week defined in the Bible comes in the Ten Commandments: "Six days you shall labor and do all your work" (Exodus 20:9). Six days of work! In an agrarian economy that could easily translate into an 80-hour week!

Perceptions of how much work is too much vary from culture to culture and situation to situation. For instance, all of us have heard stories from our parents and grandparents about the depression, how people worked double shifts and on Sundays, etc., just to make ends meet. And no one complained then that parents, especially fathers, were shirking their responsibilities to their families. In fact, people argued just the opposite: Hard work was a sign of responsibility toward one's family.

But times and circumstances change. That is why I suggest each of us needs to consciously determine how much time he needs to spend at work.

Consider the nature of the job. In some jobs, you don't have much choice but to put in many hours. My surgeon friends who are often on-call must devote extreme amounts of time to the job. Likewise, most entrepreneurs trying to establish a business must usually put in 60- and 70-hour weeks to make a go of it. And most athletes and coaches are necessarily consumed with their sport during the season.

But in all jobs, one must count the costs involved. That is the core of my suggestion.

First, look thoroughly at what your choices are. The amount of time you must put in is often determined by such things as the nature of the work, seniority, level of responsibility, remuneration and compensation structure, and so on. You must be sure to make a realistic appraisal of the time it will take to satisfy the requirements of your position.

Consider the impact on your family. But you must also evaluate the impact of your job on the rest of your life, especially on your family. If holding down your job means sacrificing your marriage and your children, then biblically you need to reevaluate whether you are in the right job.

I know this is a complex area, and your family has to be realistic about what it takes for you to honor God in your work. But I find that many individuals who have lost their family because of a job usually have done so not because the job itself demanded an extreme and unrealistic commitment, but because their own ambition or drive demanded it. The problem was not with the job but with them.

What are the real reasons for overwork? Obviously there are tradeoffs that must occur between work and family. But so often I find people trading their marriages and children in exchange for ten extra hours of work and ambition—ten hours that are often fairly unproductive, that make only a nominal contribution to their careers.

Furthermore, when a person calls home and says, "Honey, I'm afraid I've got to work late tonight," he needs to ask himself, "Why am I working late tonight? Is it because legitimate and unforeseen work demands have come up that I must satisfy? Or is it because I frittered away a good bit of my day in unorganized, undisciplined work habits, or else let someone else keep me from getting my work done? Am I staying merely to impress my boss? If so, is that altogether legitimate? Or am I avoiding going home? Is there something there I'm unwilling to deal with?"

Everything has a cost to it. One cost of extra work is a loss of leisure, which usually results in feeling tired and grumpy. Yet for many people, shaving even an hour or two a week off the schedule makes little difference in their productivity but a major difference in their physical and emotional health.

One of the major weapons in the battle to keep work in perspective is a serious evaluation of what kind of time it takes to get the job done. Having determined that, it is much easier to start setting limits so that work does not eat up the rest of one's life.

3. Set a come-home time.

I find it helpful to predetermine a time when I plan to leave work. If I don't, a project or meeting I start late in the afternoon can take me later and later into the evening, which creates obvious problems for the family.

Furthermore, knowing ahead of time that I must leave work at a certain hour helps me arrange and prioritize my day.

Two keys to making this work are (1) recruiting your secretary or an associate as an ally in helping you to be ready to leave on time; and (2) a regular phone call home shortly before the appointed departure time, so that you start the mental process of leaving on time.

4. Schedule non-work areas just as you would work areas.
I once visited the office of a CEO and began admiring the efficiency with which his business appeared to be running. At that he pulled out a large three-ring notebook with several dozen pages of neatly typed goals and objectives, each with its own action plan, carefully organized and cross-referenced. I had never seen such careful planning and obvious strategy. The executive explained that this sort of foresight accounted for his company's envied efficiency and ultimately for its impressive success.

We chatted for a while until the conversation turned to his family. He began expressing considerable anxiety and a sense of failure about his relationships there. So I asked to hear about his goals for his family life. He just looked at me blankly. He didn't have any.

I challenged him with the fact that since he had displayed such brilliance and wisdom in planning out his company's direction, he needed to consider putting the same effort and planning into the other areas of his life. This came as a revolutionary idea to him.

We don't plan to fail; we fail to plan. But that executive is not alone. If you are like me, what doesn't get planned doesn't happen. All week long I'll tell my kids that on Saturday we'll do something. But if I don't think through what we'll do, we'll often end up doing something pretty boring.

Consequently, in our date books we need to put more than just work-related appointments and reminders. We need to add family times, church and ministry commitments, community involvements, and personal plans.

In fact, you would do well to take an hour each week to sit down with your spouse and review the upcoming week, as well as any major plans after that. This offers a real check on work that may tend to crowd out important non-work matters.

5. Guard your use of emotional energy.
For many of us, work may take up only fifty percent of our time but ninety-five percent of our emotional energy. This can be tragic because, as I mentioned earlier, we can leave work but work never leaves us.

Danger signs. Some of the signals that work may be holding you captive emotionally are when your spouse tells you something or asks you a question and you realize you haven't heard a word he or she has said; when you wake up at night with thoughts and emotions about work streaming out of your mind;

when you spend hours on the phone with an associate talking about a work situation, even though you've both talked about it all day, and you'll talk about it all day the next day; when your only friends are friends at work; when your only serious reading is work-related; when you spend a good portion of your hours after work at your place of employment, whether working or not; when in your prayer life your only thoughts are about work.

Certainly work means a great deal to us, and we should make an emotional commitment to it. And certainly times of stress at work require a good bit of emotional involvement to see things through. But God never intended for work to become psychological slavery. On the contrary, as we have seen, He desires us to be freed from emotional and spiritual dependence on work, and to find rest for our souls.

Ask why. If you find work completely dominating your emotional life, you probably need to evaluate what part work plays in your life, what importance you've attached to it. You may need to enlist someone to help you do this, someone who can ask some hard, honest questions and give you objective feedback about your answers. Such a process of evaluation will likely reveal some deep-seated beliefs and assumptions about work along the lines I mentioned earlier.

When you leave work, leave work. One small step I try to take on my way home is to mentally and emotionally disengage from work. My goal is that by the time I arrive home, I want to be in a proper frame of mind to relate to my family. This may mean foregoing the news. Or if you have a car phone, it may mean not calling or accepting calls related to work.

Instead, you might want to begin reviewing what your family told you they had planned for that day, or the things you intend to do with them that evening. All of this is a sort of psychological change of clothes in which you take off your work clothes and "slip into something more comfortable."

6. Maintain a sabbath.
Earlier I quoted Exodus 20:9 about six days of labor. The context there is that the seventh day is a sabbath, a day of rest. From the earliest days of the Church, people have debated whether a day of sabbath is still in effect.[8] Even in our day, Sunday is regarded as "the Lord's day," a day when people should be in church. Even the people who aren't in church know they "should" be.

I personally believe in a sabbath, but one that is properly understood. For one thing, a sabbath is a day of rest, a break from remunerative labor. We let go of our toil. Furthermore, we rest and let go of our toil precisely because we acknowledge that while God has given us work, He is the ultimate Provider of our needs. So it makes sense that on a sabbath we would spend some special time celebrating and worshiping God.

There are two main corruptions of the sabbath principle, though. One is to ignore it completely, to make it a day of work like the others, to fill it up with doing all the things we failed to do on the other days. The other is to turn it into a legalistic requirement, which in our culture often means filling it up with activities at church, in the mistaken belief that God demands that we give Him one day out of seven, as expressed through church involvement.[9]

Sadly, Christians today are falling into both these traps. I realize that this is all complicated by the increasing complexities of work schedules and the expectations of life in our culture. But I would challenge us to forsake all forces that would rob us of a day of celebrating our rest in God's grace.

7. Cultivate interests and commitments outside of work.

This may sound rather obvious. But all too often when I ask someone about his hobbies, he replies, "My work is my hobby." To my mind this describes a rather narrow, imbalanced life.

I don't want to be too harsh in my judgment. But let me suggest that if you have gotten work out of perspective, it may be because you have no other involvements to draw you away for respite.

I know for myself that a great deal of my work is either up in front of people or is in a consulting situation where I'm involved in problem solving. So for me to relax and disengage from work, I have to get into something where I am not in front of people and I am not solving problems.

I happen to have found bicycling, swimming, and running to be enjoyable. One strategy I use to keep work from pushing these activities aside is to sign up for a triathlon, especially if I can cajole a friend or two to enter it with me. There's no way I'll slough off if I know I'll be competing! To you this may not sound like relaxation, but for me it is a total break—mentally, physically, and emotionally—from work.

Each of us needs to cultivate interests that express aspects of ourselves that don't come out at work. I once heard of an athlete who gave a banquet speech on what he called the biblical proverb, "All work and no play makes Johnny a dull boy." Afterwards, the minister who gave the invocation approached him and said, "Son, I liked your talk. But you know that saying isn't in the Bible." The athlete looked perplexed, but finally replied, "Well, it ought to be!" I couldn't agree more.

8. Beware of watching instead of doing.

In our culture, leisure has taken on the unfortunate connotation of passivity. In other words, to take a break from work means to do nothing. I suppose this is partly because we associate rest with the suspension of activity. And partly, too, because we are sometimes too tired to do anything but sit and "vegetate."

But there is a real danger to avoid in our leisure, that we not become mere spectators. Molly Ivins, whom I quoted earlier, points out that in New York the opportunities one has for leisure are so superlative that it is easy to adopt a vicarious quality of life:

> Why would you sit down and pound the piano yourself when you could go hear Rubinstein play at Carnegie or Brubeck at the Village Gate? Why join a singing group when you can hear Pavarotti? Why paint when the Met's in town? Why cook when the greatest restaurants and finest caterers in the world are right there? Why garden when the florists shops are bursting with blooms? Why participate in amateur theatricals when Broadway is right there?
>
> We spend a great deal of our lives now being audiences, watching other people do. We go to the Mavs instead of playing Horse in the driveway with our kids. Out to Ranger Stadium instead of joining a slow-pitch team. Watch the soaps instead of having emotional lives of our own. Of course you'll never sing as well as Pavarotti or act as well as Katherine Hepburn or play ball as well as Magic Johnson—but we seem to be losing sight of the fact that it's really more fun if you do it yourself.[10]

CONCLUSION

Is God for fun? He certainly is, although you'd never know it, judging from a good many of His people. But I recommend your attention to Proverbs 8:30-31. In that context wisdom is personified and explains how she exists with God from all eternity. She climaxes her retelling of the Creation account and the part she played by saying:

> Then I was beside Him, as a master workman;
> And I was daily His delight,
> Rejoicing always before Him,
> Rejoicing in the world, His earth,
> And having my delight in the sons of men.

Three things to note here. First, if we examine wisdom in this chapter, we find that it really is a description of Christ, the wisdom of God (see 1 Corinthians 1:24). So the passage actually exalts Christ.

Secondly, the word translated "rejoicing" could also be translated "playing," so that these verses display Christ as playing around, playing before His Father and playing with mankind.

Finally, notice that this Creator-Christ is a master workman, yet also a playful God. The idea is of a Creator who both works and plays. It should be evident then that if we are created in His image, we should not only be His partners in work, but also His partners in play.

NOTES: 1. Molly Ivins, "This Article's Well Worth Reading, If Only You Can Find the Time," *Dallas Times Herald.*
2. Carl F. H. Henry, *Aspects of Christian Social Ethics* (Grand Rapids, Mich.: Baker Book House, 1964), pages 32-33.
3. Arthur Miller, "Boredom, Not Poverty, Cause of Juvenile Delinquency," *Vancouver Sun* (November 15, 1962).
4. Rudolph F. Norden, *The New Leisure* (Saint Louis, Missouri: Concordia Publishing House, 1965), pages 68-69.
5. See Georges Crespy, "Fatigue and Rest According to the Bible," *Fatigue in Modern Society,* edited by Paul Tournier (Atlanta, Ga.: John Knox Press, 1965), page 62.
6. See Matthew 6:24-34.
7. This is not to deny hard and diligent work. But it has to do with deciding who or what is *ultimately* providing for our needs. God obviously uses work as one of the instrumental means of provision, but He Himself is the final cause of our supply. See Chapter 9's discussion of "His Results."
8. Romans 14:5-6, Galatians 4:10.
9. For a fuller discussion on the sabbath and its corruptions, see Crespy's chapter in *Fatigue in Modern Society,* Tournier, ed., pages 57f.
10. Ivins, "This Article's Well Worth Reading."

CHAPTER 14

THE NEW CLERGY
Relating to Your Church

I n this book I've tried to build a case for the idea that your work matters to
God. Your work has intrinsic value, because in it you mirror the God who is
a worker, and who created you as His coworker. And your work has
instrumental value, because it is one of the primary means by which you can
love God, love others, and love yourself.

Furthermore, this truth holds profound implications for you and your
work. It should affect where you work, how you do your work, how you spend
the income you derive from your work, and even how you balance work with
non-work areas. In short, what the Bible has to say about work can transform
your entire outlook on life.

But will it really transform your outlook? Will it make a profound difference in how you live your life? Will it noticeably affect the lives and work of
people across our culture?

I think that this largely depends on how churches communicate the
Bible's message on work to workers. For the fact is that for most of us, church
is the supreme court of our spiritual experience. It interprets the Scriptures for
us. We look to our churches for an authoritative statement of what it means to
live life as a Christian.

Consequently, your local church plays an extremely strategic role in
determining how you as a Christian worker will approach your work. In this
chapter I want to examine your role within that context. I want to ask and
answer the question: What will it take to adequately equip you as a layperson
to be effective as a worker for God in the marketplace? But to get at the roots of
this issue, we need to first consider the relationship between you and your
local church.

THE ROLE OF THE CHURCH

Of course, it is exceedingly difficult to speak with any authority about the local church. As Richard Lovelace says, it is somewhat presumptuous even to try.[1] Who has enough expertise to qualify for the task, especially given the incredible diversity of individual congregations?

And yet, we can always affirm what the Scriptures say, and challenge every pastor and every layperson to do what he can to bring his church in line with that truth.

In regard to the layperson and his work, Ephesians 4:11-12 must be our point of departure. Recall that in Chapter 3, I said that this passage describes the role of the "clergy" and the role of the "laity." The laity are responsible for getting God's work done, while the clergy are responsible for preparing these workers to get His work done.

Or, in light of 1 Peter 2, I suggested that we regard the laity as a "new clergy," to function as God's agents not only in the workplace but throughout our culture. The job of the professional clergy, then, is to produce and equip new clergy.

To my mind, this is the New Testament arrangement. Naturally, I liken it to the flight room I mentioned at the beginning of this book. A flight room is marked by two things: camaraderie among the pilots and preparations for the mission. It's the mission, of course, that justifies the existence of the flight room. Sure, there is a sense of belonging among those who use the flight room. But the flight room is a means to an end, not the end itself. It's the place where pilots go to get equipped and prepared for the important work that takes place outside of the flight room.

Thus I take a very strategic view of the local church. It is a place for equipping. Yes, it is unquestionably a place in which we must celebrate the Lord in worship. My metaphor of the flight room is not perfect. Fellowship is indispensable, too.

But you can't fly the plane in the flight room. You can't compete in the game if you stay in the locker room. You can't win the race unless you get out of the pit stop. And you can't perform "the work of service," the work of God, in the church program alone. For much of it, you must get out of the church and onto the street.

THE ROLE OF THE WORKER

"Ministry" is something that happens *both inside and outside* of the local church. And yet let me point out, as I did in Chapter 3, that when we talk about doing God's work, we almost always understand that work to be "church work"—singing in the choir, teaching Sunday school, serving on a committee, greeting visitors. We might also have in mind volunteer work, perhaps with young people, or the poor, or the elderly, or for some cause like antipornography or a blood drive.

These are certainly important tasks in which laypeople should participate. And yet we never think of our everyday work as part of God's work. Instead, over time we have gradually equated God's work with church work. Consequently, we assume that serving God only means serving the church.

But as Elton Trueblood points out, "It is a gross error to suppose that the Christian cause goes forward solely or chiefly on weekends." In fact, "What happens on the regular weekdays may be far more important, so far as the Christian faith is concerned, than what happens on Sundays."[2]

I couldn't agree more. Some people express their commitment to Christ through the programs of a church. Others express their commitment largely or totally outside of church. Let me illustrate with three examples.

John

John is extremely grateful to God for bringing him to salvation. He knows how easily he could have followed in the steps of his alcoholic father. Instead, John trusted Christ as a teenager and has grown in the Lord ever since.

Nearly all of this growth has been the result of his involvement in Baytown Community Church. John and his family attend Sunday morning and evening worship services and Wednesday night prayer meetings. He also helps teach a Sunday school class, so that he can influence youngsters toward God just as he was influenced.

One of John's main responsibilities at church is his involvement on the board. As a board member, he concentrates on the spiritual direction at Baytown, on the problems a growing congregation faces, on the budget, and on how to make the overall program more effective and attractive to the community.

It would not be too much to say that almost all of John's social life and emotional energy are dedicated to his church. This is more than a product of his heavy commitments and responsibilities there; it is a reflection of his commitment to Christ.

As might be expected, John is not as comfortable relating to nonChristians as to Christians. Not that he is unfriendly. On the contrary, associates at work and in his neighborhood know him as a man with a ready smile. But all of his friends are believers. He doesn't back away from mentioning his faith to nonChristians, but these conversations never lead to long-term relationships.

One barrier here is the attitudes and behavior of many of John's neighbors and coworkers. He is offended by their secular mind-set, their off-color jokes, their cigarette smoke, and the like. He tolerates these things, but they do make it hard for him to enjoy the company of these people.

How totally different John feels when involved with Christians! It is a delight for him to stand among his friends at church, singing God's praises and hearing from His Word. He is especially thankful for his pastor, a godly servant for whom he would do almost anything. Under this man's leadership, John feels he is growing ever deeper in his love for Christ and in his commitment to Christ's work in the world.

Richard

Richard became a Christian as a young businessman, thanks to the godly influence of an older coworker. Like John, he is a member of Baytown Community Church. However, he is not nearly as involved as John. He usually makes the Sunday morning service, but only on special occasions attends at other times.

Richard is very impressed with the children's program for his kids, and feels a commitment to see that they are able to participate. However, he has declined requests that he teach in this department.

Richard also feels a responsibility to be involved in the larger Baytown community. Despite his heavy work load, he serves as a volunteer in raising money for the United Way. He is also a Rotarian. Contacts like these place him in close proximity to unbelievers, as well as Christians from other churches.

These social relationships are very enjoyable for Richard. People know he is a member of Baytown Community Church, and treat him accordingly: Christians ask him to prayer breakfasts and golf; nonChristians ask him to golf! But he has never been embarrassed in any social situation.

He feels that all of these relationships are healthy, both for him and for others. He believes that as a Christian he exerts a positive influence on society. At the same time, he feels that it is critically important to participate in a local church for teaching, fellowship, and worship.

His perspective is summed up in a comment he made to a golf partner one day: "I figure when I get to heaven, God's going to ask me what kind of man I've been as a husband and father, as a Christian, and as a citizen. These are the areas I try to make priorities in my life."

Steve

Steve is a lawyer in Baytown, and his wife, Darlene, is a fashion consultant in a nearby town. They came to faith in Christ through the influence of Robert, an acquaintance of Richard. It's a long story, but after being introduced to Steve by Richard at a health club, Robert and his wife, Sharol, got together with Steve and Darlene.

Steve had many questions about Christianity that Robert was able to answer. And Darlene was immediately attracted to Sharol's poise and self-confidence, which she attributed largely to her faith. In time, Steve and Darlene committed their lives to Christ.

One of the first things Robert encouraged these new Christians to do was to find a church where they could get some sound instruction and encouragement in their faith. Among the several churches mentioned was Baytown Community, and Steve and Darlene soon began attending.

Naturally, they were well received at the church. The old-timers like John were always eager to recruit a handsome young couple like Steve and Darlene. However, the couple seemed hesitant to become involved more than on a Sunday morning basis.

The couple kept coming to the church, however, because they valued the teaching so much. They rarely attended every Sunday of a given month, but when they missed they would get a tape of the message. If the truth were known, they often attended a different church from another denomination in a nearby town. They felt that although the teaching wasn't nearly as helpful as at Baytown, the atmosphere of worship was better and more conducive to communion with God.

Obviously, Steve and Darlene take a somewhat casual attitude toward church membership. In fact, when asked why they hadn't joined Baytown after several months of attending, Steve explained, "We went to the membership classes to find out what joining was all about. It seemed to us that all it meant was you have a vote in choosing a new pastor or building a building or something. When we read all the passages in the New Testament, it seemed to us that just being a Christian makes you a member of the church. So why formalize it?"

One might think that Steve and Darlene have very little ministry, but in fact just the opposite is true. Few if any of their involvements are directly involved with Baytown Community Church. But Steve has started a Bible study with some of the other lawyers in his firm. This has resulted in two men coming to faith in Christ.

Steve also donates some time to a legal clinic in a poor section of the community. This experience has obviously helped that area, which in turn has had a significant impact on a little church there. Steve and Darlene occasionally visit that church and enjoy the cultural differences displayed, as well as the commonness shared in Christ. The pastor always points out to the congregation the contribution Steve makes in that community.

Darlene, meanwhile, has found a burgeoning ministry in her own network. As a fashion consultant, she is involved with many professional women. In discussing their fashion needs, she often learns some of the "inside" information behind these women, and has seen that many have tremendous spiritual and personal needs and questions that go unaddressed. Darlene has tried to meet some of these needs through a variety of creative, well-planned luncheons and discussion groups.

The response has been staggering. A week never goes by that she and Steve don't have at least one couple over for snacks or dinner. The conversation almost always turns to spiritual matters.

Perhaps the best summary of Steve and Darlene has come from a doctor whose wife had consulted Darlene and had accepted Christ, though her husband had not. He said, "I can't buy all this stuff about Jesus for myself, but that couple is for real! I mean, lots of people are religious and go to church and all. But these people really live it! Steve is really a genuine guy, and a crackerjack lawyer, too. And I owe my marriage to Darlene. If she hadn't spoken with my wife, I can't say where we'd be now. I'll tell you, these people have redefined the word 'Christian' for me!"

DOING GOD'S WORK—WHEREVER IT NEEDS DOING

Three dedicated Christians. Each is unquestionably committed to Christ. By "committed" I mean that each takes his relationship with Christ seriously. None is "playing religion." But they each express their commitment in very distinctive ways and consequently see their involvement with the church very differently.

I'm sure some would like to see Steve and Darlene show a stronger loyalty to a local church. And others would prefer that John overcome his uncomfortable feelings around nonChristians, so that he might have a stronger impact on them.

But the main point that John, Richard, and Steve demonstrate is that while much of God's work happens inside the local church, much of it also happens outside of it. Inside the church are organized programs that meet human needs, plus certain "housekeeping" chores, such as ushering, counting the offering, and taping the sermons.

Meanwhile, outside the church are a great many more opportunities for serving God. There are, of course, the organized programs of various parachurch ministries and nonprofit, volunteer organizations. But there are also many informal things happening, such as small prayer meetings among coworkers, or even chats over coffee. And if we also perceive daily work as an important opportunity for the believer to serve Christ, then ministries outside the church expand dramatically.

What does all of this mean for you? This says that you need to evaluate where you can best serve God. You may be like John, in that most of your service will happen at church. If this is the case, I'd encourage you to serve there faithfully. But keep in mind that God's work also extends beyond the programs of the local church.

However, my hunch is that for many Christians in the workplace, Richard or Steve may serve as more realistic models of what it means to serve God. This is because many workers, and especially many business and professional people, spend the majority of their time in the workplace. The majority of their relationships are with coworkers and associates in their professional networks. And the majority of their emotional energy is dedicated to their careers. Consequently, it makes sense that the workplace and the community would be their primary arena for ministry.

What does this mean for the church? It also makes sense that the church should equip these workers for effective service for God in that arena.

Actually, this is simply a matter of practical necessity. For the fact is that a pastor could not find enough church work for his people even if they wanted it.

This observation is not original with me. Dr. Clayton Bell, pastor of the Highland Park Presbyterian Church in Dallas, once preached a sermon entitled, "What's a Layman to Do?" He remarked:

> According to a study which I read several years ago, no church can create enough meaningful jobs for all of its members to do something in church. In fact, only one-third of the membership of a local church can be given a job doing church work. So if you think that serving the Lord means doing some work in church, then two-thirds of you are doomed to frustration and disappointment.[3]

Two-thirds! On a national basis, that adds up to tens of millions of Christians. Ephesians 4 demands that they be mobilized for ministry—for ministry outside the church, and especially, I believe, for ministry in the marketplace. To fail to do so would be a monumental waste of a resource in the face of overwhelming human need.

And so I suggest that a church will be effective to the extent that it enables laypeople to live out their faith on the street.[4] This is another way of saying what I said in Part I: It is imperative that we as Christians jettison all distinctions between the "sacred" and the "secular," and instead bring the whole of our lives together under Christ's lordship. We cannot afford a preference for church work and a depreciation of daily work. Rather, we must do God's work, wherever it needs doing.

PURSUING THE IDEAL

This is the ideal. Having looked at the ideal, though, I think we also need to recognize the real situation in the local church. Keeping Richard Lovelace's caution about generalizations in mind, I think it is fair to say that:

> The model of congregational life in the minds of most clergy and laity is one in which the minister is a dominant pastoral superstar who specializes in the spiritual concerns of the Christian community, while the laity are spectators, critics and recipients of pastoral care, free to go about their own business because the pastor is taking care of the business of the kingdom.[5]

In other words, in most cases we are far from the ideal. Naturally, there are some notably exceptional churches from which all of us who care about laypeople and their work could learn a great deal. But it would be unrealistic to say this is the norm.

Much could be said to pastors and denominational leaders about how they contribute to this situation and what they could do to change it. But that's another book.

Our concern here is the responsibility you as a layperson have for pursuing the New Testament ideal yourself and for challenging others in your church to do likewise.

No silent contracts. First, you may need to break any unholy contracts you may have negotiated with your pastor: He does the "holy work" for you, but he also avoids stepping on your toes, avoids applying convicting spiritual truth to your personal life and work; in exchange, you help pay his salary and support his plans, but are otherwise free to live and work as you please, and yet feel religious.

If that is your condition, you must repudiate it. For nothing could be further from God's will. The work of God, according to the New Testament, belongs to you, not just your pastor. In a real sense, God has placed part of this world under your management. And like any manager, you must someday give an accounting to the One who hired you. What will He say of you?

Likewise, none of us is excused from a holy, obedient lifestyle just because we are not clergy and have not been to seminary. As we have seen,

Christlikeness is to be the goal of us all.

No little kingdom. But in addition, you must avoid the strong tendency to view your church as an end in itself, as a kingdom you are building for God. Your church need not be big for this to happen.

Three questions to ask are (1) What *power* accounts for what is happening in my church? The human power of influential personalities and substantial money? Or the power of God's Spirit at work in human hearts? (2) What is the *fruit* of my church's ministry? Is it praise for great programs, or is it people with changed lives? (3) What is the *direction* of my church's mission? Is it inward toward the needs and problems of the members of the church? Or outward toward the needs and problems of people outside the church, for instance, in the workplace?

You as a layperson contribute to how these questions are answered by how you answer them for yourself as an individual. What is your power? What is your fruit? What is the direction of your mission? To challenge only pastors with these issues is to perpetuate the myth that the key to the church is pastors.

The key to the church is Christ, who said, "I will build My church." He's built it, but I'm afraid too many of us have put a lock on it. We do that to the extent that we build our own kingdom instead of letting Christ build His in us and through us. Matthew 16 says it is in our authority to unlock the church, but we had better realize that Christ is the only Key that will work.

Make Christ the Lord of the church. This is another way of saying that some of us have equated Christ with the institutionalized, local church. We think we're serving Christ, but we're only serving the church. We think we're worshiping Christ, but we're only worshiping the church. We think we know Christ, but we only know the church.

The test is this: If Christ were to see fit to dismantle or demolish our church—He has that right as the Builder—would we have any spiritual life or ministry left? If not, then that means our Christian life begins and ends with our local church. This is not what the Lord wants.

If Christ is to be the Lord of our life outside the church, then He must be the Lord within it as well. As a church member, you can move your church one step closer toward the ideal by ensuring that you yourself make Christ the focus and source of your life.

And while serving Christ, as I have indicated, will likely include some service to and through your church, it should extend into your daily work and relationships and into your community. You should pursue this broad service to people whether or not you receive a great deal of acknowledgment for it from your church.

EQUIPPING WORKERS

However, to adequately accomplish God's work, you need appropriate preparation. How can this happen? What will it take to make you effective for God in the marketplace? I'll suggest five strategies; there may be five hundred. But in my own work with business people and professionals, I've found these five to be especially helpful.

1. You need Bible teaching that addresses specific workplace issues.

Perhaps you know that the oceans contain an inexhaustible supply of gold. If only we knew how to easily extract it! But this is exactly analogous to how most of us regard the Bible. I am utterly convinced that in the Scriptures God has given us an inexhaustible wealth of resources for dealing with the circumstances we face on the job. Yet so few seem able to extract these truths and apply them meaningfully to everyday situations.

For instance, what do you do as a believer when your supervisor recommends that you apply for a promotion, even though the deadline for applications has passed, yet you know that she will postdate your form? How do you determine whether to take a new job, knowing that it will mean increased income for your family, yet also take you away from them in more travel? How do you determine a standard of living that is appropriate and Christlike? How do you know whether or not to declare bankruptcy?

Or suppose you are a Christian woman in the workplace. How can a working mother balance the demands of work, parenting, domestic chores, and marriage (if married)? How should the female careerist handle ambition? How should the single woman regard her career in light of the possibility of marriage? And how should she respond to a marriage-oriented church and society if she never marries?

I find that questions like these have Christian workers wrapped around the axle. It's not that answers are not offered. It's just that most of them are not coming from the Church, and therefore lack a sense of being grounded in Christ and His Word.

Such practical questions point to underlying issues, such as stress, priorities, relationships, ambition, and compromise. I call these "critical issues," and my organization has identified at least ninety of them that people face on the job every day.

Your church's responsibility. So a church might equip its laypeople by speaking to some of these issues in its preaching and teaching ministry. The emphasis here must be on application. All the Bible doctrine in the world—as valuable and necessary as that is—is of no practical use unless we can apply it to the situations workers confront every day.

A pastor I know in Baltimore, Jim Dethmer of Grace Fellowship Church, has a reputation for just this sort of practical preaching. In his sermons he first makes sure that listeners clearly understand the biblical text—what it meant to its original audience, and what principles we can derive from it today. He then applies these principles to the lives of the people in the congregation, many of whom are workers.

Consequently, Jim's sermons are punctuated by lots of illustrations from the work world. He displays a real insight into normal human emotions and responses. As a result, what he says has a ring of authenticity, both to the truth of the Scriptures and to the truth of how people really live. He derives this relevance, I believe, from his disciplined study of the biblical text and from his frequent visits to the workplaces of his people. He sees their world and listens to their concerns.

Your responsibility. I could mention other leaders like Jim. But whether or not your pastor or adult education teachers do all they can to speak to your issues, you as a layperson still have a responsibility to allow God's Word to inform your work. It certainly helps if your church addresses these concerns. But whether or not it does, you need to learn how to extract truth from the Bible and apply it to your situation.

I can only offer a few suggestions along these lines in this book. But you might start by asking, "What are some of the situations I face on my job that I wish the Bible addressed?" Perhaps conflict with a superior. Or a questionable business practice. Or a problem handling enormous and relentless demands. Or boredom. Each of us can likely point to two or three.

Define the issue. Having done that, you'll need to define the actual problem you are facing. Though the details of a situation at work usually get the most attention—the specifics of what happened, or who said what, or the likely consequences of a decision—the situation usually reflects an underlying issue that is far broader than the situation at hand.

For example, a friend of mine came to see me once about one of his salespeople. He had hired the fellow and, to help him out, loaned him some money on the condition that his commissions would later be used to repay the loan. But after three weeks of employment, the salesperson quit—without having sold a dime, and with no intention of repaying the loan. What was the employer to do?

These were the details of the situation. As we discussed it, however, we put our finger on two or three issues that seemed critical for my friend. One was the issue of whether or not he had a right as a Christian to sue this person to regain his money, inasmuch as this salesman claimed to be a Christian.

Another was the issue of confrontation: how he might approach this man face-to-face and deal with him.

There could have been other issues involved, such as anger, contracts, loan agreements and arrangements, hiring policies, perhaps even salary and commission structures. But these didn't seem to be at issue for my friend, though they might have been for someone else.

The point is to take the time to clarify and define the underlying issues you face in a given situation. Having done that, it's time to turn to the Scriptures. But where do you start? I'll suggest three ways; you can likely think of others.

Use a concordance. First, you should become proficient at using a concordance. This is a popular tool among those who frequently study the Bible. It lists all the words of the Bible and where they are found in the text. So you may find a number of verses that speak to the issue you face.

For instance, under "lawsuits," the concordance to the New American Standard Version of the Bible refers you to 1 Corinthians 6:7. If you turn to that verse and look at the context, you'll find that it addresses lawsuits.

Of course, a concordance won't always have an entry under the issue as you describe it. For example, you won't find any references for "compromise" or for "ethics." In that case, looking under a related word might help, such as many entries under "give" for compromise, or "integrity" for ethics.

Even so, using a concordance will only get you started in uncovering some of the Bible's teaching on issues you face. Fortunately, many editions of the Bible include notes and references in the margins that may refer you to related verses, and hence to additional material.

Consult others. But even that may not lead you to all the valuable passages that speak to your issue. So a second suggestion is to draw upon the expertise of others. I'm thinking of pastors and Bible teachers, as well as other laypeople you know.

Those who study and teach the Scriptures often know of important sections in the text that will speak to your issue. So a phone call to them may guide you to some valuable passages, especially some you might not initially think of.

For example, if you called your adult Sunday school teacher and asked him where you might find some verses on compromise, he might refer you to the story of Joseph and Potiphar's wife (Genesis 39). We usually think of this passage as relating to sexual temptations, but the context reveals that it was actually an employer-employee relationship. Consequently, this story holds a number of valuable principles that likely speak to your situation.

But don't assume that only pastors and Bible teachers can help. One of your most valuable resources is other laypeople, particularly those who struggle with the same issues you do. For instance, one of the great issues for many small business owners is debt structure. Too often decisions in this area are made purely on the basis of acquired business wisdom and common sense. This is not necessarily bad. But as Christians we should also consider what God has to say in matters like these. Thus, it may prove instructive to consult other Christians who are also small business owners and see whether they could suggest some biblical passages and principles regarding debt, and how they deal with that issue.

Form a small group. This brings us to a third suggestion, that you consider forming an on-going group of associates who purpose to bring biblical principles to everyday work situations. I'll discuss this more below.

Look for principles. In all of your Bible study, however, always be on the lookout for *principles* in the text, that is, the basic truths that the text either clearly teaches or strongly implies.

For example, in Proverbs 10:4 we read:

Poor is he who works with a negligent hand,
But the hand of the diligent makes rich.

At first you might see this verse as a guarantee of wealth in exchange for hard work. However, other passages of Scripture would not allow such an extreme interpretation. Still, the principle that emerges here is that, in the main, honest labor performed in a prudent manner tends toward profit. This verse would not cover every contingency, but would be a support for faithful work. That is the principle being taught here.

Act on what you learn. Having extracted principles of godly living from the Scriptures, look for practical ways to apply them to your life and work. That's the goal of all Bible study: life-change. It would obviously be silly to go to the kind of trouble I've described unless you intend to respond to the truth you discover.

By "applying" scriptural truth, I mean acting on it, bringing your life into accord with it. This may involve doing or avoiding specific behaviors, behaviors mandated or prohibited by the Word of God. It should certainly involve your decisions, in that as you weigh your choices, you evaluate the extent to which your alternatives may lead you toward or away from pleasing God. And it should also influence your values and attitudes, which color everything you do.

Naturally, I cannot promise that after studying the Scriptures and consulting others, you'll always come to a satisfactory decision or always do the best thing. The issues of the workplace are far too complicated for that.

Reaping the riches of Bible study. But I do find a world of difference between the person who floats through his work life, carried along by the collective opinions of his associates, swayed by some very unbiblical ideas, essentially leaving God out of his thinking and decisions; and the person who, despite limited acquaintance with the Scriptures, purposes to try to do God's work, God's way, trusting God for the results. This person will increasingly discover and enjoy the wealth of resources God has provided in His Word:

> The law of the LORD is perfect, restoring the soul;
> The testimony of the LORD is sure, making wise the simple.
> The precepts of the LORD are right, rejoicing the heart;
> The commandment of the LORD is pure, enlightening the eyes.
> The fear of the LORD is clean, enduring forever;
> The judgments of the LORD are true; they are righteous altogether.
> They are more desirable than gold, yes, than much fine gold;
> Sweeter also than honey and the drippings of the honeycomb.
> Moreover, by them Thy servant is warned;
> In keeping them there is great reward. (Psalm 19:7-11)

2. You need training in apologetics and evangelism.

I find an amazing correlation between the ability of workers to articulate to coworkers what they believe and why, and their ability to live out their faith on the job. The issue here is confidence.

Take Lisa, for instance. Lisa is an account representative in an advertising agency. She's intelligent, winsome, and very professional. She is also a Christian.

One day Lisa is meeting with the art director of her agency to discuss a project. They toss ideas back and forth, until they realize that it is past time to leave work.

At that point the art director says, "Hey, are you going to Steve's party tonight?"

Lisa replies, "Oh, is it tonight? I'm sorry, I can't."

"Oh, you don't want to miss this one. Everybody'll be there! In fact, about half our clients will be there."

"Well, I'd sure like to go, but I can't."

"Why not?"

"Well, I've got this group I meet with every week."

"Group? You mean like a therapy group or something. Are you seeing a shrink?"

Lisa smiles. "Oh, no, nothing like that. It's a group from my church. We get together and discuss, uh, spiritual things, and read the Bible, and stuff like that."

The art director blinks and pauses. "You're going to blow off the best party of the year to go read the Bible?!" he asks incredulously.

Lisa nods. She doesn't quite know what to say.

Finally the art director says, "I forgot, you are into religion, aren't you? You know I'm curious, how can you believe all that stuff?"

"Well, because it's . . . it's true."

"True! How can you say the Bible's true? I've actually done a lot of reading on that, and from what I can tell, it's anything but true! It's all derived from folklore and myths. Why would you want to discuss that?"

A fool for Christ—or just foolish? Lisa is beginning to feel very much like a fool. That's because she's looking more and more foolish as the conversation develops. Her associate has asked a legitimate, honest question, backed up by whatever reading he's done on the subject. She, on the other hand, has articulated, or at least implied, a belief for which she can offer no reasonable explanation.

Now I ask: after this experience, how likely is it that Lisa will share her faith with other coworkers, to try to persuade them to consider the gospel? How likely is it that she will live a distinctive lifestyle on the job, one informed by biblical values, one resistant to temptation and compromise? And how can she fail to go away from this experience without a subtle seed of doubt planted in her mind, doubt about the Bible's authenticity and authority?

You may be like Lisa, in that you sincerely love Christ, believe in Him, and want to serve Him. Yet you may hide this allegiance in front of coworkers for fear of getting shot out of the saddle by a barrage of questions for which you have no answers.

If so, then one of the most valuable things you could do for yourself would be to pursue rigorous training in apologetics and evangelism. Apologetics would help you clarify what you believe and why. Training in evangelism would help you communicate the gospel message to nonbelieving coworkers. The two obviously go hand in hand.

Training in apologetics. One organization that specifically helps people in this regard is Search Ministries, based in Baltimore.[6] Over many years of research, Search has found that there are only about a dozen basic questions nonChristians typically ask in regard to Christianity. Consequently, Search helps people in the apologetics that answer those questions.

The art director, for example, asked Lisa one of them: Is the Bible true? If Lisa had thought through this issue herself and knew what she believed and why, that might have leveled the playing field. She might have challenged the art director's contention that the Bible derived from myth by offering some facts of her own. She certainly would have discussed the matter from a posture of confidence.

And that is extremely important if you are a business or professional person. All day long you are called upon to demonstrate expertise and proficiency in your career. So if questions about your faith make you appear to be a fool who doesn't know what you're talking about, you'll learn to avoid questions about your faith.

Training in evangelism. Of course, one of the main reasons for answering the questions of unbelievers is to surmount the intellectual barriers that keep them from deciding for or against Christ. You still need to make a clear and accurate presentation of the gospel.

So in addition to apologetics, you need training in how to explain the gospel. Again, Search Ministries is a resource in this regard, among many other organizations.

I'll have more to say about evangelism among coworkers in the next chapter. But let me add here that one of the most fruitful starting points for evangelism is the list of critical issues I mentioned earlier. For the fact is that nonChristians struggle with the same issues at work that you do as a Christian: issues of integrity, justice, balancing work and family, and so forth.

Consequently, discussions around issues like these often lead to open doors for the gospel—especially if you can demonstrate that the Bible speaks relevantly to these topics. I mentioned earlier that many people hold a skepticism toward the faith, and think that it cannot stand the rigors of the street. But when they discover that just the opposite is true, it changes their opinion of Christianity. And that will often change their openness toward the gospel.

3. You need to cultivate personal holiness.
Suggestions 1 and 2 above are what I call training in skills. Applying biblical principles to everyday work situations, apologetics, evangelism, and the like are all skills, in that they involve tasks and performance. I believe they are vital skills in making workers effective for God on the street.

Training in righteousness. But married to training in skills must be training in righteousness. "How to" books and programs become vacuous and self-defeating if they fail to affect character. We are mistaken if we think that God's only interest is that we do good. Obviously He desires that. But His great passion is that we also become good.

This is why Peter writes:

Like the Holy One who called you, be holy yourselves also in all your behavior; because it is written, "You shall be holy, for I am holy."
(1 Peter 1:15-16)

Peter says we are to be holy in "all" our behavior. I presume that this includes behavior at work. So it must be possible to sell life insurance with holiness. It must be possible to serve in the military with holiness. It must be possible to work in construction with holiness. It must even be possible to do investment banking, to run for political office, or to coach college athletics with holiness. That is, to do it as Christ would do it, with His character.

But since we are not naturally like Christ, we must be trained in holiness. That begins when we lift up Christ, not only as the One we celebrate in worship, but also as our model, as our example, as our pattern. After all, our goal as Christ-followers is Christlikeness. That is what holiness is: being like Christ in our character and conduct.

Truth that makes a difference. So churches need to challenge workers to pursue holy character and conduct in the workplace. But you as a worker must take an active role in this process. For example, in Philippians 2, Paul presents the humility of Christ. In verses 3 and 4 he writes:

Do nothing from selfishness or empty conceit, but with humility of mind let each of you regard one another as more important than himself; do not merely look out for your own personal interests, but also for the interests of others.

This passage is often preached, yet rarely applied to the workplace. And yet nowhere else in our culture do we face a greater battle with issues of ambition, power, politics, and self-interest. Our need, therefore, is not for simplistic, sentimental platitudes; those will never help us reflect the humility of Christ in our work.

Instead, we need to correctly perceive the dynamics of the work world: that we likely work among people who labor together as a team in the success of the enterprise, and yet who often compete against each other; that we often face a tension between the need to maintain the profitability and viability of our business and the need to service our customers with equity and honesty; that our own career path and its advancement (which has a direct impact on our ability to provide for our family) competes with the interests of others who have identical needs, but who often play the game by very different rules.

In light of such relationships in the marketplace, what is legitimate self-interest? At what point does that self-interest become selfishness? When does diligent performance become empty conceit? What is a biblical view of success? How can we balance the sometimes competing needs of our employer, our customers, our coworkers, and ourselves? Like Christ, how can we serve these various people? Is there any place for self-defense in these relationships? What does Christlike humility look like in such a setting? What are some practical steps we could take to acquire it? What might we have to give up?

Unless the challenge toward humility penetrates to questions like these, we have little hope of seeing such humility in the workplace. Consequently, when we hear a speaker teach a passage such as Philippians 2, we should start barraging the text with such questions. Even if the teacher never addresses them, we should take what he does say and search for ways to apply the text to our situation.

Once again, then, we see the critical need to bring together the living truth of God's Word with the day-to-day concerns of the workplace.

One writer who consistently proves instructive in this regard is Chuck Colson. His messages are consistently marked by timely and prophetic insights into very weighty theological truths. Yet he punctuates these discussions with real-life illustrations of people who practice these truths in the real world. Such a blend is extremely helpful in training us in righteousness.

A strategy toward holiness. Of course, lifting up the person of Christ and seeing how His character might transform us are merely the beginnings of the process. In order to practice such righteousness ourselves, we must make choices and take steps.

This is usually very hard to do, especially if we work in isolation from other believers. No one is there on the job to challenge us in our conduct and character. And so, too often, we leave church with the best of intentions on Sunday, only to leave those intentions at home on Monday.

In light of this, we need to devise a personal strategy toward holiness. This begins by taking an inventory of our lives, in which we review our habits and behaviors in light of God's expectations.

Taking spiritual inventory. (1) In your *personal life,* what is the status of your spiritual disciplines—disciplines well-known to correlate with spiritual growth, such as Scripture reading and study, or Scripture memory, or prayer, or the reading of devotional literature? What about your physical condition and habits of eating, exercise, sleep, and rest? What behaviors do you especially desire to overcome: a temper, or deception, or sexual lust? Or what behaviors do you especially desire to establish: patience, or hospitality, or perseverance?

(2) In your *family life,* do you have a set come-home time that your family

can count on? Do you "date" your spouse regularly? Do you disengage emotionally from work in order to spend unimpeded time involved with your children? Are you upholding your responsibilities to your parents, to your spouse's parents, and to other relatives?

(3) In your *church life*, how often do you place yourself under the instruction of the Scriptures? Do you faithfully, generously, and joyfully donate money to the cause of Christ? Are you praying regularly for your pastor and other church leaders? Do you know what your spiritual gift is, and are you using it?

(4) In your *work*, do you give an honest day's labor to your employer? Do you follow through on commitments you make to your customers? Do you read about and otherwise stay up on new developments, ideas, and methods in your field? To the extent that you can, do you hold a steady job by which your needs and those of your family are being adequately met? Do you have a family budget, and do you stick within it?

(5) In your *community*, do you regularly exercise your right and responsibility as a United States citizen to cast an informed vote? Do you pay your fair share of taxes? What is the status of your driving record? Do you maintain your property within the statutes of your community? Are you in any way conscious of and involved with the poor and their needs?

And so forth. There are hundreds of other questions that could be asked. The point of such an inventory is simply to help you evaluate yourself critically to determine areas in which you need to grow with respect to holiness. All of these specific applications flow out of specific Scriptures and scriptural principles that instruct us in holy living.

Setting goals. No doubt you will find several areas for growth. My suggestion is that you come up with *one* goal from each of the five areas mentioned. For example, you might determine to spend an evening with your wife, doing whatever she wants, one night each week. Or you might purpose to take six weeks to set up a family budget. Or you might decide to spend five minutes each workday morning praying specifically for your business partner.

The idea is that you set your own goals, rather than someone enforcing standards on you. This is absolutely critical. Too often exhortations to holiness are hopelessly legalistic and unrealistic. The expectation is that the individual will transform himself into a model of disciplined spirituality virtually overnight, through some simple three-step process. But that is impossible. Obviously God wants to bring us to ultimate perfection in Christlikeness. But that process happens slowly for most of us—painfully slowly at times.

A man I know, for example, purposed to pray with his wife just one time during a month-long period. That may not sound like much of a goal, but for this couple that was major progress. Before the month ended, they managed a brief, three-minute prayer one night before they went to sleep.

Naturally, he and I enthusiastically celebrated this victory. So the next month, he proposed to do the same, and again achieved his goal. And so it continued in the ensuing months. Then, after several months, they upped their goal to two prayers a month.

Tiny steps like these may seem to some to be painfully and needlessly slow. However, as I read the New Testament, the emphasis seems to be less on the relative size of our spiritual victories than on our faithfulness in the process; less on the velocity of our progress than on the direction of it.

Accountability. Of course, once you set your goal, then comes the hard part: accomplishing it. If the goal is constructed properly to begin with—if it is specific, measurable, achievable, and compatible with your schedule and means—then the issue becomes one of follow-through.

I have found that one important way to ensure that for myself is to mention my goal to someone who knows me well and is concerned for my growth in holiness. I then know that that person will likely ask me how I'm doing in the execution of my goal. That doesn't always mean I follow through, but it does prevent me from sloughing off on my commitments.

This kind of accountability (which is voluntary) could happen through the various kinds of small groups your church may have in its programs. Or, if you are not part of such a group, you might enlist one other Christian you know as a partner in prayer: you agree to pray for and/or with each other about your needs and goals on a weekly basis.

The objective is Christlikeness. The ultimate goal of these strategies, of course, is Christlike character and conduct. You may prefer alternative means of arriving at this objective. But by all means you must not ignore the process of transformation commanded in the New Testament. As with a set of worn-out clothes, you must take off the old, unholy self and instead "put on the new self, which in the likeness of God has been created in righteousness and holiness of the truth."[7]

4. You would greatly benefit from a small group.
So far I have suggested three strategies that you could use to prepare for serving Christ in the marketplace. One of the most effective vehicles for accomplishing these strategies is the small group.

Many churches already have in place a system of small groups, perhaps in their adult education ministries, home Bible studies, or some type of fellowship groups that meet during the week. Groups like these have an obvious advantage in addressing individual needs that may go untouched by programs designed for a congregation as a whole.

Consequently, I believe that small groups can be invaluable in helping workers prepare for living their faith on the job. In Chapter 16, I will say much more about how you can use small groups among your coworkers. But if your church wants to develop a small group ministry among its workers, I would make five suggestions.

First, I believe small groups will work best if they are led by laypeople, but strongly supported by the pastoral staff. I hold an obvious bias in favor of lay leadership in light of Ephesians 4. But I also find that laypeople too often resort to the "right" answers when a pastor leads the group. This can happen when a lay leader leads as well, but a perceptive leader will immediately spot this and tend to force the discussion into more realistic responses.

Second, such groups are best suited to discussion rather than lecture. The greater the involvement of participants, the more learning will take place. I encourage this discussion to focus on the *application* of scriptural principles to specific workplace situations. Case studies and problem-solving exercises help in this regard.

Third, the discussions will tend to work better when the groups are homogeneous. This is often difficult to arrange in a church, where workers from many different situations tend to come together. But it will obviously be easier for a secretary to think through what it means to serve Christ as a secretary with other secretaries and clerical workers than with vice presidents and CEO's.

Fourth, for groups like these to promote true life-change, some level of accountability needs to be devised. This could easily be arranged for workers who happen to work in the same company, or who meet together during the week anyway. Others might consider establishing partnerships in which the two partners call each other, or perhaps meet for a breakfast or lunch during the week, for mutual support and encouragement.

Finally, while most church-sponsored small groups will tend to meet in the church, *I would suggest relocating some of these groups to the workplace, if at all possible.* This is because a greater transfer of learning takes place when the learning environment closely resembles the environment of application. Board rooms, conference rooms, even offices, are only steps away from the arena in which you must apply the truth you have been discussing.

5. You need lay heroes.

Too often church leaders convey the impression that God's "first team" consists of outstanding preachers, Bible scholars, evangelists, and missionaries. Certainly I would take nothing away from the contribution of these people. But in the spirit of Ephesians 4, we must recognize that laypeople are in fact the front-line troops in the cause of Christ.

Consequently, you will be far more motivated to live your faith on the job if you can point to someone else who actually does. Again I would mention Chuck Colson in this regard, for his books mention many workers who have won various victories for God in their spheres of influence.

In a similar way, a pastor could weave into his sermons plenty of illustrations of workers, including some in his congregation who exemplify biblical truth. He need not embarrass people by using their names. But he does need to indicate that it is possible to live truth on the street.

But you as a worker should also participate in this modeling. Many churches arrange for times when members are encouraged to share some testimonial that would benefit the congregation. You should use such an opportunity to describe your participation in God's work. Don't worry so much about calling attention to yourself; call attention to God, and what He is doing in you and through you. And encourage other workers to do the same.

Perhaps someone can relate an unusual instance of God's grace at work through his business. Perhaps a coworker has trusted Christ for salvation. Or a person could relate a personal victory in holiness. Or someone could explain how he is serving Christ in the larger community, perhaps through a volunteer program.

When workers see and hear from you and other workers, they are far more likely to believe that they, too, can be effective for God. As someone has wisely perceived, "Most words of a clergyman are minimized simply because he is supposed to say them. . . . The contrast in effect is often enormous when a layman's remarks are taken seriously, even though he says practically the same words. His words are given full weight, not because he is a more able exponent, but because he is wholly free from any stigma of professionalism."[8]

CONCLUSION

Thirty-five years ago, Elton Trueblood called for a second Reformation in the Church. The first Reformation returned the Word of God to the people of God. Now we need a second Reformation to return the work of God to the people of God.

I wholeheartedly agree. But, of course, reformation implies significant change. Is such change possible? Is it even desirable? I suppose that this all depends on your opinion of the Church.

I happen to believe it is both very possible and very desirable. It is very possible because the Church has already undergone radical change at least twice in her history: once (for the worse) between the New Testament era and the beginning of the Middle Ages; and once again (for the better) at the time of the Reformation. And, of course, there have been other setbacks and break-throughs along the way.[9]

So to my mind, there is no reason why the Church could not once again take a step forward by restoring the layperson to a front-line status in the cause of Christ.

But is this desirable? I think it is not only desirable but indispensable, because unless the Church undergoes such a transformation, she may well undergo expiration.

In the beginning of this book I suggested that we have allowed a chasm to grow between the world of work and the world of the Church. We have labeled the one "secular" and the other "sacred." As a consequence, we as Christians are rapidly conceding the field, with the result that the workplace grows more unholy, while the Church grows more irrelevant.

But Christ is never irrelevant. In fact, I think one of His greatest passions today is to be brought back into the workplace. But of course it is up to us as His followers and workers to bring Him back, to invite Him to be the Lord of our work, and to do our work as unto Him. If that were to happen, it would mean a reformation in the Church.

To many, such a reformation seems impossible, or highly unlikely. But I liken it to landing a man on the moon. At one time that seemed beyond possibility, too. Yet it happened. Reforming the Church, of course, is considerably more difficult. So difficult, in fact, that only two people could make it happen: Christ, who has the power to do it, and you, who have the choice of letting Him start to do it in you. To make that choice would be the spiritual equivalent of setting foot on the moon, one small step for man, but one giant leap for mankind.

NOTES: 1. Richard F. Lovelace, *Dynamics of Spiritual Life: An Evangelical Theology of Renewal* (Downers Grove, Ill.: InterVarsity Press, 1980), page 209.
2. Elton Trueblood, *Your Other Vocation* (New York: Harper & Brothers, 1952), page 57.
3. Sermon preached at Highland Park Presbyterian Church, Dallas, Texas, September 22, 1985.
4. I use the word "effective" here, not "successful." A "successful" church today has come to mean one that has a large attendance, a large budget, a large campus of buildings, a prestigious pastor, and many well-attended programs. However, such a church may or may not be "effective." "Effectiveness" means doing the right things. A church can do the "right things" to get a crowd together, and yet fail to do the things God desires for a church. Programs and budgets are inevitable. But the "right things" that God desires are the things that make for laypeople who live out their faith outside of the church context. This is the point of Ephesians 4. Consequently, a church will be "effective" to the extent that she accomplishes this goal.
5. Lovelace, *Dynamics of Spiritual Life*, page 224.

6. See "For More Information."
7. Ephesians 4:24; see also Colossians 3:5,8,10,12.
8. Trueblood, *Your Other Vocation*, pages 40-41.
9. This is the point G. K. Chesterton makes in his chapter, "The Five Deaths of the Faith," in *The Everlasting Man* (New York: Dodd, Mead, & Company, 1944).

CHAPTER 15

EVERY CHRISTIAN A LEADER!
Relating to NonChristian Coworkers

I t remains for us to discuss what difference a biblical view of work will make in your relationships with coworkers. In this chapter, I want to concentrate on your involvement with nonChristians, and in the next chapter on your interaction with Christians. In both cases, I want to stress that you have a vital role to play as a Christ-follower. Let me begin by explaining why.

WORK IS THE MOST STRATEGIC ARENA

I once spoke at a conference in Boston about some of the ideas presented in this book. After one of the sessions, a middle-aged gentleman approached me. We chatted at some length about the implications of these concepts.

This man worked at one of the high-tech firms that ring Boston along Route 128. He also served as an elder in his church. He wanted to know how his faith could make a difference in his day-to-day work.

Finally I challenged him: "Why don't you recruit some of the other people who work along 128 to get together and develop a strategy for impacting this sector for Christ."

He paused for a moment. "You mean an evangelistic strategy?" he asked.

"Sure," I explained. "Both that and building up each other as Christians."

Again he paused, "You mean do this at work—away from the church?"

"That's right!"

Again he paused, obviously thinking this proposition over. Finally he smiled. "Gee, I never thought of that!" We discussed how this could happen for a while. Later I related the conversation to Bill.

"I'm not surprised," he said. "You have to understand how a lot of people here perceive evangelism."

"What do you mean?" I asked. Bill had spent ten years in Boston, and had worked on the pastoral staff of a church during part of that time.

"Evangelism for so many people means a special event at church, or maybe hospital or prison visitation," he explained. "They never think about the workplace as a forum for the gospel."

I was stunned! I had read statistics that suggested that as many as forty percent of all Americans will *never* darken the door of a church or synagogue for any reason. And I knew that in a culture of rear-entry garages, police locks, and high transience, most of us don't even know our neighbors, let alone discuss our faith with them.

Thus, work may be the only place many people will ever be exposed to Christians. In fact, I believe the workplace has become the most strategic arena for Christian thinking and influence today.

CLOSET CHRISTIANITY

Yet, as I pointed out in Chapter 1, that influence seems not only to be weakening but vanishing altogether. An enormous gap has opened up between the world of religion and the world of work. Consequently, not only is religion having a diminishing influence on the workplace, but through the workplace, secularism is having an increasing influence on religion.

I think that the elder in Boston is typical of many Christian workers today. Like him, they see evangelism in the workplace as a novelty. Like him, they say, "Gee, I never thought of that!" But why not? Why have they not thought of evangelism among the people with whom they spend sixty percent or more of their time? Why are so many Christians silent about their faith when they go to work?

There are no doubt many reasons for this. But let me suggest a major one: I believe many Christians have bought into a very prevalent idea in our society—that no one has the right to "foist" their beliefs, and especially their religious beliefs, on others; that people should be "left free" to make up their own minds; and that no one point of view has the right to claim to be the final and authoritative view (as Christianity does).

I hope you can see the inherent foolishness of such a perspective. It is predicated on so many preposterous assumptions that it is hard to believe anyone could accept it. And yet it is quite common in our culture. And a Christian who accepts this idea will be a Christian who becomes cowed into a sort of "closet Christianity."

The main thing to say in response is that in our culture one not only has a right but a duty to tell the truth, even if it conflicts with what others think or say. It is when the truth remains unspoken and unwanted that we take the first step toward spiritual and cultural suicide.

YOU CAN LEAD OR YOU CAN FOLLOW

But let me state the matter much more forcefully: As a Christ-follower you must become a leader for Christian thinking and influence in your workplace. Let me explain.

The fact is that the workplace is far from a neutral setting. It is a marketplace, some would say a battleground, of ideas, beliefs, and influences as well as of goods and services. I'm not thinking only of the influence of corporate culture, though that is certainly involved. Nor am I thinking only of the ideas inherent in the creation and delivery of products, though again that would be involved.

Instead, I'm thinking more of the influence of people on other people in the workplace, an influence felt in a thousand ways in day-to-day situations, decisions, and conversations. People bring their values, their perceptions, their beliefs, and their assumptions to work with them. Let's call this set of ideas, convictions, and opinions their worldview. In the routine of daily work, they act and communicate from that worldview, and this influences not only what happens on the job, but the values, beliefs, perceptions—in short, the worldview—of their coworkers.

This prevents the workplace from being a neutral setting. This has nothing to do with the nature of work. It has everything to do with the nature of workers. People cannot help but act from their worldview. This is not why people work, but it happens at work.

In this competition of ideas, there will be winners and losers, leaders and followers, influencers and influenced. I'm suggesting that too many Christians have allowed themselves to become the losers, the followers, the influenced.

You may feel that this overstates the case. But it must be seen in light of a much larger picture. For our society and our world are likewise far from neutral. Worldviews and philosophies are vying for influence as never before. And what is their strategic point of impact? The workplace.

For example, the Marxists have for many decades been infiltrating the work world of countries throughout Africa and Latin America. And as we are now discovering, they are meeting with great success. As a former Marxist explains:

Capitalist society presents the Communist with, maybe, scores of thousands of people as a ready-made audience, not just once, but every day. This audience is presented to him free, at the enemy's expense. The capitalists provide the building, they get the people together and give him the opportunity to be with them for six, seven, maybe eight or more hours a day. He stands amongst them at his machine as they work, he eats with them in the canteen at lunch time, chats with them during the morning and afternoon tea breaks.

The most important part of the Communist's day is, or should be, that which he spends at work. He sees his work as giving him a wonderful opportunity to do a job for the cause.[1]

Likewise, the ideas of New Age philosophies like est and Scientology are being actively promoted in corporate America. Werner Erhard, the founder of est, has set up a consulting firm called Transformational Technologies, Inc., which services influential clients, such as Ford and NASA.[2] And at Pacific Bell, 67,000 workers were trained in seminars "loosely based on the teachings of G.I. Gurdjieff, an early 20th century Russian mystic."[3]

In short, the influencers of the world are discovering that the workplace so greatly dominates our culture that it has become the distribution point for change.

EVERY CHRISTIAN A LEADER

For this reason I repeat: As a Christ-follower you must become a leader for Christian thinking and influence in your workplace.

Here's what I mean by a leader:

The task of making leaders is really one of creating an attitude of mind. When some new situation arises, the reaction of most people is to ask: when is someone going to do something about it? The spontaneous reaction of the trained leader is at once to ask himself: what do I do in this situation?

He comes before his fellows and says: We should do this and that and the other. And they follow him. Partly because he speaks with authority, they respect him and look up to him, but also because they have learned from experience that he has something to offer . . . .

The Christian . . . might profitably ask: What do I do as a Christian? Then act accordingly. Something in the nature of a social revolution and a moral regeneration would occur in the life of the West if every committed Christian we already have were to acquire, or to be given, this attitude of mind and start to think in these terms.[4]

Do we need a social revolution and a moral regeneration in our culture today? I believe we do. But whether or not you or I think so, what matters is something Jesus said 2000 years ago:

> Jesus came up and spoke to them, saying, "All authority has been given to Me in heaven and on earth. Go therefore and make disciples of all the nations, baptizing them in the name of the Father and the Son and the Holy Spirit, teaching them to observe all that I commanded you; and lo, I am with you always, even to the end of the age." (Matthew 28:18-20)

These three verses express the "last will and testament" of Christ, and they sanction the type of leadership and influence described earlier and its results. In them, Christ summarizes an end, a process, an agency, an extent, and an authority that define your impact on coworkers.

The end. When Jesus said, "Go . . . and make disciples of all the nations," He did not have in view the remaking of cultures but the *remaking of people.* He wants your coworkers to share in His life, to be transformed in their conduct and character, to become like Him.

The process. The key command here, as I pointed out in Chapter 4, is to "make disciples." The process that results in Christlikeness is *discipleship.* To be a "disciple" means to be a learner, a follower of Christ. This involves baptism (a sign that one is trusting Christ for his salvation) and obedience (doing what Christ has commanded). Christ wants your coworkers to become people who follow Him in order to become like Him.

The agency. To accomplish the discipling process, Jesus uses *people* who are already His disciples. This is obvious from the fact of who this commission is addressed to: His original disciples, and ultimately to every Christ-follower today.[5] The idea is not that Christians recruit coworkers to become their disciples. Rather, Christ wants to use you to influence your coworkers to become His disciples. If a person follows you, he will only become what you are. But when a person follows Christ and relates to Christ, then he will become like Christ.

The extent. The process of discipleship is to extend "to all the nations," literally "to all the peoples or people-groups."[6] In other words, every human needs to have the opportunity to respond to Christ's call to follow Him. Furthermore, the promise of Christ's presence "even to the end of the age" implies that the process must go on until He returns. In other words, *it is still in effect today.* However, as you think about this, don't think only of reaching "the unreached millions and billions"—though certainly they must be reached. Instead, start by realizing that Christ wants to disciple the coworker in the office next to you.

The authority. The beginning of the Great Commission is a statement of lordship. I mentioned before the fact that the workplace is not a neutral setting, but a marketplace or battleground of ideas, beliefs, and influences. Jesus comes into this venue not as a disinterested bystander, not as a spectator, not even as an active participant, but as the *Lord of creation.* He comes in to take over, to have the final say—not over the workplace, but over people. It is *His* authority that sanctions your intention to influence coworkers.

TRANSFORMATION, NOT DOMINATION

But note: It is precisely His authority, not yours.

> The purpose of Christian leadership training is not just to help ambitious men to the top, or to make little men who have done leadership courses feel bigger than they really are. Still less is it to produce führers, either large or small.
>
> It has much more to do with the making of integrated people. Ones who understand what they believe, are deeply dedicated to it, and who try unceasingly to relate their beliefs to every facet of their own lives and to the society in which they live.[7]

It is critically important that we understand this point. There is a growing movement afoot among some Christians to "reclaim America for Christ." These "reconstructionists" believe that God wants America to be a Christian nation, and the way to achieve this goal is to elect Christians into government, and place Christians at the head of corporations and institutions, and to set laws and policies that will promote Christian values.

If you are a Christian, this idea can't help but sound somewhat appealing. The question is, is this what God wants? Is this what He has instructed His people to be about? Obviously, the reconstructionists believe it is.

But I think they misunderstand our Lord's instructions. His primary goal is to make new people, not new societies. His principle means is the discipleship process, not the electoral process. His agents are Christians who compel, not Christians who control. His plans extend to all peoples, not just to Americans. And, perhaps most importantly, the authority that people obey must be His authority, and this is not an authority He has delegated to Christians or to any Christian government.

Beyond all of these, a fundamental flaw in this view is that it misunderstands the nature of change. Christ intends to make new people, but this transformation happens not from the outside in but from the inside out. Christ goes to work on the thinking, the attitudes, the values, and the character of people in order to produce behavior that pleases Him.

This is not to say that external constraints, such as laws, are unnecessary. Indeed, as long as sin is in the world, laws are indispensable. But as Romans 7 shows, no amount of law can transform the heart, because laws are unable to do away with sin. Only Christ can do that.

I do not question that Christians should exert social and political influence. But the clear teaching of Scripture, as well as history, is that Christian activism wins limited (though valuable) objectives. When Christ returns, He will set all things right in the macro-economy of the world.

In the meantime, our task is to influence people around us, including coworkers, to accept a relationship with Christ (to accept the gospel), and if they do, to influence them to follow Christ. In the rest of this chapter, I'll discuss the first part of this objective. In the next chapter, I'll discuss the second part.

INFLUENCING NONCHRISTIAN COWORKERS

Believe it yourself. If you expect to persuade people to accept the gospel, then the place to begin is to make sure that you yourself believe that Christianity is true. This may sound obvious. But unfortunately, too many of us don't know what we believe or why.

For instance, most of us believe that God exists, but why? Furthermore, we think that God is loving and yet just, but why? How do we know that He is all-powerful or all-knowing? And what about Jesus? Was He God? Or merely a good man? Did He really rise from the dead? Or is it just resurrection as an idea that matters? Is the Bible true? Does it have any authority? Is it mostly the stories and ideas of humans about God, or is it God's Word to humans?

And what about the gospel? What is it? What is this condition called sin? What does it have to do with our relationship to God? How did Christ deal with it? What happened at the Cross? And how can someone come to know God today?

And finally, what does any of this have to do with life in this culture today? How can anything that happened in an obscure province on the outposts of the Roman Empire nearly two thousand years ago make any practical difference in this generation?

One need not have tight answers to all of these questions to be a Christian. But these are the kinds of questions that must be answered intelligently if one is to be convinced that Christ and the Christian faith are true. Not just true for a few, or true for a while, but true for all in all places at all times.

Of course, one must not only believe *that* Christianity is true, but also believe *in* it as well.[8] That is, it is not enough to give mental assent to the facts of Christianity. One must also commit himself personally to Christ in order for those facts to have application to him.

It is the person who understands what he believes, is deeply dedicated to it, and who tries unceasingly to relate it to every facet of his own life and his society, who will be a leader for Christ. This is why I say that if you want to influence nonChristian coworkers to accept the gospel, you must believe that gospel yourself.

Believe that people want Christ. But you must also believe that people really want to find Christ. That they need to find Him is indisputable, given the message of the New Testament. But what keeps many Christians silent is that they do not realize how badly many people want to find Christ. People today are looking for many things: for an explanation to life; for meaning and purpose; for relief from anxiety about the outcome of this world; for hope; for healing; for some sort of power that will bring about change in their personal lives; and for joy. They will find these and more in Christ. In fact, whether they realize it or not, they are really seeking Christ and not just these things. As one who knows Christ, you are in a position to point them toward finding Him.

THE GREAT CONVERSATION

How can this happen? If you believe in Christ yourself and you want to help others find Him, then you must engage in a conversation with your coworkers. Let me explain.

In the work world, quite aside from the work itself, everyone is holding a sort of conversation with each other. We all communicate with each other in thousands of ways. Naturally, our values and beliefs and worldview get communicated in this conversation. This is the process of influence that I mentioned earlier.

For instance, suppose you are on a coffee break with several of your coworkers. Suddenly one of them drops his voice and relates a dirty joke that he has heard the day before. Everyone laughs. This whole incident communicates something, something about the joke teller, and something about each member of the group.

Again, suppose you overhear your supervisor correcting one of your coworkers. He is firm and to the point. Yet he never raises his voice, never tears down the dignity of the person. Then as the conversation concludes, the two shake hands before parting. This tells you something about the supervisor.

This conversation goes on all day long. People say something by the hours they keep, by their punctuality or lack thereof, by the way they deal with their spouse on the phone, by the comments they make about customers or coworkers after they leave, by the way they fill out reports, and even by their personal appearance and habits. This conversation is far more involved than mere personalities. It is a conversation loaded with value statements.

This conversation always has two aspects: the verbal and the nonverbal. The verbal conversation obviously includes statements and questions that expressly communicate ideas and values. But as you can probably guess, it is the nonverbal messages that communicate the most.

In order for you to be a leader for Christian thinking and influence among your coworkers, you must participate in the conversation at both these levels. As opportunity permits, you must make verbal statements that communicate the truthfulness of Christ's life. And in your nonverbal statements, you must communicate the authenticity of your own life as a Christ-follower.

By the way, it is often what you say with your actions that will lead to inquiries about your faith. One executive, commenting on the lifestyle and workstyle of Christians in his firm, said, "There is a serenity and a deep self-confidence, an inner peace, I have noticed in some of these guys. They are very able, very confident. They don't tell you about it, but you can't miss it. It's not a cosmetic thing and it can't help but have a beneficial effect on the business community."[9]

1. Build relationships.
How then can you take part in this conversation and have a very influential impact on coworkers? The most natural way is to carry on this conversation in the context of a relationship. I suggest that you start by identifying people with whom you already have relationships at work. Or, if you are new on your job, identify potential relationships.

Think about people with whom you already have an affinity or "chemistry," people with whom you seem to get along naturally. Often these friendships develop along horizontal rather than vertical lines. In other words, as a vice president of a bank, you would be much more likely to associate naturally with other vice presidents and executives then you would with a teller or a secretary. Likewise, a nurse is more likely to get close to other nurses rather than doctors or administrators.

If you cannot think of anyone with whom you could have at least a potential relationship, this should give you some concern. Sure, there might be a handful of jobs in which you as a worker are totally isolated. But if you work in the presence of others, it is only natural that associations will develop. God has designed humans that way. So if you cannot think of even one such relationship, you should ask whether you are bringing some unhealthiness to the situation that prevents you from interacting normally with others.

2. Pray for coworkers.

But assuming you can identify those significant others in your workplace, I suggest that your next step be to start praying for these people. Obviously, pray that they might discover Christ as their Savior. But pray, too, for the rest of their lives: their decisions, their families, their successes, their problems, their conflicts, their relationships, their work. This is exactly what the New Testament says we are to do.[10]

3. Seek common ground.

Then, as you pray for these people, week after week and month after month, let your relationship with them emerge and grow. This obviously happens when you work side by side with people on various work projects. You get to know each other well in such settings.

But also get involved socially with work associates. A friend of mine rides horses every few months with about fifty of the other executives in his firm. Everybody dresses up in cowboy gear, complete with chaps and pearl-handled revolvers. Needless to say, things get pretty rowdy! But the interaction between the men on such an outing is priceless. Situations happen in which relationships can go very deep, and the real person becomes apparent.

Another level of interaction with associates is the intellectual level. The same man I just mentioned regularly trades books and articles with some of his coworkers. In fact, in the process of exchanging ideas, they discovered the extent to which his Christian worldview affects his perspectives on life.

This intrigued them, because most had written off Christianity long ago as mindless nonsense. So they began plying him with their questions and comments about life and God-issues. This led to a weekly discussion of some of the philosophical foundations for the faith.

4. Remain honest and authentic.

Building healthy relationships like these will take time. So be realistic; you cannot rush friendship. People need time to "warm up" to you. They need to discover whether you share some of their values and dreams. They need to know that they can trust you over the long haul, especially when conflicts and crises develop. Likewise, you need time to get to know them.

Consequently, I encourage Christians in the workplace to watch and wait for opportunities to verbally explain the gospel message to coworkers.

Here's why. So many relationships in our culture, and especially on the job, are utilitarian: We "use" people to accomplish tasks. In the work world, this in unavoidable. But where the gospel is concerned, we never want to "use" a relationship as a pretext for evangelism.

Unfortunately, in their zeal, some extremists have done precisely that. They have cut short the relational process. They have built contrived relationships. Their main interest is in "selling" Jesus as though He were a product, not in a friendship for the sake of friendship.

But this is dishonest! It uses friendship as a pretext, communicating messages of acceptance, when in fact the objective is conversion. NonChristians quickly perceive this and respond appropriately with mistrust and anger.

Instead, Christians ought to pursue healthy relationships. This means allowing the natural chemistry of human interaction. We need not "force" a relationship where none would otherwise develop, simply to fulfill an unhealthy obsession with witnessing.

5. Do what is appropriate.
Rather, as we cultivate friendships, we should encourage coworkers to consider the claims of Christ out of a genuine interest in them as persons. We ought to ask, "Will I continue to accept and be a friend to this person, even if he rejects the gospel?" If we cannot answer yes, we should ask whether our witness—and perhaps the relationship—is contrived.

Therefore, watch, wait, and as situations arise, say and do what is appropriate. Remember that your character and conduct on the job are under constant observation. This doesn't mean that you need to project an image of spirituality—only that you be yourself and live as best you can under God's power.

But you want to be especially sensitive to the needs of others. Times of change or crisis often reveal what some of those needs are. In such moments, you may be able to move in with whatever is appropriate: a listening ear, a word of encouragement, a statement of what is true or important, perhaps a prayer, or perhaps a presentation of the gospel—whatever the situation calls for.

6. Tell what you know.
How you explain the gospel to coworkers is largely a function of your personality. You may be bold and outspoken; you may be reserved and subtle. The main

thing is that you be honest and clear. Unfortunately, many Christians, especially some who hold a Mainstream view of life, convey the impression that only direct, unequivocal, perhaps confrontational approaches are valid.

Confrontation has its place—*but* it is inappropriate for most opportunities in the workplace. Instead, I recommend an ongoing dialogue that preserves the dignity and respects the intelligence of your coworkers. Over time, your beliefs will emerge and pique the interest and curiosity of others.

But then comes the problem of *explaining* those beliefs. This is a problem, because some people are excellent at explaining almost everything; others can't explain anything! My suggestion is that you start by telling what you know—that is, speak from *your* experience about *your* relationship with Christ, and what He has done for *you*. If you can then clearly explain the biblical basis for your faith and experience, do so.

But if you cannot, say "I don't know," but offer to find out. You might also offer to put the person in contact with someone you know who can explain things. Just make sure that indeed the person desires an explanation, and also that your contact is able to explain the gospel clearly and sensitively.

7. Hurry up and wait.
By the way, be realistic in your expectations about how quickly a person will respond to the gospel message. Obviously, you will be eager to see your friend embrace it with immediate acceptance.

But this is unlikely. After all, you are not offering a free trip to Disneyland. You are confronting a person with very bad news (his own sin) and explaining very good news (the work of Christ on the Cross) that will redirect the whole course of his life and eternal destiny. These are weighty matters!

Therefore, be patient. Give the person time to think it all through and come to his own conclusions. And never forget that he must make his own choice, and that he must be left free to do so.

8. Your reputation is everything.
Again, whatever you tell your associates about your experience with Christ should be consistent with your life and reputation. I've known Christians who told everyone what a difference Christ made to them, but whose integrity and values were a laughingstock.

On the other hand, I've occasionally met people who make no pretense to perfection, moral or otherwise, but who will gladly tell anyone that their very failures are what drive them back to Christ's grace. Your coworkers will instinctively recognize the difference between the repulsive hypocrisy and the refreshing honesty of these two kinds of Christians.

CONCLUSION

You can be a leader for Christian thinking and influence in your workplace. You need not be pushy or preachey or pious—just yourself as a follower of Christ. But don't stop with nonChristians. You can also have a profound impact on the other Christians in your network. In the next chapter, I'll show you how.

NOTES: 1. Douglas Hyde, *Dedication and Leadership* (Notre Dame, Ind.: University of Nortre Dame Press, 1966), pages 97-98.
2. Peter Waldman, "Companies Seeking Advice Spawn Host of Consultants," *Wall Street Journal* (July 24, 1987), page 17.
3. Peter Waldman, "Motivate or Alienate? Firms Hire Gurus to Change Their Cultures," *Wall Street Journal* (July 24, 1987), page 17.
4. Hyde, *Dedication and Leadership*, pages 156-157.
5. This is implied by the words, "Lo, I am with you always, even to the end of the age."
6. See Donald A. McGavran, *Understanding Church Growth* (Grand Rapids, Mich.: Eerdmans Publishing Co., 1970), page 56.
7. Hyde, *Dedication and Leadership*, page 157.
8. My appreciation to Dr. Norman Geisler for this crucial distinction.
9. Nathaniel C. Nash, "Businessmen Who Pray Together," *New York Times* (February 15, 1981).
10. 1 Timothy 2:1.

CHAPTER 16

YOU CAN MAKE AN IMPACT!
Relating to Christian CoWorkers

I n the last chapter, I explained that you must become a leader for Christian thinking and influence in your workplace. As we saw, this leadership role begins with doing whatever you can to persuade coworkers to accept a relationship with Christ, to accept the gospel.

But it also involves challenging and assisting those who know Christ to follow Him. In this chapter, I'll suggest some ways that you can do that. But before we discuss strategy, let's consider some of the needs that Christians bring to the workplace.

THE NEEDS OF CHRISTIAN WORKERS

As I mentioned in Chapter 1, Christians bring a number of unique needs to their work, needs that all too often go unaddressed. This results in countless problems both on and off the job, problems that seriously undermine the leadership they ought to have in the marketplace. Let me review four of these areas.

1. Every Christian worker needs to be known, accepted, and understood.
Perhaps nothing is more terrifying to the human spirit than to feel alone in a hostile world. Yet this is exactly how so many Christians tell me they feel when they go to work. "I'm the only one," they say. And although the slogan, "You and Jesus always form a majority," makes a nifty bumper sticker, it never quite works out that way on the job.

Ethical loneliness. Many Christians feel not only an emotional loneliness, but an ethical loneliness as well. I don't think Christians are any stronger emotionally than anyone else. We feel the same insecurities, the same anxieties, the same frustrations. But in addition, we feel the tension of living between two worlds, between two sets of values.

I recall an internship I served as an intelligence officer in Ubon, Thailand, in the early '70s. I hopped off the transport plane and met my commanding officer, who informed me that I would be living downtown during my stay.

"Downtown, sir?" I queried. "I thought we were in a war zone?"

"I wouldn't worry about that, lieutenant," he explained. "We've fixed up a room and supplies and a girl for you and for each of the other men downtown."

I began to grasp the situation—and its implications. I knew that as a Christ-follower, I could not participate in living with a girl. So I replied, "Sir, I cannot do that."

You can well imagine the officer's response! We "argued" back and forth for a while, until finally he said, "Lieutenant Sherman, I'm giving you a direct verbal order to live where we tell you to live. Do you understand what a direct verbal order is?"

A direct verbal order is the highest priority command a senior officer can give a subordinate. To disobey or ignore it is considered the ultimate breach of authority. This was his warning, then, that if I didn't go along with the plan, I might as well hop back on the plane and call it quits.

I remember how I stood there and saw my whole career waiting on my next words. I felt so alone. I was in a strange culture, thousands of miles from home, and light years from those who had challenged me to grow as a believer. And I was face-to-face with a very frustrated and angry commanding officer, who awaited my reply.

Finally I spoke. "Yes sir, I understand what a direct verbal order is."

"Then you'll be staying downtown?"

"No sir, I cannot."

In rage, the officer turned and stormed off, leaving me standing on that enormous tarmac by myself. Eventually I found quarters on the base and reported to my assignment. But for days I felt so completely isolated and alone. In fact, when I finally ran into a group of Christians on the base, I nearly wept for joy.

The need for support. Over the years, I have found that this situation and my feelings in it are typical of what many Christians face at work on a day-to-day basis. They come up against enormous ethical challenges and temptations. And they feel the hostility of those who repudiate their values.

I've concluded that Christian workers need to find other Christian workers who understand their world. They need to know not only that they are not alone, but that they actually have a solidarity with others who share their convictions.

Lay affinity groups. This need may explain the rise of more than two hundred lay affinity groups during the past twenty years. These are organizations such as the Christian Medical Society, Nurses Christian Fellowship, and the Fellowship of Christian Athletes.[1] One of the values of such groups is that they offer participants a point of identity and association with other believers and a sense of belonging.

2. Every Christian worker needs to be inspired to moral excellence.

As Americans we pride ourselves on our rugged individualism and self-sufficiency. Indeed, we tend to honor the entrepreneur as the ultimate American hero. And yet all of this is less fact than fancy. The reality is that the overwhelming majority of us take our cues from others long before we "make up our own minds." Nowhere is this more true than in the realm of values.

In the situation in Thailand I described before, I managed to hold on to the courage of my convictions. But that courage came largely as the result of many months of being nurtured and trained by some Christians at the Air Force Academy. Had I not been through that process, I can't say how I might have compromised in Southeast Asia.

All of us need other believers to inspire us to moral excellence. This is a matter of both encouragement and accountability. We need encouragement from others to make choices and commitments that we believe will please God. We also need others to help us follow through on those decisions with action. Otherwise, it is too easy to waffle when things get tough, too easy to lose our "ethical edge."

3. Every Christian worker needs resources for decision making and problem solving.

Consider the investment a large company makes in its decision-making process. It pays big bucks to top management, who are the primary decision makers. It surrounds these leaders with a board of directors, who meet to advise and ask questions. It often hires consultants to study the particulars of a situation and make recommendations. And it may even sink hundreds of thousands of dollars into pilot programs and tests as an indication of an idea's potential for success or failure.

Why go to such expense? The answer, as Peter Drucker points out, is because one good decision can save a company millions of dollars and earn it millions more. Likewise, one poor decision can cost millions, and may even jeopardize the survival of the enterprise.

If it's good enough for IBM, it's good enough for you. So making sound choices is prized at the corporate level. But this is not always the case for an individual. Unfortunately, in their own decisions, many people prefer to play Lone Ranger. Yet, are the costs and the risks really much different for an individual than for a company?

In Chapter 11, for instance, I discussed the matter of integrity, and said that while holding on to your integrity may cost you, it will cost you far more if you don't. So what is true in business is true for you: one good decision can make all the difference in the outcome of your life.

Consequently, each of us needs resources, just as a business does, to help us make sound choices and to confront the problems we face. Again, I'm thinking especially of other Christian workers, those who know the issues we face and the implications of our various alternatives. Such people can offer wisdom, advice, caution, suggestions, creative alternatives, and objectivity, as well as prayer.

Without such a group of confidants, too many of us will continue to fly by the seat of our pants at work. Some of us are excellent decision makers. And all of us can probably make at least some good decisions. But none of us, no matter how wise we may be, can always make the best decision. So if we choose to go it alone, we may be taking a needless and foolish risk. That is why Proverbs 15:22 advises us, "Without consultation, plans are frustrated, but with many counselors they succeed."

4. Every Christian worker needs resources for growing in Christlikeness on the job.

In many ways this is a summation of everything I've said in this book. It should be apparent by now that your work matters deeply to God. He has given it to you. And He wants you to be distinctive in it. But that won't just automatically happen. It takes a conscious resolution and effort to grow in Christlikeness as a Christ-follower on the job.

It also helps to have resources that promote such growth. In this book I've mentioned a wide variety of resources that God has already provided: a view of work in Scripture that gives dignity and meaning to everyday work; the many Bible passages that speak to particular issues you face on the job; the example of godly workers in Scripture and history, as well as the moral champions and lay heroes of our own times; books and other materials that have been prepared; and of course the resource of prayer and the presence of God with us as we enter the workplace each day.

But in the remainder of this chapter, I want to concentrate on what to my mind is one of the most valuable and yet most ignored resources we have as

Christian workers: other Christian workers. I've mentioned this resource throughout the book, but here I want to discuss one specific strategy by which Christians can impact other Christians in their networks. What we'll find is that most of the needs we have as workers can be met largely through our fellow Christians on the job.

SMALL GROUPS

First, a bit of history. Several years ago I began to work with business and professional people, trying to help them integrate their faith into their work. I did consulting, luncheons, seminars, and so forth. But the format that really seemed to help people the most, that produced the deepest and most significant life-change, was the small group.

Here's how these small groups would work. I would show up to meet with six or eight people about a work-related issue. The topic of success was popular. So was the idea of balancing competing time demands. In time, I discovered at least ninety "critical issues" that Christians face on the job each day. And these groups came alive when they discovered that the Scriptures speak to these areas.

First, I would generate discussion of the subject by throwing a case study on the table. These would come directly from the workplace and would surface the issues, the dynamics, and the tensions of the topic at hand. Under each case study, I would have four or five discussion questions designed to examine the issue and then personalize the discussion to each person's own situation.

After twenty minutes or so of discussion, I would then offer one or two principles from Scripture that speak to the issue. The group would then spend the rest of the time applying these principles both to the case study and to their own situations.

Of course, this idea of small groups is nothing new. Nor is the use of case studies, which Harvard has been employing for years in its esteemed MBA program. But I knew I was onto something dynamic when small group participants began to use the term "life-changing" to describe the benefits of this experience to them.

It wasn't just my teaching, though I think that helped. But there was something much more important happening through the dynamics of the small groups themselves. The participants became a resource to each other. In fact, the relationships extended beyond the groups into everyday work situations.

My suggestion to you, then, is that you consider forming a similar small group of Christians in your network to discuss work-related issues.

A PERSONAL BOARD OF DIRECTORS

A forum for discussion. Consider the value of such a group. First, it offers you a distinctive opportunity to address the critical issues you face on the job every day. You may be fortunate enough to attend a church that speaks to these areas. But whether or not you or your coworkers do, the chance to interact with a group of peers who know each other's world, share each other's values, and will help each other to apply biblical principles to workplace issues is a rare privilege.

Accountability. Furthermore, consider the benefits of such a group for encouragement and accountability. We all could use more of that. When I was in college I was on the wrestling team. At the end of each season, our coach would prepare us for a tournament. This tournament was a grueling series of matches on Friday night and all day Saturday.

To prepare for the tournament, we had a practice routine that went something like this. First we would warm up with stretches and calisthenics. Then we would run two miles. After running, the first-string wrestlers would all get on the mat. This included me.

I would wrestle for nine minutes with the second-string man. Then the third-string man would come in, and I would wrestle for nine minutes with him. Finally, the fourth-string man would wrestle me. Needless to say, by the time we were done, I was nothing more than a puddle of protoplasm!

But then we would get up and run for two more miles—only to come back and do two more matches! Finally we would loosen up and head to the showers. We followed this exhausting routine every day for two weeks prior to the tournament in order to prepare for the strenuous challenge of capturing a championship.

I can honestly say I've never worked out so hard in my life—and never will! I was probably in the best physical shape I've ever been in. But why did I work so hard? Why did I push myself so far? For the championship? Sure. But on a day-to-day basis what kept me going was the presence of my teammates. It's very difficult to quit or slack off when you're involved with a group of peers.

And that's the value of a small group. Human nature being what it is, we all need some kind of accountability and encouragement. Going it alone, it's too easy to slack off in our personal and spiritual commitments.

Decisions and problems. An additional benefit of such a group is its value in decision making and problem solving. Should you take a particular job offer? Should you hire this or that person? Your wife's career calls her to relocate to another city: How can she and you determine what's best? One of your partners is being investigated for criminal activity: What should you do?

Your supervisor makes life difficult for you because of your Christian convictions: How should you respond?

These are the kinds of practical questions in which the people in your group could help each other. This would be an invaluable resource. In fact, some of the groups I helped start have become so close that the members refer to each other as their personal board of directors. And they won't make a major decision without consulting the board! No wonder so many of the people who have participated in groups like these report them to be life-changing!

GETTING STARTED

Sounds great. But realistically, how can this happen? How could you form such a group and make it work? Let me suggest four principles you could use to get started.

1. Recruit a homogeneous group of peers from your network.
In our experience, people who share similar values, goals, worldviews, status, etc., seem to relate to each other more naturally. That's why your network of peers is your most likely source of potential participants.

2. Be sure that everyone in the group agrees with the purpose for meeting and the expectations involved.
You may have a clear idea of how the group should operate. But make sure you explain your concept clearly to each person, and allow each one to decide whether or not the group is for him. By the way, I recommend that you ask potential members to commit to only six weeks at a time. This gives people a chance to disengage if they need to.

3. Use a tool that will promote a lively discussion.
I've already mentioned how I used case studies to accomplish this. A similar idea would be for group members to trade off on being responsible to prepare a case for each discussion.

For instance, in a six-week series on integrity, each person can likely recall a situation he or someone he knows has faced that illustrates some aspect of integrity. He would prepare the case by typing up the salient details on a sheet of paper. Then he could propose two or three discussion questions that investigate the issue raised and help the group apply biblical thinking to the situation. Obviously pertinent Scriptures should be brought in as well.

The point is to get the group talking about how the Bible applies to real life as we find it in the workplace.

4. Place the emphasis in your group on application of God's truth.
So often discussions can get lost in hypothetical or esoteric questions. These may be intellectually stimulating. But your goal should be *life-change*. Remember, as Os Guinness says, the problem with Christians today is not that they are not where they should be, but that they are not what they should be where they are.

The point of your small group is to produce men and women who live a life that is so unique and so distinctive, coworkers will want to know why. That's impact!

CONCLUSION

Christ wants you to have a significant impact on coworkers, to be a leader among your peers. Leaders are those who understand what they believe, are deeply dedicated to it, and who try unceasingly to relate their beliefs to every facet of their own lives and to the society in which they live. If you want to make a difference for Christ in this generation, the best place to begin is with the handful of coworkers God has placed in your network.

NOTES: 1. For more information about some of these groups, see the listing in John A. Bernbaum and Simon M. Steer, *Why Work?: Careers and Employment in Biblical Perspective* (Grand Rapids, Mich.: Baker Book House, 1986).

AFTERWORD

We have come full circle. In Chapter 1, I described the gaping chasm that now exists between the world of religion and the world of work. And I said that it lies with you, the worker, to somehow bridge that gap.

This led to a review of three inadequate approaches to this problem that many, perhaps most, Christians are now trying. Then I suggested an alternative view of work that I believe is more faithful to the Scriptures and more realistic about people and their work.

Finally, I highlighted some of the many implications that this view holds for you and your job. This section concluded by stressing the important role you can play in impacting your world for Christ. Let me dwell on this point.

As a Christ-follower and a worker, you are perhaps the most strategic figure in the cause of Christ right now. That is a bold statement. So let me offer a basis for it.

THE END OF CHRISTENDOM[1]

For years, indeed for decades, two themes have been articulated again and again by thinkers and observers throughout our society: the declining importance of Christianity and the Church on public life, and the declining moral and spiritual condition of our culture.[2] Over a century ago, Henry W. Beecher, a clergyman and speaker, addressed the Chamber of Commerce of the State of New York on the topic, "Merchants and Ministers." His thesis was:

> There are three great elements that are fundamental elements. They
> are the same everywhere—among all people and in every business—

261

truth, honesty and fidelity. [Applause.] And it is my mission tonight to say that, to a very large extent, I fear the pulpit has somewhat forgotten to make this the staple of preaching. It has been given too largely, recently, from the force of education and philosophical research, to discourse upon what are considered the "higher" topics—theology—against which I bring no charge. [Laughter.][3]

As a result, he continued, people throughout society were giving way to compromise at the moral pressure points:

How is it that pious men are defrauding their wards? That leading men in the Church are running off with one hundred thousand or two hundred thousand dollars? In other words, it would seem as if religion were simply a cloak for rascality and villainy. It is time for merchants and ministers to stand together and take counsel on that subject. I say the time has come when we have go to go back to old-fashioned, plain talk in our pulpits on the subject of common morality, until men shall think not so much about Adam as about his posterity [Applause], not so much about the higher themes of theology, which are regarded too often as being the test of men's ability and the orthodoxy and salvability of churches.[4]

Though a hundred years old, Beecher's comments sound remarkably relevant for today. Church historian Martin Marty points out that in this same period, institutional religion in America thrived, yet it became increasingly alienated from public life.[5] Since then, nothing much has changed: Religion has become privately engaging, but socially irrelevant.

In fact, Henry Steele Commager described the Church in America as something of a country club, as having "largely forfeited its moral function and assumed, instead, a secular one—that of serving as a social organization."[6]

And despite all the crowing over a renewed interest in religion in the '70s and the new conservatism of the '80s,[7] we have little to cheer about if we take a much broader, long-range view of what has happened to the Church and where it stands today. Francis Schaeffer, surveying evangelicalism from a lifetime of study, reflection, and involvement, growled:

Accommodation, accommodation. How the mindset of accommodation grows and expands. The last sixty years have given birth to a moral disaster, and what have we done? Sadly we must say that the evangelical world has been part of the disaster. More than this, the evangelical response itself has been a disaster. Where is the clear voice speaking to the crucial issues of the day with distinctively biblical, Christian answers? With tears we must say it is not there and that a large segment of the evangelical world has become seduced by the world spirit of this present age. And more than this, we can expect the future to be a further disaster if the evangelical world does not take a stand for biblical truth and morality in the full spectrum of life. For the evangelical accommodation to the world of our age represents the removal of the last barrier against the breakdown of our culture. And with the final removal of this barrier will come social chaos and the rise of authoritarianism in some form to restore social order.[8]

This message sounds so bleak that we are inclined to write off the messenger as a disillusioned old pessimist. But Schaeffer is warning us that the house is on fire.

A similar alarm comes from H.R. Rookmaaker. Dr. Rookmaaker was the late Professor of the History of Art at the Free University of Amsterdam. After surveying modern art and what it tells us about Western civilization, he concludes:

We may study the present situation, point to the fact that our culture is collapsing, notwithstanding its technical achievement and great knowledge in many fields. . .yet we must never think that it is just "they," the haters of God. We must realize that we Christians are also responsible. Much of the protest of today's generation is justifiable. But why did not Christians protest long ago? Why were we not hungering and thirsting for righteousness, helping the oppressed and the poor? To look at modern art is to look at the fruit of the spirit of the avant-garde: it is they who are ahead in building a view of the world with no God, no norms. Yet is this so because Christians long since left the field to the world, and, in a kind of mystical retreat from the world, condemned the arts as worldly, almost sinful? Indeed, nowhere is culture more "unsalted" than precisely in the field of the arts and that in a time when the arts (in the widest sense) are gaining a stronger influence than ever through the mass communications.[9]

Dozens of similar quotes could be summoned. But the point is that despite repeated warnings, Christianity has become insignificant as a force of influence on American life.

At the same time, the culture of the world as a whole appears to be sinking in the quicksand of spiritual stupor and nihilism. According to the brilliant historian Arnold Toynbee, cracks in the very foundation began to be noticed soon after the one-two combination blows of World War I and the Great Depression:

> The year 1931 was distinguished from previous years—in the "post-war" and in the "pre-war" age alike—by one outstanding feature. In 1931, men and women all over the world were seriously contemplating and frankly discussing the possibility that the Western system of Society might break down and cease to work . . . . In 1931, the members of this great and ancient and hitherto triumphant society were asking themselves whether the secular process of Western life and growth might conceivably be coming to an end in their day . . . . The catastrophe, however, which Western minds were contemplating in 1931 was not the destructive impact of any external force but a spontaneous disintegration of society from within; and this prospect was much more formidable than the other.[10]

One could argue that America rallied and rose to meet the challenge of this "incipient failure of will and wisdom and vitality." After all, did she not overcome Hitler and Japan and embark on an age of unparalleled progress and prosperity? Yes, but did the spiritual fiber of the culture grow as well? Not according to Carl F.H. Henry:

> A marked deterioration in American society, indeed in Western society generally, has arisen at the very time when evangelicals have been emerging from the subculture into the culture . . . .
> Simply stated, American culture is at a fateful crossroads. The fortunes of all the West are now enmeshed with those of the Bible, as are the fortunes of this entire planet, in fact, to which the West carried the message of the self-revealing God. Indeed, much of Western civilization may already have made its decisive turn . . . .
> Only the most stupid of souls will fail to see how bleak is America's prospect if she opts ongoingly for sensual gratification and crass self-fulfillment. As John Wesley put it, "a studied inattention to the invisible, eternal world, an indifference to death and its consequences" leads to the tragic unhallowing of human life. Tightrope maneuver two: *The rampant moral iniquity of our era brings us perilously near a civilizational endtime.* Our nation continues to be spared from ruin—believe it!—not by technological genius, not by political wisdom, not

by economic expertise, but by the forbearing mercy of God despite those who no longer "glorified him as God nor gave thanks to him" (Romans 1:21).[11]

Such a pessimistic theme of impending doom does not play well in a culture that is "amusing itself to death." It certainly did not play well at Harvard in 1978 when Nobel laureate Aleksandr Solzhenitsyn articulated a similar version of the decline of modern civilization. As an outsider observing Western society, the esteemed author confessed himself shocked by the impoverished spirituality of the West.

At the conclusion of his address, Solzhenitsyn reiterated the root of the problem, and then he threw down the gauntlet of a challenge for broad cultural and spiritual change:

We are now paying for the mistakes which were not properly appraised at the beginning of the journey. On the way from the Renaissance to our days we have enriched our experience, but we have lost the concept of a Supreme Complete Entity which used to restrain our passions and our irresponsibility. We have placed too much hope in politics and social reforms, only to find out that we were being deprived of our most precious possession: our spiritual life. It is trampled by the party mob in the East, by the commercial one in the West. This is the essence of the crisis: the split in the world is less terrifying than the similarity of the disease afflicting its main sections . . . .

Even if we are spared destruction by war, life will have to change in order not to perish on its own. We cannot avoid reassessing the fundamental definitions of human life and human society. Is it true that man is above everything? Is there no Superior Spirit above him? Is it right that man's life and society's activities should be ruled by material expansion above all? Is it permissible to promote such expansion to the detriment of our integral spiritual life?

If the world has not approached its end, it has reached a major watershed in history, equal in importance to the turn from the Middle Ages to the Renaissance. It will demand from us a spiritual blaze: we shall have to rise to a new height of vision, to a new level of life, where our physical nature will not be cursed, as in the Middle Ages, but even more importantly, our spiritual being will not be trampled upon, as in the Modern Era.

This ascension is similar to climbing onto the next anthropological stage. No one on earth has any other way left but—upward.[12]

THE DAY OF THE LAYPERSON

A dying culture. An irrelevant religion. This is the world that confronts you and me as workers. Three things need to be said in response.

1. You must act.

The tragedy of our situation is exceeded only by our appalling disregard of the warning signs. Our culture is not facing a new or sudden calamity. The foghorn has been sounding for so long that many of us have never known life without it. Indeed, you may have expected a chapter like this, since it is now commonplace to decry American life:

> Self-criticism is a popular genre, like self-help. Being lampooned is one of our favorite forms of entertainment, and a cautionary book can be as much fun as a horror movie. We love warnings—and we love ignoring them. Buying a book is a prophylactic act: to read about a problem is magically to solve it. Reform is one of the archetypal romances of American life.[13]

Is it possible that we have not only become accustomed to guilt, but addicted to it as well? That we want our religion to flagellate us, to prophesy disaster, to inveigh against our culture—not because we have the slightest intention of changing, but because doom and gloom preach so well? To feel guilty is to feel good. We studiously avoid the "sorrow unto repentance," which requires change, and rather prefer a "sorrow unto rejoicing."

In this chapter, as in this book, I have no interest in playing such a game. I have quoted many Daniels who, with remarkable and prolonged consistency, have interpreted the handwriting on the wall. It is time, not for feigned tears, but for a purposive change in the way we look at life and the way we live life.

In other words, I ask you to do something about what you have read in this book. I hope you have found it to be interesting, to be readable, to be thought-provoking, to be practical and relevant to your world. But I have written it in the hope that it will make a difference in your life, that it will spark *life-change* in you; that you will not simply buy it, read it, smile, and put it on the shelf, but that you will act on it. I've made many suggestions for you, and I'll make three more. But first we need to consider two crucial concepts.

2. Christ will build His Church.

G. K. Chesterton, Christian essayist, critic, and novelist, wryly noted that at least five times throughout history, "the faith has to all appearance gone to the dogs. In each of these five cases it was the dog that died."[14]

In other words, never count Christ out. American culture must inevitably pass. Christendom is probably sighing its final death moan. Humanism and secularism will collapse under the weight of their own self-defeating assumptions. But Christ will never again die. His enemies tried that once, only to discover that He was "a God who knew the way out of the grave."

This same Christ said, "I will build My church." And if the gates of hell cannot prevail against it, then our modern society cannot either.

This should result in two things. First, it should guard us against thinking that the end of America is the end of the world. I certainly have no desire to see such an end. Indeed, I think we as Christians should do what we can to steer our country back toward God. But we must remember that Christ is building His Church, not America. And if America proves to be an impediment to the Church, Christ can easily do away with America.

But secondly, this should give us hope, not despair. Hope for the Church, hope for the truth, hope for justice and righteousness, hope for people who fear God. If our lives are built on the truth that Christ is building a people who are like Him, then we can have great confidence that He will do whatever it takes to complete that task. Of course, if our confidence is in the American economy and the American political system, then we are building our lives on sand.

3. The worker has a strategic role to play.
It is always dangerous to try to describe exactly what God is up to. If we say that He is about to bring down the curtain on American life, we may instead find that He is only completing the overture before Act I. On the other hand, if we proclaim that a new era in the Church has begun, we may be simply polishing the brass on the *Titanic*.

Nevertheless, I am not certain that we are at the end just yet. Instead, I perceive our day as a crossroads. With Aleksandr Solzhenitsyn, Malcolm Muggeridge, Carl Henry, Os Guinness, Francis Schaeffer, Charles Malik, Richard Lovelace, and many others, I believe God may be presenting us with a choice. We're Americans; we demand options; so God may be giving us one: We can either turn away from secularism and turn instead toward Him, or we can forsake Him and live very secular lives apart from Him.

This is where the thinking and the action of the worker is absolutely critical. It is evident that the culture needs renewal and that the Church needs reformation. But as I pointed out in Chapter 1, a wide gulf has opened up between these two. The Church as she is commonly regarded is irrelevant, for example, in the workplace. And the secular values of the workplace are writing

268

AFTERWORD

the script for Christians and the Church.

But suppose God had a double agent, a person who could slip back and forth between these two worlds, not as a schizophrenic but as a change agent, a leader influencing others toward God.

The worker who is a Christian can be such an agent. That is why I said earlier that as a Christ-follower and a worker, you are perhaps *the* most strategic figure in the cause of Christ right now. Because:

You are the only person who has unimpeded access to both your workplace and your church. You live with a foot in both these worlds, no matter how divergent they may have become. So you are in the best position to influence either one of them in light of your involvement in the other.

In the workplace, you have a chance to demonstrate a lifestyle and workstyle so unique and so distinctive that coworkers could come to regard you as a leader, along the lines suggested in Chapters 15 and 16. In your church, you have an opportunity to influence your pastor, your leaders, your teachers, and others to apply biblical truth to the entirety of life in very practical ways, as I suggested in Chapter 14.

You are the person with the most credibility in the work world. Boston University sociologists Dianne Burden and Bradley Googins surveyed 1500 workers and concluded that "the workplace is becoming the main community for people." Today's workers most often turn to coworkers and supervisors instead of relatives or community agencies for advice and help.[15]

This means that as a Christ-follower in the marketplace, you have more leverage than ever before to impact your coworkers for Christ. Your values and convictions, and especially your reputation and personal involvement, can open the door to persons seeking advice and help.

You are the person to whom God has delegated His work. As we have seen earlier in the book, you are the new clergy. You have been given God's work to do, wherever it needs doing. Yours is not second-class status, but front-line status in the cause of Christ.

If the Church has failed to influence the culture as she should, it may well be because she has failed to equip workers to do the work of God in the culture. Not simply to teach Sunday school classes, or to oversee church finances, or even to volunteer in ministries to the poor or the elderly—tasks that certainly must be done. But to be Christ-followers and Christ-bearers in driving trucks, practicing law, making travel reservations, processing insurance claims, writing novels, constructing houses, ringing up sales, issuing traffic citations, repairing cars, etc.

Christ either does or does not make a difference in such work. If He does, then you as a worker need to know what difference He makes. If He does not, the ball game is over except for the write-up: The secularist will walk away with the culture.

For these reasons, I suggest that we have come to the day of the layperson, the day when the key operative in the Church is not a pope or a saint or a monk or an evangelist or a missionary or even a "highly committed" churchman—but the everyday worker who simply puts Christ first in his or her career, as in the rest of life.

Thirty years ago, Elton Trueblood predicted the same thing. It is hard to see that much has happened since then. But as I have suggested, this may be because work, the key to the layperson's life, has gone virtually unaddressed in a day when careerism has stolen the show.

Nevertheless, the key to bringing the culture and the Church back together; to renewing the workplace and reforming the Church; to choosing Christ as the Lord of life, rather than leaving Him out of the system—may well be a movement of people who are known for their hard work, for the excellence of their effort, for their honesty and unswerving integrity, for their concern for the rights and welfare of people, for their compliance with laws, standards, and policies, for the quality of their goods and services, for the quality of their character, for the discipline and sacrifice of their lifestyle, for putting work in its proper perspective, for their leadership among coworkers—in short, for their Christlikeness on and off the job. What could an army of such workers accomplish?

IT BEGINS WITH YOU

For these reasons, I sometimes dream of an entire generation of people living and working "as unto the Lord." But as Christ and the apostles showed, influencing a generation happens one person at a time. *It must start with you.*

In a moment I'll suggest three things you can do to get started. But first let's be certain about the goal. Changing the culture and reforming the Church is ultimately Christ's responsibility, not ours. He may use us in that process. But at the individual level He has one ultimate goal: to transform us into Christlike people. That should be our main focus.

I point this out because the culture may not change; it may drift further into moral chaos and godlessness. And the Church may not be reformed either; she may grow more detached, more mystical, more irrelevant. But whether or not the Church or the culture changes, you must. Even if, like Noah, you were the last righteous person on earth, you would still have a responsibility to fear God and obey Him. You cannot wait for others to act; you must make the first move. Here's what you can do:

1. Nail down your own perspective about work.

Here is the crux of this book: Unless you can make a connection between what you do all day and what you think God wants you to be doing, you will never find ultimate meaning in your work or in your relationship with God. If you are an insurance salesman, you have to be convinced that you are selling insurance because God wants insurance to be sold. If He does not, then you are wasting your life.

What is your view of everyday work? You need to come to some conclusions about this, because work is so central to life. Does your work matter to God? Or are you firmly convinced that everyday work has little if any value to Him, and that He really would prefer most people to be in the professional ministry? Or do you still believe that your main goal at work should be evangelism? Or do you feel that work is really none of God's business? You must evaluate the Scriptures and the workplace and yourself and come to some convictions about this issue.

By the way, you may disagree with much of what I have said in this book. But if you value the New Testament, I cannot imagine that you would reject my underlying premise that Jesus must be the Lord of all of life. You may feel that that holds different implications for work than those I have suggested. But even that I could accept if I were certain that you intend to make Christ the focus and driving passion of your life.

2. Put together a career manifesto.

Every successful business began with a business plan. Many have long since abandoned or lost theirs. But someone, somewhere, at some point sat down and thought through what the business would be, who its customers would be, how it could service those customers, and how it could achieve a profit.

Likewise, football teams play according to game plans. Armies fight according to battle plans. NASA spent millions of dollars and man-hours simply planning to put a man on the moon. Teachers write lesson plans. Authors come up with outlines. Cities hire planners to map out development. Producers work from scripts. Architects devise blueprints. Even Leonardo da Vinci worked from sketches.

The point is that thinking through what one intends to do seems commonplace and natural in the world of work. Yet I could probably count on one hand the number of people I know who have thought through their careers in light of their relationship with Christ. The difference between them and most workers is profound. They bring a sense of purpose and resolution to their work, which gives them confidence, direction, meaning, wisdom, and perspective, among other things.

If you desire such a sense of purpose, I suggest that you put together a career manifesto. A manifesto is a statement of purpose, intentions, and motives. It is a chance for you to think through what you intend to accomplish with your life and your career, and why.

A few of the many questions you might want to consider include: Why am I in the career I'm in? How does my work accomplish something that God wants done? What resources has God given me to do His work? How does my work show my love for God? How does it serve others, including my employer, employees, and customers? What is my plan for assisting the needy? How does my work serve myself and my family? What is the relationship of my work to non-work areas (family, church, community, etc.)? What is my purpose as I interact with the people who work around me? What do I intend to do with the income I gain from my work?

There are scores of other questions you could consider. The point is to devise a comprehensive strategy and foundational principles that will help you handle the day-to-day situations that arise. Operating from a manifesto, you will be able to respond to such developments, not react to them. You will be moving ahead with an overall direction for your life, not operating with a come-what-may attitude, at the mercy of momentary expediency.

So you might say: "As an architect, I purpose to design my projects to the glory of God. I intend to pursue certain kinds of projects and to avoid certain others. I intend to treat my clients, employees, and sub-contractors with certain kinds of values. Here are my convictions about my debt structure. And here is what I intend to do with my profits. An here's why."

And so forth. Writing or dictating such a document would probably fill several pages and be fairly extensive. It might even be worth a weekend's retreat to put it together. But the idea is that you set forth in a comprehensive, written form how you intend to be different as Christ's employee in your job.

3. Discuss God's view of work and its implications with your associates.
Throughout this book I have stressed that people who work alongside of each other can have a profound influence on each other. And in Chapters 15 and 16 I said that as a Christ-follower you must be a leader for Christian thinking and influence among your coworkers.

If you want to see a change in the culture and in the Church, this is the place to begin. Don't think in terms of big media campaigns or marches or conventions or legislation. These all have their place. But the biggest step you can take is to talk with the coworker in the office next to yours. This is where Christ wants you to start. Why talk of changing a generation if we can't influence those already within our network?

IN CONCLUSION

We stand at a crossroads. Which way will we go? The choice is not so much the Church's as yours. We're never going to take a vote in our congregations, in which everyone who wants to follow Christ raises their hands, and everyone who wants to leave Christ out raises their hands, and then we tally the results. It doesn't work that way.

Instead, you will make the choice a thousand times this next month, and millions of times over the course of your life. You will decide whether or not you will live and work for Christ. Millions of other Christians will do the same. As a generation, we will thus decide which way we will go.

"Who is wise enough for this moment in history?" someone once asked. I pray that you will be wise enough to determine that your life and work please God. That will make history. That really matters to God.

NOTES: 1. This subtitle is borrowed from Malcolm Muggeridge's Pascal Lectures on Christianity at the University of Waterloo in 1987 (Grand Rapids, Mich.: Eerdmans Publishing Company, 1980).
2. Obviously, Christians think these trends are related.
3. Henry Ward Beecher, "Merchants and Ministers," *The World's Great Speeches*, edited by Lewis Copeland and Lawrence W. Lamm (New York: Dover Publications, Inc., 1942), page 669.
4. Beecher, "Merchants and Ministers, page 670." I am not certain that I altogether agree with Beecher's comments about "theology," though I cannot speak definitely, not being familiar with the context. However, if the past century should have taught Christians anything, it is that we must have *both* right doctrine and right practice. Either one without the other is disastrous.
5. Martin E. Marty, *The Modern Schism: Three Paths to the Secular* (New York: Harper & Row, 1969), pages 9f.
6. Henry Steele Commager, *The American Mind: An Interpretation of American Thought and Character Since the 1880's* (New Haven, Conn.: Yale University Press, 1950), page 426.
7. For instance, John Naisbitt's prediction that the current "national revival" will continue, *Megatrends* (New York: Warner Books, 1982), pages 269-270; or Jeremy Rifkin's view that we are witnessing a second Protestant reformation that will replace the theology of Luther and Calvin and "the liberal ethos which grew out of it" with "a new covenant vision," a "Protestant 'conservation' ethic," *The Emerging Order: God in the Age of Scarcity* (New York: Ballantine Books, 1979), pages 281-355.
8. Francis A. Schaeffer, *The Great Evangelical Disaster* (Westchester, Ill.: Crossway Books, 1984), page 141. I disagree with Schaeffer that there have been no clear voices speaking. Carl Henry, Elton Trueblood, Joe Bayly, C.S. Lewis, and many others have spoken clearly and relevantly. With tears, we must say that they have not always been listened to—or rather, that God has not been listened to or obeyed.
9. H.R. Rookmaaker, *Modern Art and the Death of a Culture* (Downers Grove, Ill.: InterVarsity Press, 1970), page 222.
10. A. J. Toynbee, *Survey of International Affairs, 1931* (London: Oxford University, for Royal Institute of International Affairs, 1932), pages 1-6.
11. Carl F.H. Henry, *The Christian Mindset in a Secular Society* (Portland, Ore.: Multnomah Press, 1984), pages 14-20.
12. Aleksandr I. Solzhenitsyn, "A World Split Apart," *Solzhenitsyn at Harvard*, Ronald Berman, ed. (Washington, D.C.: Ethics and Public Policy Center, 1980).
13. Anatole Broyard, "Down With Ignorance, Long Live Ontology," *The New York Times Book Review* (July 26, 1987), page 12.
14. G. K. Chesterton, *The Everlasting Man* (New York: Dodd, Mead & Company, 1944), pages 319-320.
15. Study cited in "Labor Letter," *The Wall Street Journal* (August 25, 1987), page 1.

FOR MORE INFORMATION

The organizations listed below may be of help regarding particular issues raised in this book. Many others could have been mentioned, but the ones listed here were specifically mentioned in the text as resources. (See Bernbaum and Steer, *Why Work?*, for an excellent list of additional sources of help.)

Intercristo
P.O. Box 33487
Seattle, Washington 98133
800-251-7740
Intercristo positions itself as "the Christian career specialists," and the claim is not without merit. Its most impressive resource is *The Career Kit*, an extremely useful and affordable notebook and set of tapes that attempt to help one find a rewarding career. The assessment tool in the package is itself worth the price of the notebook. Intercristo also holds seminars across the country on the same topic, along with an individualized career consulting service called CareerWorks. Intercristo's Christian Placement Network (CPN) is a comprehensive listing of work opportunities in Christian non-profit ministries worldwide. Intercristo's sister ministry, Tentmakers International, helps Christians integrate their faith and life-work by using secular employment to be a witness for Christ overseas. If your issue is job selection, don't overlook Intercristo. If you are in college, graduate school, or an entry-level position, contacting them is a must.

People Management, Inc.
10 Station Street
Simsbury, Connecticut 06070
203-651-3581
If you are an executive and facing a career change, People Management may be of help. They offer a highly specialized inventory of motivated abilities that is

foundational to a variety of consulting services. Two of the principals, Ralph Mattson and Arthur Miller, have authored the excellent book, *Finding a Job You Can Love.*

Search Ministries, Inc.
P.O. Box 521
Lutherville, Maryland 21093
Search Ministries specializes in equipping Christians to present the gospel to their nonChristian associates in clear, relevant terms. They also have done extensive research in apologetics, and have excelled at helping laypeople address the common questions unbelievers ask about Christianity. They have staff across the country, and are especially interested in assisting churches in the area of evangelism.

Probe Ministries
1900 Firman Drive, Suite 100
Richardson, Texas 75081
214-480-0240
Probe Ministries is another organization to consider contacting if you have questions pertaining to apologetics. In many ways a Christian "think tank," Probe excels in addressing the many philosophical and sociological tensions Christians confront in our culture. By the way, Probe publishes a helpful newsletter specifically for business and professional people called *Spiritual Fitness in Business.*

Career Impact Ministries
711 Stadium Drive East, Suite 200
Arlington, Texas 76011
817-265-3441
Our own organization, CIM, exists to challenge people with a biblical view of work and provide resources and services to help them live out that view. A few resources worth mentioning include: *On Your Way to Work*, a growing series of cassette albums on specific workplace topics; *Standing Out in Your Workplace*, a series of case history discussion notebooks for executives; and *Christianity at Work*, a monthly newsletter addressing the faith and work of the urban center.

SUGGESTED READING

Bernbaum, John A. and Steer, Simon M. *Why Work?: Careers and Employment in Biblical Perspective.* Grand Rapids, Mich.: Baker Book House, 1986.

Written in conjunction with InterVarsity's Marketplace '86 conference, this book is a good preparation for anyone considering career selection. Most helpful are the appendices at the back, which list Christian professional and academic associations, vocational guidance resources, and other resources on the subject of work.

Friesen, Gary. *Decision Making and the Will of God.* Portland, Oreg.: Multnomah Press, 1980.

Friesen's book proved controversial when it first came out, and it is not without problems. But overall, he sets forth an excellent foundation for sound, biblically informed decision making. The need for such an ability in the workplace is self-evident.

Henry, Carl F. H. *Aspects of Christian Social Ethics.* Grand Rapids, Mich.: Baker Book House, 1964.

Chapter 2, "The Christian View of Work," is an extremely helpful summary of biblical teaching on the subject by the "dean" of evangelical scholars. It is unfortunate that this seminal essay should have been buried in a book entitled *Aspects of Christian Social Ethics.* Had it been developed as a book in its own right, the world of work and the world of religion might look much different today.

Hyde, Douglas. *Dedication and Leadership.* Notre Dame, Ind.: University of Notre Dame Press, 1966.

A communist-turned-Catholic, Hyde applies the lessons and strategies he learned as a party worker to the Church. We were hard-pressed not to reprint his chapter on the workplace, "You Must Be the Best," in our own book. His final chapter, "Leaders for What?" also sparked our thinking about how Christians ought to impact coworkers.

Johnson, Harold. "Can the Businessman Apply Christianity?" *Harvard Business Review,* Volume 54 (1957), page 68.

LaBier, Douglas. *Modern Madness: The Emotional Fallout of Success.* Reading, Mass.: Addison-Wesley Publishing Company, Inc., 1986.

A Washington, D.C., psychiatrist, LaBier investigates the dark side of careerism and its impact on the human frame. His well-researched analysis embarrasses the success-oriented, you-can-have-it-all hype of popular magazines and pop psychology paperbacks in much the same way as the little boy in the fable who cried, "Look, the emperor has no clothes!"

Mattson, Ralph and Miller, Arthur. *Finding a Job You Can Love.* Nashville, Tenn.: Thomas Nelson Publishers, 1982.

The authors, principals in the executive search firm, People Management, Inc., explain how you can find a match between your God-given design and a job or career that expresses that design. Especially helpful is Chapter 6, "Discovering Your Design," and the appendix on the System for Identifying Motivated Abilities (SIMA).

Peabody, Larry. *Secular Work Is Full-Time Service.* Fort Washington, Penn.: Christian Literature Crusade, 1974.

This little paperback is a fine affirmation of the dignity of everyday workers and their work. It would be a useful tool for small group discussion.

Sayers, Dorothy. *Creed or Chaos?* London: Harcourt and Brace, 1949.

Her address, "Why Work?" makes for provocative reading in that it indicts the Church for failing to respect and speak to the secular vocation. Sayers comes at the topic from a reformed position theologically. Unfortunately this book is now out of print.

Sherman, Doug. "Toward a Christian Theology of Work." Th.M. Thesis, Dallas Theological Seminary, 1984.

This represents Doug's initial effort at articulating a theology of work. Many readers have found the extensive bibliography to be especially helpful in their own research and study.

Sproul, R.C. *Stronger Than Steel: The Wayne Alderson Story.* San Francisco: Harper & Row, 1950.

Alderson is presented as a gutsy executive of Pittron Steel, and stands as a lay hero worth emulating. The sub-text of the story is the idea that Christ can penetrate the arena of management-labor relations.

Terkel, Studs. *Working.* New York: Pantheon Books, 1974.

If you want to hear what work means to people in their own words, this is the book to read. It's a photograph of the American worker.

White, Jerry and Mary. *On the Job: Survival or Satisfaction.* Colorado Springs: NavPress, 1988.

Yankelovich, Daniel. "The Work Ethic Is Underemployed." *Psychology Today* (May 1982), pages 5-8.

General Index

Scripture Index

285

Luke (cont.)
  16:10 **62n**
  18:1-8 **168n**
  18:22 **45**
John 4:34 **80**
  5:17 **86n**
  6:27 **45**
  15:18-19 **148**
  17:14-15 **107**
Acts 2:42 **74n**
  2:44-45 **198n**
  4:32-35 **198n**
  8:4 **74n**
  13:2 **136**
  16:9-10 **136**
  18:3 **74n**
Romans 1:1 **136**
  1:1,6 **136**
  1:21 **265**
  7 **245**
  8 **102, 103**
  8:19-21 **110**
  8:20 **102**
  8:21 **112**
  12-14 **206**
  12:1 **61n**
  12:1-2 **168n**
  12:2 **168n**
  12:9-21 **149**
  13:8-10 **168n**
  14:5-6 **213n**
1 Corinthians 1:1 **136**
  1:24 **212**
  1:26 **146n**
  3:5-9 **62n**
  4:1 **62n**
  4:1-5 **62n**
  5:9-10 **117n**
  6:7 **226**
  7:17 **86n**
  7:20-22 **145**
  9 **73**
  9:1-23 **74n**
  9:14 **194, 198n**
  9:16,23 **74n**
  10:9 **197n**
  10:31 **62n**
  10:32-33 **94n**
  12:18,25 **62n**
2 Corinthians 4:7 **62n**

  4:18 **62n**
  5:9-10 **62n**
  5:17 **116**
  11:12-15 **198n**
Galatians 1:11-17 **137**
  2:6 **62n**
  2:10 **198n**
  4:10 **213n**
  5-6 **206**
  6:6 **62n, 194**
  6:10 **168n**
  6:16 **198n**
Ephesians 1-3 **114, 137**
  1:6,12,14 **69**
  1:18 **146n**
  2:8-10 **74n**
  2:10 **114**
  4 **221, 235, 236, 238n**
  4-6 **137, 206**
  4:1 **114, 137, 146n**
  4:11-12 **56, 216**
  4:24 **238n**
  4:28 **86n, 92, 95n, 114, 116, 168n**
  5 **168n**
  5:15-17 **133**
  6 **114, 146n**
  6:5-6 **126**
  6:5-8 **70-71**
  6:7-8 **100, 113**
  6:8 **62n**
Philippians 2 **232**
  2:3-4 **231**
  2:15 **117n, 168n**
  3:7-8 **197**
  4:12 **197**
  4:19 **198n**
Colossians 2:16-17 **78**
  3 **114, 146n**
  3-4 **206**
  3:5,8,10,12 **238n**
  3:9 **168n**
  3:17 **68, 114**
  3:22-24 **113**
  3:27 **62n**
  4:1 **113**
1 Thessalonians 4:11 **107n**
  4:11-12 **95n**

  5:12-13 **62n**
2 Thessalonians 3 **73**
  3:6-12 **91**
  3:6-15 **182**
  3:12 **74n**
1 Timothy 1:9 **146n**
  2:1 **251n**
  2:1-2 **164**
  3 **143**
  5:8 **91**
  5:17-18 **62n, 198n**
  6:3-5 **198n**
  6:6 **146n**
  6:6-8 **186**
  6:6-10 **197n**
  6:9-10 **186**
  6:17 **198n**
Titus 1:10-11 **198n**
  2:9-10 **129**
Hebrews 1:3 **86n**
  3:1 **146n**
  5:8 **169n**
  12:1-13 **146n**
  12:11 **167**
  13:5 **184**
  13:17 **62n**
James 1:2-4 **150**
  1:17 **146n**
  1:17-18 **198n**
  1:27 **198n**
  2:14-17 **198n**
  5:4 **182**
1 Peter 1:15-16 **231**
  2 **216**
  2:9-10 **57**
  2:12 **57**
  2:13 **57**
  2:13-15 **168n**
  2:18 **126**
  2:18-20 **169n**
  2:18f **57**
  3:1f **57**
  4:3-4 **117n, 168n**
2 Peter 2:1-3 **198n**
  2:18-21 **146n**
  3:10 **44**
  3:11-12 **62n**
1 John 3:17-18 **193, 198n**
Revelation 21:1 **62n**

The Navigators are able to provide assistance and training in the use of this material through their Business and Professional Ministries in the U.S. and Canada.

This service is offered with the sole aim of helping to stimulate and broaden the ministry God wants you to have in your sphere of influence. If you would like to know more about how we could assist you in the success of your ministry, or if you would like to have more information about the Business and Professional Ministries, please contact us at one of the following addresses:

In Canada:
The Business and Professional Ministry
The Navigators of Canada
55 Queen Street East, Suite 207
Toronto, ON M5C 1R6
Phone: (416) 362-5851

In the U.S.:
The Navigators Business and Professional Ministries
Attention: Mr. Lorne Sanny
P.O. Box 6000
Colorado Springs, CO 80934
Phone: (303) 598-1212, After 3/5/88 (719) 598-1212